From Centennial to
World War

The
History of American Society

EDITED BY JACK P. GREENE

WALTER T. K. NUGENT

From Centennial to World War

American Society 1876–1917

THE BOBBS-MERRILL COMPANY, INC.
Indianapolis

The Bobbs-Merrill Company, Inc.
4300 West 62nd Street
Indianapolis, Indiana 46268

First Edition
First Printing 1977

Library of Congress Cataloging in Publication Data

Nugent, Walter T K
    From centennial to world war.

    (The History of American society)
    Bibliography: p.
    Includes index.
    1. United States—Social conditions—1865–1917.
2. United States—Politics and government.   3. United
States—Intellectual life.   I. Title.   II. Series.
HN64.N83   309.1′73′08   76–15164

Contents

Editor's Foreword

The historian's traditional preoccupation with political history, a noted French historian has recently suggested,* is traceable to an understandable fascination with great public figures and noble deeds and events. Because the realm of politics in all its aspects— "theoretical politics, practical politics, politicians"—is by definition and in virtually all societies "the realm of the elite," political history, he has observed, is necessarily history in the "aristocratic style," inevitably preoccupied with the study of the public stage and the most prominent actors upon it: kings and presidents, ministers and senators, diplomats and generals. In view of the elitist orientation of political history, it is perhaps somewhat ironic that historians of the United States, the first large modern republic that has never had a true aristocracy, should have persisted in their emphasis upon political history far longer than those of any other major Western nation. That "economics, society and culture seem to have monopolized historians' attention for the last half-century" is probably true for every other group of national historians; it does not, however, apply to those of the United States, where, despite some impressive shifts of attention over the past decade, politics continues to be the central object of concern.

The *History of American Society* series is an attempt to break free from this emphasis. It represents an effort to look at the American past from the wider perspective of the development of American society as a whole. It proposes not to neglect politics, and the other familiar aspects of the history of American public life, but to put them in their broad social context. Because so few specialized and dependable studies have been made of the many complex components of American social development—values, economic and religious organization, aspirations, social structure, and internal tensions—this series is obviously somewhat preliminary in character. Without the kind of precise information about aggregate social behavior and long-term social developments that can only be

*Jacques Le Goff, "Is Politics Still the Backbone of History?" *Daedalus* (Winter, 1971), pp. 2–3.

supplied by an enormous amount of detailed study, the volumes in the series will necessarily be highly impressionistic and illustrative, more speculative analyses of the meaning of contemporary social perceptions than confident syntheses of hard data with firm conclusions about the changing character of the American social system. Despite the tentative nature of this undertaking, the series may at least provide an expanded conceptual framework for viewing the American past, one that will focus not merely upon elites and their public activities, but also, and primarily, upon the preoccupations, behavior, and drift of American society as a whole. Each volume in the series outlines in broad strokes for a specific period the main thrust of American economic, social, and cultural development and the interaction between that development and American political and public life; each also provides the reader with a guide to the specialized historical literature on that period.

The third volume to be published is Professor Walter Nugent's comprehensive and penetrating survey, *From Centennial to World War: American Society, 1876–1917.* The author treats the forty years from the Centennial of the United States in 1876 to the eve of the country's entry into World War I in 1916 as years of extraordinary and rapid change for American society, as it passed from being essentially rural and agricultural to being more and more urban and industrial. Rapidly increasing segments of the population lived in towns and worked at blue-collar or white-collar jobs instead of upon farms. The shift from a rural to an urban society was accompanied, moreover, by increases in size, scale, and sometimes even efficiency in many areas. Business, industrial, and professional organizations; transportation networks; organs of mass communication; educational institutions; and the armed forces—all grew in extent and sophistication to meet the needs of an increasingly integrated national economy that, complete with colonies and protectorates, came more and more to resemble those of the most advanced European countries. In some areas—size of gross national product and amount of capital exported—the United States had already surpassed or was in the process of surpassing all of its European rivals. With the urban-industrial revolution came a much more varied ethnic population, the result of massive emigration from southern, central, and eastern Europe;

a drop in the size of families; and an improvement in the lot of women. The unmitigated individualism of the mid-nineteenth century was gradually being superseded by evolutionary pragmatism and a growing sense of social responsibility. Although poverty and propertylessness remained, the decades following the depression of the early 1890s witnessed, the author argues, a modest increase in social mobility for whites and perhaps even for the few blacks who found their way from the rural South to the urban North. In general, however, the position of the blacks declined, as the virulent racism that underlay so many aspects of America's new colonial policy found ever more effective legal expression throughout much of the United States. Despite these many changes, the urban-industrial revolution in the United States was, of course, still incomplete in 1916. Over the previous four decades, however, the United States had passed through the most difficult stages of that revolution and—the author emphasizes—with a minimum of dislocation in any sector of American life. The complex interaction between the changes wrought by this revolution and the traditional organization and values of American society are the central themes Professor Nugent uses to guide his readers through this rich and engrossing chapter in the *History of American Society*.

Jack P. Greene

The Johns Hopkins University

Preface

This book is a history of American society from the 1870s to 1917. In those forty years the United States underwent the several profound social processes collectively called modernization, as also happened between about 1840 and 1950 to the other countries of the world which are now regarded as "developed": chiefly Germany, France, Britain, Japan, and the Soviet Union. Modernization in each of these countries, and in others less heavily populated or not affected in every region (Canada, Australia, South Africa, Italy), had certain common characteristics. It also had historical uniqueness in each case. Perhaps the following discussion of the American case will shed light on what happened at that time to the societies of the other now-developed countries, and on what may happen to "developing" countries in the future. Perhaps not. In any event, the history of American society during its years of modernization was complicated and interesting, involving such things as a shift in social ideology from the social ideas current in the seventies and eighties to those of the immediate prewar years; a constant interplay of social ideas with economic and demographic change, in a pattern reminiscent of the DNA double helix but without as much regularity and predictability; and the importance both of ethnocultural factors and of business cycles.

The first chapter describes the society as it existed in the 1870s, the decade of the Centennial and also of depression. The next two chapters describe how the benchmark situation of the seventies changed in unanticipated and often unfruitful ways during the interdepression years of 1878 to 1893, Chapter two dealing with ideas and institutions and Chapter three with demography and economics. The fourth chapter discusses a cultural crisis, the near-disaster that occurred between 1893 and 1901, when the depression of the 1890s reacted with the uncoordinated society which emerged during the preceding fifteen years. Chapters five (ideas and institutions) and six (demography and economics) describe how Americans devised and proposed solutions to their problems in the years from about 1901 to 1910, and, Chapter seven, how they instituted changes through law and politics from about 1901 to 1916. An epilogue makes explicit the major differences in the society as it was in the 1870s and as it was on the eve of World War I. The basic scheme of the book is thus a movement across time from fragmenting to crisis to coordination.

Throughout that basic plot marched certain people and groups. The most important of these was the American middle class. Others in the cast included businessmen, workers, farmers, blacks, and immigrants, but those whom I call the middle class are critical to the story. As one reader of the manuscript correctly perceived, "the book is about how the class in power managed to keep in power in a period of widespread economic and demographic dislocation. . . . The class in power, not strictly in Marxist terms, realized that without some action they would lose their power, and so they reshaped the social and political environment as little as possible, but sufficiently to keep their power." The term "middle class" appears so often in the following pages, and has been used and abused so much, that I owe the reader some explanation of how it will be used here.

The most basic point is that the middle class, like everything else, changed across time. During the forty years under discussion, it became decreasingly rural in residence and agricultural in occupation; it became increasingly urban in residence (though by no means entirely in the largest cities) and white collar in occupation. In general, whether its members were rural or urban or early or late in the period, the middle class signifies here property owners, either of real or personal property, and those who for reasons of education, ethnicity, religion, color, and luck were on their way to becoming property owners, or at least could reasonably expect to do so. The native white middle class almost had to be winners, and dominant. They held all of the cards: not only property, but white skins, Protestant affiliation or background, British-stock ethnicity, and access to education. Their dominance was not just a matter of money. So greatly was the deck stacked in their favor that it was predictable that those not a part of it would usually aspire to such a condition and would make every reasonable attempt to acquire middle-class coloration in such things as occupation and ideas.

The middle class was thus quite inclusive. Even those with very substantial property were, in the all-important ideological and identificative sense, middle class. Compared to other industrializing nations, there were hardly any "upper classes" in America, no hereditary nobility or aristocracy as in Britain, France, Germany, Japan, Russia, or Italy. To be sure, certain East Coast families had enjoyed wealth and social position for several generations, and wanted to keep it that way through private preparatory schools, private colleges and universities, family businesses, or exclusive clubs and societies (and many of these institutions were founded in the nineties and early twentieth century to insure continued high position). But to an unusual degree, compared to the mobility patterns of other advanced, modernizing societies, someone new could enter that elite if his color, ethnicity, and religion were correct.

Although the middle class thus lacked a ceiling, because of the functional absence of an upper class, it certainly possessed a floor. Below that floor, certain people were not middle class. If one of the constants in the definition of middle class is property-holding of some sort, then those without property, and without good prospects for acquiring very much of it, were the outs. They included, throughout the period, the great bulk of the black minority. They included also the great bulk of the "newer" immigrants who began arriving in the relatively prosperous eighties: people separated from the native white middle class not only by lack of property or prospects but also by language or accented English, by their Catholic or Jewish backgrounds, and by the assumption on the part of the native whites that these new arrivals were genetically inferior. American Indians were not middle class. Also, the non-middle class included, during the whole period but especially before 1900, many of the older immigrants (especially Catholic Irish), as well as native stock whites, rural or urban, who were farm laborers, tenant farmers, manual laborers, or were otherwise rootless because of mental or physical disabilities or criminal associations.

Thus the contant features of the middle class, over the forty years, were property holding or the reasonable prospect of it; white color; British-stock ethnicity; Protestant background: a combination of economic and social characteristics. The changing features, those features which made the middle class different (and larger) in 1916 than it was in 1876, were its increasing likelihood of being urban in residence and white-collar in occupation. These features were less important than the constants, in both the long and short runs. Indeed the ways by which those in possession of the constants were able to solidify their dominant position, especially through the cultural crisis of the 1890s and during the progressive period which followed, are a central part of the story that follows.

As should now be evident, this is not a textbook history—that is, a basic introduction to the main facts and trends of United States history during the forty years before World War I, which would include many things not discussed here, and would leave out many that are. It is an extended essay about the development of American society, from the Centennial and the close of post-Civil War Reconstruction to the close of the "progressive era" and the onset of World War I. These were the years during which Americans came to grips most intensely with urbanism and industrialism, during which it modernized, and during which it became very unlike the spacious rural society which preceded it, and became surprisingly like the America of the middle and late twentieth century. Historians are often tempted to claim too much importance for their subjects, and perhaps I succumb to the temptation here; but probably no other period of equal length in the history of the United States brought so many fundamental changes, at least of a social or economic sort. And yet through it all, certain basic ideas, laws, and social structures not only survived but were accorded more solidly dominant roles.

I would like to acknowledge the help of a number of people who contributed in various ways to the researching and writing of this book. Tony Freyer and Peter Curtis were able research assistants, and I thank them as well as the Office of Research and Advanced Studies of Indiana University, which supported them. Annette Atkins and Susan Wladaver read the manuscript carefully and provided critical comments of exceptional value to me. Students in my graduate colloquium over the years were first captive auditors, then refiners and contributors to many of my ideas; they all helped, but I wish to thank especially Robert G. Barrows, Brenda Berkman, Sheila M. Cooper, Marcia Hatch, Boyd James, Timothy Sehr, Fred Stielow, and Allan Teichroew. I am indebted to Jack P. Greene, and Gerard F. McCauley for intellectual support and morale from the earliest stages of the enterprise. I benefited greatly from conversations with other historians, particularly Michael Les Benedict, Lee Benson, Robert Berkhofer, Rogers Hollingsworth, Robert Kelley, and Robert Wiebe. Other scholars whose writings I found especially influential, and whose ideas are probably not acknowledged adequately in the notes, include Otis Graham, Robert Higgs, Richard Jensen, Paul Kleppner, Thomas Kuhn, Benjamin Rader, David Thelen, Brinley Thomas, Morton White, R. Jackson Wilson, and Clifton K. Yearley. For their many contributions I thank all these people; for my use or misuse of them I am of course responsible.

I also thank the Indiana Historical Society, and especially Gayle Thornbrough of its staff, for permission to reprint in chapter one substantial portions of my paper, "Seedtime of Modern Conflict," which appeared in the Society's *Lectures 1972–1973: 1876, The Centennial Year.* Finally, I am deeply grateful to Robert and Golda Werman, and the clear air of their city, Jerusalem, for providing me with a lucid atmosphere at a critical instant in the formulation of this book.

W.T.K.N.

Indiana University

From Centennial to
World War

1

American Society at the Centennial: An Overview

Much had changed in the hundred years since Thomas Jefferson and the Continental Congress declared the independence of the United States at Philadelphia on July 4, 1776, making the Fourth of July forever the new nation's prime patriotic date.

So mused many Americans, in a rare reflective mood as the hundredth Fourth approached in 1876. Washington, Jefferson, and the other Founding Fathers could not have predicted in 1776 that steam power would soon be practically applied, and they would have marveled, as many people did in 1876, at the giant Corliss Engine which drove the machinery for the Centennial International Exhibition at Philadelphia. In fact they probably would have been surprised that there was an exhibition, and that it was international. They would not have expected a transcontinental railroad: where would it have gone and why? They were about to have enough trouble proving the independence of the thirteen Atlantic Coast colonies. After the Revolutionary War did prove that independence, the peace treaty of 1783 located the new country's western boundary at the Mississippi, only a third of the way to the Pacific. Even then most of the territory was wilderness, and Spain still claimed a considerable part of it. They would have been disturbed at how their offspring had produced over two dozen cities larger than fifty thousand (none were that large at the time of the Revolution), and, within fourteen years from the Centennial, would produce three monsters of over a million. Washington and Jefferson might have been saddened that their fellow Virginians no longer numbered one of every five Americans, but instead, fewer than one of every twenty-five; and that the Virginians of 1876 lived in a Commonwealth no longer among the richest, but one of those

1

most devastated by Civil War. But they might have been happier to know that the political society they had helped create still survived, and that it revered them and the other Founders. Whether it could be called "flourishing" at the time of the Centennial is doubtful.

Many nonetheless thought it was flourishing, at least in certain basic and important ways. July 4, 1876, the "Centennial Fourth," was appreciated as such very generally, by celebrations not only at Philadelphia, throughout the summer, but in places like Indianapolis and San Francisco and Chicago, places not much on the minds of the members of the Continental Congress. In many parts of the country it was celebrated as an official three-day holiday, a rare thing in those days. At any rate, the Centennial Fourth provided a punctuation both pleasant and patriotic. Preparations began on Sunday, July 2. Activity accelerated on Monday the third, especially Monday evening, and climaxed on Tuesday the Fourth, the anniversary of the adoption by the Continental Congress of the final draft of the Declaration of Independence by Jefferson's committee. Across the country, celebrations took place over the three days. The epicenter was Philadelphia, site of the Exposition, where a half-million people lined the sunny streets to cheer on a triumphal parade which included ten thousand torch-bearing workingmen and five thousand Civil War veterans, members of the Grand Army of the Republic, still straight-backed and black-haired only eleven years and three months after Robert E. Lee surrendered to General Grant. The leading spectators were the new presidential candidates, the Democrats' Samuel J. Tilden and the Republicans' Rutherford B. Hayes, both nominated not many days before; Dom Pedro, Emperor of Brazil, and a number of other foreign dignitaries; and several governors and mayors. All of them watched the procession march beneath triumphal arches which had last been used in 1824, when the aged and honored Marquis de La Fayette, the greatest French hero of the American Revolution, had visited the city. After the parade, the renowned lawyer and statesman William M. Evarts reminded the crowd of the significance of the occasion (through every nuance of significance: Wednesday's newspapers needed nearly four hundred column inches in three-point type to print his speech).

In Brooklyn, which was still twenty years away from becoming part of New York City, a parade brought out marching contingents of native-stock Americans, ethnic groups, workers, and benevolent societies: The Grand Army of the Republic led the Butchers' Guard, the German Centennial Union, the Order of American Mechanics, the Sons of Washington, St. Patrick's Mutual Alliance, Societies of the Irish Convention, St. Augustine's Temperance Society, the Society of Red Men, and others, though as yet virtually no Poles, Italians, Chinese, Puerto Ricans, or blacks.

In Indianapolis, not far from the geographical midpoint of the U.S. population and already "middle American" in several ways, a leading dry-goods merchant, L. S. Ayres & Co., urged the ladies to stock up on new hats and dresses for July 4, "this day of days," and an editorial preached that "those only who wind up the day in sobriety are worthy to be citizens of a repulic [sic] one hundred years old." [1] A severe lightning storm struck the area late in the evening of July 3, literally the eleventh hour of the United States' first century, but Hoosiers did not record this as an ominous symbol, only as an inconvenience. Threatening weather continued until mid-morning, but by 2:00 p.m. on the Fourth the celebrations were enjoying fair skies, westerly winds, and (had it been invented yet) a comfort index of about 72. The day lengthened into a delightful evening, with the temperature 70 degrees F. at sunset.

Decorated houses, elaborate "tableaux" (the floats of that day), and a long parade entertained the sixty thousand Indianapolis citizenry and the twenty-five thousand visitors brought in by special trains. Governor Thomas Hendricks, just nominated for the vice-presidency by the Democrats, presided over the official program, which was more than usually swollen by speeches, and over the inevitable parade. The marching order included a whole range of ethnic, veterans', benevolent, and other groups, indeed a public census of the voluntary associations then functioning in Indianapolis: first the Schwarzer Ritter Order Band, then the Veterans' Association, the Fraternité Française, the Emerald Society, the Liederkranz Society, the Turnverein, the Society of St. Joseph, the Order of Bonafacins, the Männerchor, the Free-thinkers' Society, the Beer Brewers' Association Band, and so forth. In the evening, a "monster balloon, America," was inflated and sent aloft from the Indianapolis Exposition grounds. It came down an hour later in Greenfield, about a dozen miles east (witnessed) after rising to fifteen thousand feet (estimated); during the flight, the balloonist, a Prof. Shotts, doubled as clergyman and married a young "theatrical couple."

Newspapers across the country on July 5 filled their columns with minute descriptions of the festivities and verbatim transcripts of the speeches. What were the speakers saying? "Fourth of July oratory" was already a cliché, but despite all the amply elaborated cadences and periods, all the orotundity of Evarts and the many who echoed him across the country, a bedrock of sincerity undoubtedly existed. They were all saying: *we rejoice.* Since 1776 Europe had almost universally been turbulent, but the United States had made itself a free and solid nation. "The nations of the Old World look on in wonder at our achievements," claimed an Indianapolis editorial,

> and while there is a proud victory there, all over the land a patriotic thrill stirs the American heart, as the people gather, as prophesied by the fathers of the republic, to render grateful shouts of rejoicing over the heritage that is ours. Let the day be festal for all. Let the rich and the poor, who alike enjoy the blessings of freedom, rejoice together. Let the old rejoice in the inheritance of their children. Let the young rejoice in the promises of the future. Let all render grateful thanks to the God of nations for our free and peaceful land from the Atlantic to the Pacific, from the lakes to the Gulf.[2]

These were a proud people, optimistic and confident in the future, not fearful, not shouting down the wind to suppress their own insecurities. They were expressing a commonly held and prized belief, and expressing it according to their traditions of patriotic ritual as well as their fervor of evangelical chosenness.

Nor did they do so blindly, without recognition of the facts of life in the 1870s: "It was hard times yesterday, and will be tomorrow," an editorialist noted, "but today is the Centennial Fourth of July." The Fourth was in fact a brief interlude—not by that fact unreal or escapist or false in its sentiments—which did provide an opportunity for reaffirmation of basic faith. But it was an interlude nonetheless, surrounded before and after with conditions of life which made reaffirmations often difficult.

What was it like to be an American in 1876? For that matter to be in America? The Centennial Year represented an important historical anniversary. It happened to occur at the midpoint in a difficult depression. In addition, it was part of perhaps the most gilded decade of what Mark Twain in 1873 called the Gilded Age, a time with a visual, historical, and social character which would soon be lost beneath the steaming accretion of future industrial-urban history, and yet a time which looked and felt very different, even at times unmanageably so, to those who lived through it and who yet remembered the sixties, the fifties, the forties, and beyond into the receding early-nineteenth-century past. From a later perspective (even one as close to the Centennial as the 1890s), the rural aspect still predominated in 1876: in the West, the cutting edge of the frontier sliced across northern Wisconsin and Minnesota, turned southward in the Dakota Territory and dropped forbiddingly through the Great Plains all the way to the Rio Grande. West of it, except for enclaves around Denver, Salt Lake City, Portland, San Francisco, and the Spanish-American outposts of the New Mexico Territory, American civilization had staked few claims against Indians, buffalo, mountains, and desert. To the east of the frontier line, railroads had yet to pierce the northern interiors of Maine, New York, and Michigan, or Florida's peninsula, or most of Appalachia. Nearly all of these places would hear steam locomotives by 1893. The 1870 federal census disclosed that more than three-fourths of the population lived on farms or in villages of less than twenty-five hundred; in the next fifty years the rural proportion would drop to less than half of the total. Rural isolation was common. In the Colorado Territory, turn-around time for the mail between Trinidad in the South, and Georgetown, twenty miles west of Denver, was about ten days in good weather.[3] On the Solomon River in Kansas, a fifteen-year-old girl who kept a diary after she arrived there with her homesteading family from Barre, Massachusetts, in 1871, recorded the Chicago fire when she first heard about it, which was four days after the fact. Indians meant more than President Grant, prairie fire more than the Chicago fire. But the family nourished the body on fried chicken, beef hearts, buffalo meat, and vegetables, and the spirit on the novels of

Dickens, the music of their piano, and the contesting of land claims.[4]

American excellence in landscape painting, established by George Inness and the Hudson River School before the Civil War, continued to flourish into the seventies, in part because there remained so much natural landscape to paint. Landscapes abounded at the art exhibits of the Centennial Exposition, and were seen by the Exposition's ten million visitors. Perhaps two dozen painters who deserve to be remembered described an unpolluted majesty visible not only in the mountains of the West but, still, in the Catskills, in the Delaware Valley, or at Niagara. As the art historian Lillian Miller has pointed out, these painters retained a romantic-idealist sense of nature which developed earlier in the century in England and Germany, and merged that sense with pride of country: "Nature was," for them, "a symbol of creation and a divine past; the unique nature of America, its sublime and awe-inspiring wilderness, as portrayed in Thomas Moran's *Yellowstone*, represented God's grand design for the nation, its manifest destiny in moral as well as physical terms." [5] Yet the future was at hand: Thomas Eakins' *Dr. Gross' Clinic*, that noteworthy harbinger of realism in painting, also appeared at the Centennial—in the medical section, not the art gallery. Yet it was there.

The landscape was also an attractive and still-available subject for artists-in-words. The great narrative historian Francis Parkman had reveled in the West in his first book, *The Oregon Trail*, but that was a product of the late 1840s. In the late sixties he published *The Discovery of the Great West*, the third of his magisterial seven-volume history called *France and England in North America*, and revised and republished it in the late 1870s. Parkman's excellence as a historian rested in part on the grace of his pen, in part on his thoroughness with written sources, and also on his personal observation of the country he wrote about. At one point in the *Discovery* he described the journey of Count Frontenac, the French governor, up the St. Lawrence Valley to Montreal, and then upriver to the tip of Lake Ontario and the Iroquois encampment at Cataraqui, just beyond where the shore of the St. Lawrence was (by the 1870s) "now covered by the quiet little city of Kingston."

Frontenac and his entourage left "La Salle's old settlement of La Chine," at future Montreal, and

> fought their way upward against the chain of mighty rapids that break the navigation of the St. Lawrence. As they approached the Long Saut [sic], rain fell in torrents; and the governor, without his cloak, and drenched to the skin, directed in person the amphibious toil of his followers. . . . At length the last rapid was passed, and smooth water awaited them to their journey's end. Soon they reached the Thousand Islands, and their light flotilla glided in long file among those watery labyrinths, by rocky islets, where some lonely pine towered like a mast against the sky; by sun-scorched crags, where the brown lichens crisped in the parching glare; by deep dells, shady and cool, rich in rank ferns, and spongy, dark green mosses; by still coves, where the waterlilies lay like snow-flakes on their broad, flat leaves; till at length they neared their goal, and the glistening bosom of Lake Ontario opened on their sight." [6]

It is important to note that Frontenac's journey took place in the 1670s. Two hundred years later Parkman could describe the scene almost as it looked to Frontenac. But another twenty years after Parkman wrote, the Thousand Islands were becoming an erstwhile late-Gilded-Age summer resort, where shortly, it is said, Oscar of the Waldorf invented Thousand Island dressing. In the 1970s even Parkman's creative gifts might have been hard put to subtract the cottages, cars, speedboats, and ocean ships in order to recreate Frontenac's scene; and the awesome Long Sault rapids were not even there, having vanished after the St. Lawrence Seaway was built in the 1950s. In a graphic note in the same volume, Parkman told of how, in the 1870s, from written documents and his personal observations, he was able to locate the main settlement of the Illinois Indians and the nearby site of the fort built by the French in 1682. In the 1870s a railroad ran nearby and the area was settled farmland, but Parkman could still identify such features as woodlands and meadows from two-hundred-year-old documents.

America's historic rural quality was thus still highly visible to artists like Inness and Parkman, and was strongly valued by their forty million countrymen. In general, the population was rapidly growing more dense, nearly doubling from 7.9 people per square mile in 1850 to 15.3 in 1876. In some places it seemed dense indeed. New Jersey in 1870 held over 120 people per square mile, nine times the national average, and even a "western" state like the Illinois that Parkman visited held 46 per square mile. But those future giants, Texas and California, barely qualified as settled: fewer than four people per square mile lived in them. Thus the landscape had changed. But it would presently change much more.

Even in the yet-rural seventies, new sources of national pride were rising, usually in or around the increasingly numerous cities. Americans, especially in the Northeast and Midwest, were turning away from the glories of nature and were beginning to place their ideological bets on their own granite and iron creations. The U.S. Patent Office issued over fourteen thousand patents on new inventions in the Centennial Year, more than in any other year before 1881, and more than three times as many as it issued in 1860. The network of railroads, not only the eye-catching transcontinentals but the more practically important grid of trunk, connecting, and switching lines in the Northeast and Midwest, was the most potent growth factor in the American economy of the late nineteenth century. Even during the depression years of 1874–1878 and 1894–1896, the miles of new track built per year never dipped below fourteen hundred, and in more favorable times, such as 1866–1873, 1879–1893, and 1897–1913, new trackage often exceeded six or seven thousand miles per year. In 1850 the railroads operated about nine thousand miles of track. Snaking westward, crisscrossing each other, the lines extended to 53,000 miles in 1870 and to about 77,000 miles in the Centennial Year. After the depression of the seventies they more than doubled, to 167,000 miles by 1890, and kept increasing. Highways and paved roads were virtually nonexistent, but the railroads were, as the cliché has it, banding the country together with iron. As steam power and ironclad vessels came into more common use, waterways were, more than ever, important as transportation routes. On Western rivers (chiefly the Mississippi-Missouri-Ohio system) alone, upwards of half a million tons of merchant vessels operated during the 1870s, a figure not surpassed in that watershed until 1947. It was the heyday of the river steamboat. And a curious divide was passed sometime in the seventies, one that is surely an index of modernization: in 1870, more than half (51.1 percent) of the horsepower developed in the United States still came from work animals, less than half from mechanical sources. By 1880, about 56 percent of the horsepower was mechanical, the other 44 percent animate.[7] Nearly all of the mechanical power came from steam engines to operate railroads and factories.

The visual changes occurring in the seventies in buildings, bridges, and cityscapes were often quite astonishing to the Americans who were watching them happen. The potency of the steam and railroad revolutions extended to people's imaginations and infected them with an exuberant hyperconfidence displayed preeminently in the High Victorian architecture which began to appear in the late sixties. Cast-iron spires, mansard roofs, abundant pillars, stained glass, and what today seems to be ubiquitous clutter appeared on government buildings, town houses, railway stations, summer cottages, college and university buildings, factories, nearly every kind of structure—except possibly the utilitarian grain elevators of the Midwest. Not quite French, Italian, Romanesque, or Gothic, the best new buildings of the seventies drew consciously on those traditions, and in doing so they have been criticized for being derivative. But they were no more derivative than, and were certainly different from, the Greek-revival classicism of the early and middle years of the nineteenth century. Sometimes, in their search for grandeur, architects arrived only at the grandiose, and instead of elegance arrived only at meretricious gingerbread. Sometimes they achieved beauty and splendor, at least in comparison to the architecture of the past. A. B. Mullett's State-War-Navy building, completed in 1871 just west of the White House in Washington, with its huge mansard roof and cascade of double stone columns, contrasted mightily with the classicism of earlier government buildings. Large and florid, it expressed an American *superbità*, a putting-on-the-map of the three major departments of the government, which it was to house for several decades. For its time it was a new departure not only in style but also in manifesting the grandeur of the state. Decades later, of course, it became almost quaint: the departments simply outgrew it and moved after World War II to the stark masses of Foggy Bottom and the Pentagon, themselves as different in style, and thus in ideas about the federal government, as Mullett's building was in 1871 from the Greek revival architecture of the pre-Civil War years.

The "old" City Hall in Philadelphia, at Broad and Market, was another mansarded marvel, designed in 1869 and built all through the seventies "to be the largest building on the continent, its tower the highest artificial structure in the world." [8] Government buildings were not the only grand creations; James B. Eads' suspension bridge, after seven years in construction, opened in 1874 at St. Louis, its five hundred-foot center span clearing the Mississippi by fifty feet. Made of steel instead of the usual cast iron, and supported by two huge piers sunk to bedrock beneath the water and nearly a hundred feet of shifting sand, it was a triumph of engineering as well as a critical transportation link. Henry Hobson Richardson, the most influential American architect of the seventies and eighties, planned Trinity Church in Boston in 1872 and saw its realization five years later. Dark, massive, and Romanesque, Trinity eschewed mansard roofs and turrets. But it was definitely a Gilded Age product, and through it and other designs, Richardson—who also applied his basic stylistic ideas to private homes and government buildings, just as Giuseppe Verdi composed the same kind of music for opera as for liturgies—laid out new directions to be followed by Louis Sullivan, Burnham and Root, Stanford White, and other leaders of the next architectural generation.

Of course not every architectural structure of the seventies was the work of a Mullett, an Eads, or a Richardson. Factories and the homes of industrial workers were less decorative: their mansard roofs were the product of economy not elegance. The tenement was as characteristic of the seventies as Trinity was, and although tenement styles differed in some respects from city to city, historical accidents like the size and shape of town lots or accessibility to gas and water lines, not architectural considerations, produced most of the differences. Industrialism was, in the abstract and in its material results, something of which Americans were proud; not so its visual byproducts, not now or at the time. A traveler in 1872, crossing the country by rail, wondered

whether this era of industrial activity is an unmixed blessing. Clustered about the mills, with their ugly uniformity of brick and their tall chimneys, [one] will see collections of squalid cottages, or rows of tenement houses redolent of poverty, and disfiguring the landscape like blots upon an otherwise fair page. These are the homes of the operatives. These are the structures, crowded, unventilated, undrained, infectious, which have replaced the cottages in which the labor of seventy years ago found its home.[9]

Visually, at least to some observers, Arcadian America was disappearing. The people of the 1870s were probably just as prone as people at any other time to idealize the past and to indulge in bouts of nostalgia. Their Arcadia never really was. But it seemed to them that it had existed, that the "good old days" of Jeffersonian simplicity were gone. A day such as the Centennial Fourth of July provided an opportunity to reaffirm and express their proud confidence in the American verities.

They also knew that the present and future held things which they did not clearly understand. As Walt Whitman wrote at about that time, in *Song of Myself*, "I do not know what is untried and afterward, But I know it will in its turn prove sufficient, and cannot fail." Neither Whitman nor his contemporaries were always in such an ebullient mood—both he and they could dwell on death, as well as life, and sometimes did—but the difference was that for death they kept a healthy (and well-placed) respect, while for life they held an exuberant affection.

From the hindsight of a hundred years, the American people of the 1870s display perhaps one characteristic above all: their homogeneity. They look alike. They lived with Nature, enjoying and exploiting it; they interpreted their existence, from birth through life to death (and beyond), as individuals and as a collectivity, through an intellectual lattice of Natural Laws; they were confident of the moral superiority of their republican form of government and their democratic traditions. Yet within this unity there was much diversity, a lot of it obvious to the Americans of the 1870s themselves. Whitman listed many of them, also in *Song of Myself:* girls who sing in church, whaling sailors, farmers, quadroons, Indians, women bearing children and women working, statesmen, salesmen, hunters, farmers, many others through time and across space according to the twin spirits of Nature and the Republic: "Seasons pursuing each other the indescribable crowd is gather'd, it is the fourth of Seventh-month, (what salutes of cannon and small arms!)."

There were some other diversities which Whitman chose not to discuss, diversities which sometimes involved rhetorical or even physical conflict. In and around the Centennial year, agreement was scarce between Republicans and Democrats; the Sioux and the Cavalry; greenbackers and gold-standard men; railroads and grain elevator combines versus farmers and small businessmen; Radicals and Redeemers in still a few ex-Confederate states; workers and managers on the Baltimore & Ohio and other railroads; prohibitionists and personal-liberty men in certain states; farmers and cattlemen; freedmen and whites; natives and immigrants. These and other conflicts did exist. But, to say it again, when one looks back upon those Americans of a century ago, the similarities seem more striking than the differences. The people of that time appear to be, to an extent unknown later, of a piece. It does violence to history to blur the differences too greatly, but nonetheless—in the context of what would happen later—there did exist, in the seventies, a degree of unity in such areas as cultural assumptions, ethnicity, distribution of wealth, occupational experience, religious and moral outlook, familiarity with the facts of life and of death, the commonness of moving frequently from place to place, the recent experience of the Civil War, and the honest joy over the Centennial celebrations amidst the general suffering caused by the ongoing economic depression.

Certain predominating cultural assumptions have already been mentioned, especially the pervasive inevitability of nature and the moral and historical virtuousness of the republic. Nature was good, bad, and indifferent, but in any event always there: good because it caused wheat to grow, mares to foal, the seasons to change; because Niagara and the Rockies were part of it; because, many (though not all) believed, God made it; because it operated according to discoverable, predictable laws. It was bad, or at best indifferent, when it manifested itself in grasshopper plagues, floods, earthquakes, economic depressions, or epidemics. At any rate it was unavoidable and everywhere, a context of life which had to be met, largely on its own terms, and coped with. To a people who, for the most part, lived on farms or in country villages, nature was, simply, natural—the natural order of things. In the Centennial Year, the chances were almost three to one that if you were an American you lived on a farm or in a village of less than twenty-five hundred people. And if you were twenty-five years old, or older, in 1876, the chances were six or twelve to one, depending on your age, that you had been born and raised on a farm or in a tiny village where the open countryside was a five-minute walk away.

The overwhelmingly rural character of the American population before 1920, either in actual place of residence or in outlook on life as a result of having lived in a rural setting during one's formative years, is a fact of fundamental consequence in American history. Without understanding it (which is difficult because the metropolitan America of Bicentennial days is so very different), nothing much about the America of the Centennial Year falls into place, neither its social patterns, its economics, its politics, nor its cultural assumptions. Americans of the 1870s, because of their ruralness, confronted nature—physical, biological, meteorological—at almost every turn. They could try to understand its order and obey its laws, and they could even try to control it and use it to some very small degree. But they could not ignore it. Most often, they just assumed that a natural order and natural laws existed everywhere, not just in the physical universe but also in human relations, in how society was organized, in how wealth got distributed, in how governments ought to function with regard to the general welfare. On that point, the best policy seemed to be to leave things alone and "let nature take its course." Nature, pervasive and inevitable in the minds of those rural-bred Americans, provided an ideological backdrop to resistance to change in attitudes about the function of government. The natural law idea was a conservative influence in Americans' minds, and it should be no surprise that it was present, considering that in so many ways the United States was an agrarian, traditional society.

The moral and virtuous character of the American Republic itself was another cultural assumption, very widely held. Undoubtedly there were some unregenerate ex-Confederates in 1876 who disagreed, Indians who had reason to scoff at the idea, many former slaves who already knew that republican morality and virtue would be a long time in coming to them. But for the majority, it was an unquestioned assumption that Thomas Jefferson had been right in 1776 when he wrote that life, liberty, and the pursuit of happiness were self-evident truths, and that, moreover, it was self-evident in 1876 that the American Republic had been for a century preeminent in the world as a place where the rights of man were protected, observed, and flourishing. Time and again, not only in the Fourth of July speeches at the 1876 Centennial, but in sermons, editorials, works of art, popular songs, histories of the United States, or textbooks for schools, these ideas were repeated (and widely believed): That the Republic had been founded in 1776 in the interest of natural human rights. That as the "mother of Republics" America provided to the world a shining example of what political society should be, an example taken up after 1776 by the peoples of Latin America and elsewhere. That divine Providence was especially manifest in this Republic that Lincoln had called "the last, best hope of earth." That Providence would continue to protect it. That one hundred years of existence, as of 1876, had given historical validity to the ideas and hopes of the Founding Fathers.

Republican virtue was an idea both widely held and quickly assimilable. Immigrant societies, marching in parades on the Centennial Fourth, displayed their adoption of patriotic ideals through elaborate historical tableaux. In Indianapolis, a succession of German-American organizations presented onlookers with "The Landing of Columbus," "The Landing of the Pilgrims," Washington and La Fayette, "The Goddess of Liberty," "Columbia" (according to newspaper reports, "in the form of a beautiful blond[e] with erect commanding figure and rich length of golden hair"), a bust of Lincoln, a "band of Indian Warriors, mounted, and in wagons," who "presented the noble red man in his most attractive aspect," "another Columbia in the act of loosing the shackles of a slave who was in every way worthy of a freeman's devotion." [10] The speeches were replete with rhetorical gingerbread, the counterpart in words of turrets, wrought iron, and mansard roofs. But one gets the strong impression from these pictorial and verbal arabesques on the patriotic theme that the basic ideas were believed, cherished, and culturally assumed.

Nature and republican virtue were not the only cultural assumptions made by Americans in the 1870s. There were others, but they and the way in which they changed through the 1880s and into the 1890s, will be discussed in Chapter two. At the time of the celebration of the Centennial, nature and republican virtue were particularly explicit. Despite the social problems that were already beginning to emerge in the 1870s to disturb Americans' certainty, those ideas would continue to affect American thought and action through the rest of the century.

The Americans of the Centennial Year appear unified, in retrospect, in several other ways besides their ideas. They were also ethnically cohesive, a characteristic which, like their shared agrarian origins, underpinned cultural cohesion. Of the forty-six million Americans living in 1876, about 73 percent were native-born whites, the vast majority of "colonial stock"—English, Scotch, Scotch-Irish, Welsh, plus the descendants of the small colonial groups of Dutch, French Huguenots, and Germans. Statistics on immigration and ethnicity during the nineteenth century are not as complete or as accurate as we would like, but on the basis of what we do know, it is safe to say that well over half of the Americans alive at the time of the Centennial were descended exclusively, or nearly so, from Americans alive at the time of the Declaration of Independence. The population of 1876 was also homogeneous in religion: nearly three-fourths of the total population were native-born white, and nearly two-thirds of the total were probably native-born white Protestant or at least nominally Protestant. Since many of the foreign-born and virtually all of the Negro population were Protestant too, the religious homogeneity of Americans was extensive. By no means were all of these people regular church-goers or even formally affiliated with church congregations. But their traditions were Protestant, the Scripture was more or less familiar to them, and moral precepts were agreed upon if not always observed.

The other quarter of the population was almost evenly divided in the 1870s between Negroes and immigrants. Of the roughly six million blacks alive at the time of the Centennial, the great majority were ex-slaves; just over 90 percent lived in the states that had comprised the southern Confederacy; well over 80 percent (probably over 90 percent in the South) lived on farms or in small villages. Movement from place to place, either from the South to some other part of the country or within the South itself, was minimal. For a long list of reasons, such as cultural separation from white America, economic bondage to a piece of land, and lack of education, literacy, and labor skills except for farming, the Negro in the 1870s was not very mobile, nor would he be for another forty years. In effect ghettoized on poor Southern farms, the black people of the United States could be conveniently forgotten about except for a few brief episodes between Reconstruction and World War I, and were. The mainstream of the culture flowed on without them.

Immigrants, on the other hand, were by definition mobile people. Through the 1870s the foreign-born in the United States almost exactly equaled the black population in numbers. But the immigrants were a more diverse collection. Sixty percent of them were members of two ethnic groups of about the same size, the Irish and the Germans, each of which included substantial numbers of Catholics. Canadians accounted for another 10 percent, followed by smaller groups (but each over one hundred thousand by the Census of 1880) of English, Scots, Norwegians, Swedes, French, Austrians, and Chinese. Although immigrants were already grouping in cities—77 percent of the native white population was rural in 1870, but only 47 percent of the foreign-born—the immigrants present in the seventies, compared to those of thirty or forty years later, were much more often farmers. They spread themselves around the then-settled country (especially the Midwest) to a much greater degree, and often, as was the case with the British and Canadians, they merged quickly with the culture of the numerically dominant old-stock majority.

Thus it is accurate, though a little misleading, to say that about 27 percent of the American population at the Centennial were not native stock, but were blacks or immigrants. For neither group presented problems of cultural deviance or conflict in anything like the proportion that their sheer numbers suggested—the six million blacks because of their rural Southern isolation, and many of the six million foreign-born because of their cultural similarity to the native white majority. The United States at the time of the Centennial was, in most important social and cultural respects, ethnically homogeneous: a white, Anglo-Saxon, Protestant society.

Substantial homogeneity also existed with regard to levels of wealth and income and what people did for a living. The "great American fortunes" were yet to be made, while belts of abject poverty were rare. As for the very wealthy, the situation had already changed somewhat from the 1850s, when the John Jacob Astor's reputed fortune of ten million dollars was regarded as quite the largest of any American's; some "fortunes" had been made during the Civil War, as has tended to happen as a result of all modern wars, but the number of dollars was puny by twentieth-century standards. For example, the most successful banker in the country, Jay Cooke of Philadelphia, had profited from the Civil War, and quite legitimately. Cooke's firm had served as the agent of the Union government for the sale of war bonds. Yet the assets of Cooke and his business partner, William Moorhead, were later estimated at about $650,000 at the beginning of the Civil War, and at about $2 million when the war ended:[11] a modest increase by later standards. And these were assets of their company as well as themselves; owners and firm were not clearly separable, which is in itself a commentary on the relatively primeval state of accounting and business practice at that time. Some large fortunes were in the making during the 1870s, to be sure. John D. Rockefeller was already well entrenched in the oil business, the Vanderbilts were running railroads, and Andrew Carnegie was making steel rails; eventually these people, and a few others, would amass fortunes in the hundreds of millions of dollars or even more, greater by two, three, or four orders of magnitude than the fortunes of the few dozen millionaires of the seventies.

But if there were not many people at the extreme of great wealth, there were likewise not many at the other extreme of dire poverty—not, at least, the visible, grinding poverty of urban slums, which would be apparent twenty years later. Certainly there were considerable numbers (we cannot be very accurate now as to just how many) virtually or completely without property and with very low, precarious incomes, especially after the Panic of 1873 and, in the rural Midwest, the grasshopper plague of 1874. But once again one has to remember the rural context of life in the seventies: the large majority of the people lived in small villages or farms, and in such a setting a person at least had some assurance, most of the time, that he or she could eat. Not well, but sufficiently. The farm family mentioned earlier which moved from Massachusetts to the Kansas frontier in 1871 owned probably an average amount of land and personal possessions for families in that part of the country at that time, and they consistently put meat, vegetables, and salads on the table, according to the records we have, and almost certainly picked their own strawberries, apples, plums and cherries as well. That represented a standard of living superior to that of many people, rural or urban, in much of the world today. No doubt it was also superior to that of the "lower class" of farmers in the United States then—that is, the tenants and farm laborers, especially in the South (thus including most of the black population), who did not own land. But even they survived; mass famines have not been a prominent feature of American history.

Sometime during the early 1870s Americans quietly crossed a significant statistical line. For the first time, and permanently, less than half of all the people who earned a living were doing so by farming. A decline in the proportion of the working force engaged in agriculture is a key indicator of economic development, since it implies a shift away from subsistence farming, greater output per farm and farm worker, and more people therefore involved in urban-industrial kinds of work. The crossing of the 50 percent line in the seventies occurred without fanfare for several reasons. In the first place, the proportion of farmers was not much below 50 percent; to be precise, 53 percent of the 12.9 million workers reporting an occupation to the census takers in 1870 said they were farmers, while 49.4 percent of the 17.4 million workers in 1880 reported that they were farmers. Also, many people who still lived in rural environments (farms or small villages) were not actually farmers; "farming" as an occupational category involves fewer people than "rural" as a residential category. The United States was still an agrarian society, by birth and upbringing and it would not be until 1919 that fewer than half the population actually lived in rural settings. But the slight change in what most people did for a living, to just under 50 percent in farming, with corresponding slight increases in the proportion involved in railroading, trade, construction, and especially manufacturing, was a tip-off as to what was coming in the future. The trend away from farming and toward more urban-located occupations would accelerate. From the standpoint of its occupational distribution, as in so many other ways, the decade of the 1870s was the final one for the old order of American society.

Thus the Americans of the 1870s were homogeneous, by future standards, with regard to the ways by which they made a living and the proceeds they received for their work. Again we should not overblur the differences: even in a small town, the social distance between the brick mansion of the leading local banker or merchant or factory owner, with its high windows and wrap-around porch, and the three or four-room cottage of an artisan or factory worker, was much greater than the geographical distance of the two or three blocks which separated them. The social distance between the shack of the Southern black farm laborer and the nearby plantation house was practically the same as it was before the emancipation of the slaves. It was far easier in either case to walk the geographical distance than figuratively to stride across the social distance; horizontal mobility was much easier than vertical mobility. Nonetheless, the facts of economic and social life did not vary much among most rural and small-town Americans.

They also shared certain facts of physical life. In the 1870s, compared to our own day, people were on the average younger, and they were born, married, bore children, and died at faster rates. Mobility of populations can be defined in a number of ways, but in this grimmest of ways—turnover of population by rapid birth and death—mobility was high. The median age of the American people during the seventies was twenty to twenty-one years (and for the black minority, about eighteen). In the 1970s, by comparison, the median age was twenty-eight to twenty-nine. The fact that the median age at the Centennial was eight years younger than at the Bicentennial reflects the presence of many fewer older people and many more children and teenagers, proportionately, at that time. On the average, fewer people lived past middle age, and many more died as infants or children. In the late 1870s, a baby born in Massachusetts (the state which has left us the best vital statistics from the late nineteenth century) could be expected to live forty-two to forty-four years—on raw averages. Today the comparable figure is close to seventy. A person who had survived to the age of twenty, however, could expect, again on raw averages, to live until sixty-two or sixty-three. The problem was to survive the first five years of life, especially the first year. The death rate in Massachusetts in 1875 for infants of under one year was 226.6 per thousand, and for children aged one through four, 74 per thousand. The combined death rate for people under twenty was 322.8 per thousand, nearly one out of three. To bury infants or children was an experience common to most families, and was frequently repeated many times over. It was no different elsewhere in Western civilization; life expectancy and infant mortality rates in England and France were very close to those in America. In Sweden and Denmark people lived a little longer, in Germany and Austria not quite so long.[12] Medical technology, or the lack of it, was at a common level in Europe and America. The most frequent causes of death in Massachusetts in 1875 were tuberculosis, diphtheria, and typhoid, in that order, and no one as yet had any clear idea how to treat them effectively. Thus despite a national birthrate in 1880 of 39.8 per thousand, about the same as India's during the 1960s and over two and one-half times that of the United States in the early 1970s, population turnover was frequent. The median age was fairly young, as is usually the case in "developing" countries, which the United States was then; total population increase was substantial but not overwhelming.[13] Youth, birth, and death, according to the unavoidable dictates of nature, were common features of existence in the United States in the 1870s, facts which one could take for granted or take into account.

In one other important way, Americans shared something at the time of the Centennial, something that also divided them: the recent memory of the Civil War. For those living in Union states, the war had brought good results despite the 140,000 killed in battle, the 224,000 who died of disease or other non-battle causes while in uniform, and the 281,000 wounded; the Union had been reunited, and, as a sort of by-product, slavery had been abolished. Over a million-and-a-half Union veterans were alive at the time of the Centennial, most of them in their thirties, and the occasion was especially gratifying to many of them because of the knowledge that without their handiwork there would have been a much truncated Union to celebrate. Without them the Republic founded in 1776 would not have survived its first century intact. For Southerners, the results of the War had obviously been far less satisfying. Deaths and wounds were even more abundant than among the Yankees; the economic system, agrarian and otherwise, had been disrupted and devastated; and the "redemption" of the ex-Confederate states—that is, the restoration of native white rule in place of the Reconstruction governments—was only just finishing.

At the Centennial, attempts to join hands "across the bloody chasm" did occur, as when the mayor of Montgomery, Alabama, sent a telegram to the president of the Centennial Committee at Philadelphia, saying "the people of Montgomery, the birthplace of the confederate government, through its city council, extend a cordial and fraternal greeting to all the people of the United States, with an earnest prayer for the perpetuation of concord and brotherly feeling throughout our land." [14] The mayor could afford to be generous. In Alabama and six of the ten other former Confederate states, Reconstruction was a thing of the past, as it would become in the remaining four states in the next eight months. The Reconstruction "era," the period in Southern history beginning with the Reconstruction Act of March, 1867, when the right of freedmen to vote was generally protected and when some freedmen actually were elected to office, lasted for as little as two or three years in some states, and in none more than ten. Conservative Democrats, often called "Bourbons" or "Redeemers," returned to control of most Southern state governments in the early 1870s. They did so through the ballot box, as the Radicals' resolve weakened and organizations such as the Ku Klux Klan intimidated many freedmen into staying home on election day. The establishment of Redeemer governments in the Southern states, after the brief interlude of Radical Reconstruction, simply reflected the fact that in national politics Reconstruction was a moribund issue, vivid and compelling though it may have been in 1866 or 1868 or even in 1870. The split in the Republican party in the election of 1872, between the Liberals supporting Greeley and the former Radicals who tended to support President Grant's re-election, further reduced the fervor of Republican reformers with regard to the South. By 1876 it was clear that Radical Reconstruction was dead, even in the three or four ex-Confederate states where some federal troops were still stationed. It was clear to the freedmen; it was clear to the tired remnant of pre-Civil War abolitionists, some of whom had supported the Radical effort for a while and then had grown disillusioned; and it was clear to the white Southern Redeemer Democrats. Their time had come again, and it was to last far longer than the "era" of Radical Reconstruction. So, as the mayor of Montgomery stated, concord and brotherly love could prevail. The nation had indeed been reunited.

To recapitulate for a moment. The festive celebrations of the Centennial Fourth were general throughout the country, even touching the recently defeated Confederate states, and by all odds the celebrating and the patriotic rhetoric were heartfelt. Whitman's *Song of Myself* could have been entitled, more prosaically, "Song of Myself and all other Americans and we are metaphysically one and unique." Whitman was not always so exuberantly happy—his *Democratic Vistas* of 1871 is full of dourness and doubts about the present and future state of American democracy—nor were those other Americans for whom he tried to be the poetic exemplar. Yet he was in some sense correct in asserting that, happy or fretful, Americans exhibited a kind of oneness. Maybe not his transcendental kind of oneness, but at least a degree of unity in cultural assumptions (Nature, the Republic), ethnic and religious background, ruralness, rough equality in worldly possessions, familiarity with the uncertainties of life and death, and fresh memory of the Civil War whose outcome had ratified that Union created in 1776 on behalf of the unalienable and self-evident rights of Man.

On these ideas and experiences there was some agreement in 1876, as there was on the notion that July 4 of that year was a very special occasion. There was also agreement that it was definitely a holiday, a punctuation in what was "hard times yesterday, and will be to-morrow." Hard times indeed; and mean and dangerous times. The same newspapers that described the Centennial festivities so proudly also reported that in late June, near the Little Big

Horn River in Montana, Major General George Armstrong Custer and a sizable detachment of the U.S. Seventh Cavalry had been wiped out by the Sioux under Crazy Horse and Sitting Bull.[15] The Sioux victory was taken as a major defeat by the United States, the most depressing of over two hundred military engagements against the Indians during the Grant administration. Despite President Grant's good intentions with regard to Indian affairs, the Army counterattacked, and the decisive U.S. victory on the Northern plains took place in the closing months of Grant's Presidency.[16]

Another news story on July 4, 1876, disclosed that the Chicago Common Council had been forced to terminate the Boards of Health and Public Works of the city because they were costing $2 million more than expected tax revenue. A classified advertisement announced that Drs. Johnson and Laubach, of the "American Opium Institute," would "cure the opium habit in ten days," with "no charge whatever until the patient says he is cured." Imports of crude opium to the United States rose rapidly during the seventies, with imported morphine quickly following.[17] Another story reported civil disorder: a horde of two hundred "tramps" had infested Milwood, Illinois, thirty miles south of Springfield, and "sundry depredations have been committed at various points," including a passenger train wrecked because a switch was thrown the wrong way. "The train men on the Toledo, Wabash, and Western railroad," said the newspapers, "are supplied with arms, and the company guarantees the legal expenses of defending any of its employees who are obliged to use force in defending the property of the company against the tramps. There is no doubt that some vigorous action is necessary to protect farm houses, small villages and railroad trains against this late development of villainy."

In still other ways the Centennial celebrations were a diversion from an otherwise unprepossessing national scene. Party politics proceeded in a vigorous if tawdry way in that election year. The Republicans, with the Liberalism of 1872 dead and the Radical Reconstruction of the late sixties even deader, were forced to give attention to the need for a "reform" candidate because the scandals of the Grant administration would not down. They nominated the virtuous and empty-headed governor of Ohio, Rutherford B.

Hayes, who subsequently would be remembered for two acts of his Presidency: allowing his wife to abolish alcoholic drinks in favor of lemonade at White House functions, and vetoing the only significant piece of legislation which a divided Congress put before him in his four years, the Bland-Allison Act of 1878. In the periodic rankings which historians make of presidential performances, Hayes has not received his due: he was awful. The Democrats, on the other hand, smelled victory in 1876. In 1874 they had won control of the U.S. House of Representatives for the first time since before the Civil War, as a consequence of Republican disarray over monetary policy and the widespread disgruntlement over "Grantism"; they did not lack for issues. They nominated Samuel J. Tilden, governor of New York and hero of the successful prosecution of the Tammany Hall boodler, William M. "Boss" Tweed. Some months later the irony became apparent that Tilden and Hayes, the two paragons, had headed the only presidential election in American history in which the will of the voters was almost certainly thwarted by outright vote fraud.[18] The ideals of the Centennial were seldom less manifest.

Congress, despite the upcoming campaign, remained in session until mid-August, bedeviled by unusually sweltering Washington weather and by debate over a new and compelling issue, the question of whether and how to employ silver in the American currency system. The intensely divisive silver question already had a substantial history, though most of it had happened within the closed chambers of Congress and the Treasury. From the summer of 1876 and for another twenty years, until the climactic Bryan-McKinley presidential campaign of 1896, it remained a perennial and intractable problem in American politics. The precise questions which Congress argued about in the summer of 1876 were whether to repeal the Specie Resumption Act of January, 1875, which had promised (among other things) that United States notes ("greenbacks") would again become fully convertible with gold in January, 1879—in other words, a resumption for practical purposes of the pre-Civil War gold standard—and whether to regard the silver dollar once more as a standard of value, as it had been from 1792 until passage of the Coinage Act of 1873, a law which silverites were just beginning to call the "Crime of '73." These two interrelated questions were, on their face, bloodless and technical, and certainly seem so now. But as was generally the case with questions of public finance in the late nineteenth century, the actual bills before Congress reflected and represented a Byzantine compound of ideas, attitudes, and economic interests. Was bimetallism (the use of gold and silver simultaneously as monetary standards) theoretically sound or should the United States emulate Britain and use the gold standard solely? Would greenbacks work? Would not specie resumption mean a windfall for creditors? Would not silver dollars allow debtors to repay their bills on the cheap? Would not New England and the Middle States make colonies of the West and South through specie resumption and the gold standard? Which standard was *honest* and *moral?*

Homogeneity was certainly not characteristic of Americans when it came to the money question. The emotion with which congressmen in 1876 and later argued their conflicting views on silver and specie resumption derived from their much deeper disagreements over the correct relations of social and economic groups; whether economic progress ought to be encouraged for farmers, industrial workers, or manufacturers; whether banking and other capitalist elites would be subsidized and entrenched by "sound money" (i.e., the gold standard and deflation); and whether bimetallism, the gold standard, and/or greenbacks would best achieve and perpetuate such shared American values as democracy and individualism. The money question was not the only serious issue which reflected and demonstrated social tensions, and surely public issues always do to some extent. But on no other question in politics between 1870 and the early 1900s were moral overtones so resonant, the perceived consequences so great, and the argumentation so rigid.[19]

Thus the festive celebration of the Fourth of July, 1876, had a context. That context included many elements of relative homogeneity, already described. But it also included elements of unhappiness and conflict, among them unsatisfactory relations between whites and Indians; a disastrously poor resolution of the problems of the freedmen, as a result of the retreat from Reconstruction both by Northern Radicals with dwindling regret and by Southern Redeemers with dreadful alacrity; reflections of some degree of

drug abuse; instances of semi-organized violence against persons and property, both by "tramps" and by the vigilantes encouraged by property interests to attack them; political corruption, not only in executive agencies, tarnishing the mighty figure of General Grant, but in the presidential election of 1876; and finally, profound disagreement over the future shape of society and the proper and moral relations of social groups, disagreement which had its specific focus in debates over the money question.

The context of the Centennial included one other critical element, one whose effects were shared by nearly all Americans, and which at the same time divided them. This element was the economic depression of the 1870s. It was the first general depression since before the Civil War, the longest since that of 1837–1841, and the first phase of a worldwide deflationary slump which lasted from 1873 until 1897 and which from then on, until the greater disaster of 1929–1941, was called "the Great Depression." In the United States this first phase lasted from the fall of 1873 until the closing months of 1878. Financial panics, and ensuing depressions lasting four or five years, had struck in 1819, again in 1837, again in 1857 (with depression foreshortened slightly by the onset of the Civil War in 1861), then in 1873. There would be another in 1893. Economic developments displayed a cyclical pattern, or more accurately a spiral pattern, since growth did take place and the size and complexity of the economy was greater at the end of each cycle of (roughly) twenty years. The segments of these cycles were, at some point, a few years of prosperity when investment, construction, employment, and trade proceeded at high rates and without much inflation; then an inflationary heating up of the economy and increasing skittishness on the part of investors, merchants, and bank depositors; then the abrupt collapse of one or several major banks or trading firms or a commodity market—a "panic"; then depression; then after three to five years a gradual return of a measure of confidence and revival of trade; and then prosperity again.

These cycles of prosperity-inflation-panic-depression-recovery-prosperity took about twenty years, except when some cataclysm with profound economic consequences, such as the Civil War, telescoped the process by a few years. The Civil War, like the two world wars fifty and eighty years later, pulled the economy rapidly out of depression and shortened the usual recovery stage, and then produced a few years of very vigorous and highly inflationary activity centering on high demand for goods and services with which to carry on the war. A recession from wartime inflation lasted for three to four years after the end of hostilities (as would also happen in 1919–1923 and 1945–1949), gradually settling in 1869 and 1870 into fairly widespread stability and prosperity involving solid investment and economic growth.

That growth was manifested in such activities as the long cattle drives from Texas to Kansas (1866–1873), intensive mining development in Nevada and elsewhere in the Mountain states and territories, expanded foreign trade, and the advance of farming settlements into the Great Plains. But by all odds the most important activity, in dollar terms, was a surge of railroad building. The nation's first transcontinental railroad, the Union Pacific-Central Pacific, was completed in 1869, and investors and entrepreneurs were already thinking of building other routes. Railroad building required federal aid, which the government willingly provided in the form of land grants from the public domain, and it also required cash. The cash was to come from the sale of bonds by investment banks. Investment banks would normally underwrite the bonds of the railroads in the expectation of selling the bonds at a profit to domestic and foreign investors. The banks might also, if they wanted to or thought they had to, lend funds directly to the railroads in anticipation of selling the bonds. Such cash advances had the advantage of speeding up railroad construction and thus bringing closer the date when the newly built railroad would start earning money out of freight and passenger operations and the sale of its land-grant dowry to settlers. It also had the potential disadvantage and danger of tying up the funds of the bank, and funds of the bank's commercial depositors, too tightly in the railroad company. (A large bank could carry on, quite legally, both investment and commercial functions; the two were not required to be separate until the Banking Act of 1933.)

Precisely these dangers overtook Jay Cooke & Co. of Philadelphia, regarded then as the foremost banking house in the United States. Cooke had become interested in 1869 in financing the

Northern Pacific Railroad, a new transcontinental which would open up the whole Northwest from Minnesota to Puget Sound. But the vision of 1869 became a nightmare by 1873. The inflationary economy caused skittishness among potential buyers of railroad bonds. Cooke's vaults remained crammed with unsold Northern Pacific securities, and short of the cash needed to meet depositors' demands. Jay Cooke & Co. closed its doors on the morning of September 18. The demise of Cooke's banking house meant the death of many other hitherto solid and respected firms which were tied to it financially, and it meant a vital blow to business confidence. The Panic of 1873, touched off by Cooke's failure, precipitated the depression which lasted for another five years until late 1878.

The story was not simply an economic tale of the overenthusiastic misjudgment of Jay Cooke, or the failure of businessmen and economic theorists at that time to discern and give heed to cyclical patterns, or the dangers of a banking system which allowed investment and commercial functions to be intermingled. These were all part of it. But the episode also carried a moral and ideological lesson: the panic and depression were perceived as another example of the inexorability of natural laws in human affairs. After all, Cooke's bank was headed by a thoroughly moral man who had carried on the patriotic work of keeping the Union Treasury going through the traumatic emergency of the Civil War; who had promoted American economic progress through railroad building, the grandest means then available; and who had always tithed a tenth part of his earnings even in the worst of times. Cooke was no get-rich-quick speculating buccaneer like Jim Fisk and Jay Gould, who cornered the gold market in 1869 and departed hastily with their own selfish profits while the markets crashed behind them.[20] If disaster could strike Cooke, whom the Lord had, and apparently should have, rewarded, who might it not strike?

Financial hardship or outright disaster did strike many people besides Cooke between 1873 and 1879, and unfortunately the worst effects of the depression of the seventies were visited upon those least able to withstand them. The economic events of the 1870s fortified the prevailing conviction of the time that panics and depressions, like tornadoes or crop failures, were natural and thus inescapable calamities. Nature behaved capriciously and indifferently, and nothing much could be done about it. Moreover, the depression of the 1870s was felt in such a peculiar way as to disguise the crisis and its lessons for some, yet to make it especially hard on others. Retained profits and dividends were not greatly disturbed; total national output in mining, manufacturing, and agriculture actually increased rather than decreased; the Gross National Product, as reconstructed for the period, shows that growth through the seventies was higher (about 5.5 percent per year) than it would be in the eighties or nineties; the balance of international trade improved, since the depression was less severe in the United States than it was in other countries, notably Britain, the leading economic power at the time; and the currency continued to stabilize, eventually allowing specie payments to be resumed as planned in January, 1879. Consequently, two key groups, capitalists (people with money to invest) and economic policy-makers in government, although they were certainly aware that business conditions were not favorable, could take the view that the depression was not all that bad in certain important respects, and that it was actually having a desirable effect in shaking out reprehensible tendencies toward speculation and overspending that had, in their view, infected much of the public during the Civil War and postwar years.

In the meantime, however, many members of the middle and lower economic classes were suffering. Manufacturing production in 1876 was off 10 percent from 1872, and the rate of unemployment in 1876 was off 12 to 14 percent. Railroad workers suffered pay cuts and extensions in working hours while roads kept stockholders' dividends steady, a combination of practices which precipitated widespread strikes and violence in 1877. For the near-majority of the working force who were farmers, the seventies brought increases in output but falling prices for livestock, corn, wheat, and cotton worst of all, and in the Midwest farmers were already buckling under the burdens of drought and grasshoppers. Thus the impact of the depression of the 1870s was oddly distributed. Consequently, those who were in a position to make economic decisions for the society did not gain from the depression the knowledge that productivity and wealth were becoming spread about in a dangerously uneven way. On the other hand, for farmers and industrial workers the experience of the depression was direct indeed.[21]

The depression of 1873–1878, like other panics and depressions in American history, was a catalyst of certain social and economic changes, and intensified and made other changes more visible. Because it was so selective in its effects, its lessons were lost on important segments of the public who ought to have learned them if the changes then taking place were to be well understood and coped with. But they were not; rich and poor alike simply waited for a return of "good times," the restoration of the tranquil agrarian America of predepression days, including the patterns of thought which surfaced during the brief respite of the Centennial celebrations of July 1876. The Centennial Fourth was a day of patriotic reaffirmation, and quite properly so. It was not an occasion for pointing out, much less harping upon, the changes and problems taking place within the context of those depression years. Unfortunately, however, those problems and changes remained unrecognized and ignored on other days as well. The point which was generally missed was that the decade of the 1870s was in important respects the last of that older America that was so homogeneous in its rural-centered culture, and the first of a newer kind of society whose thrust and whose problems centered around cities, industry, different types of people, and unfamiliar ideas. If the magnitude of the changes already underway in the seventies had been recognized by Americans at the time of the Centennial they might have despaired. As it happened, the depression of the seventies was simply endured, and the lessons it involved were mostly unlearned. The experience was to be repeated in harsher and more threatening terms twenty years later, when panic and depression returned in the 1890s.

What were some of these crucial and largely unrecognized changes? Several were particularly important; some have already been touched on in this discussion. The demographic and economic fact that sometime during the decade farmers ceased to be a majority of the gainfully employed was important in itself and also was symptomatic of coming changes in cultural as well as occupational patterns. It would be another forty years before any other single occupational group (factory workers, as it happened) outnumbered farmers, and before more Americans lived in towns and cities rather than on farms and in country villages. Rural aspects of life still dominated. Yet a different social order was in the offing, indicated not only because farmers were outnumbered by other workers for the first time, but also because manufacturing began to generate, in the seventies, a larger share of national income and national product than agriculture did. Also, the minority of the population living in towns and cities (over 12 percent of the total lived in cities of a hundred thousand or more in 1880), directly experiencing urban life, was growing more rapidly than the rural population, even in the depressed seventies. The dynamics of further urbanization were already almost irreversible. Fourteen cities each contained over a hundred thousand people in 1870, six more by the Census of 1880. Eighteen of these twenty cities were located in the Northeast and North Central states, which also contained almost two-thirds of the labor force and three-fourths of the national income[22]; only one metropolitan city had emerged in the West (San Francisco), and only one in the South (New Orleans). Over eight hundred thousand people lived in Philadelphia when the Centennial was headquartered there, and New York and Brooklyn held about a million and a half. Almost five hundred cities of five thousand or more were scattered across the country, mostly in the Northeast and Midwest, in 1880; urbanism was not completely exotic. By 1890 the proportion of urban to rural population was about the same in the United States as it was in France; less than in Britain or Germany; more than in Scandinavia, Ireland, Austria, or Russia.[23] And in the rough parallelogram whose outer points were St. Louis, Milwaukee, Boston, and Washington, the number of urban places and the proportion of people living in them were not greatly different from the urban-industrial parts of Britain and Germany, which, together with France and the United States, were the leading "developed countries" of the late nineteenth century—except that in the United States the land area and numbers of people were larger. The demographic and economic facts of the 1870s already portended the world leadership which came within the next twenty-five years. The American people, still so rural in so many ways at the time of the Centennial, were creating for themselves an urban-industrial country, especially in the Northeast and the older Middle West, without fully understanding what they were doing or how they were supposed to live with it and take their place among other industrialized nations.

Another novelty of the seventies involved problems of law and order. Disorder and violence did not originate in the seventies, to be sure; witness the earlier record of chronic wars and skirmishes with Indian tribes, rioting (or worse) over taxation and local government (the Regulator movement, the Whiskey Rebellion, Shays' Rebellion, the Dorr Rebellion), street gangs in New York and elsewhere, slave uprisings such as Nat Turner's in 1831, and of course the Civil War itself. But the seventies brought some new twists to the record of violence, in addition to the Seventh Cavalry's difficulties with the Sioux, or the gunfight at the OK Corral several years later. The appearance of railroad tramps during the depression has already been mentioned. They came back in greater numbers in the 1890s, and in 1893 the Populist governor of Kansas, Lorenzo D. Lewelling, was damned as an anarchist for instructing law enforcement officers to treat them sympathetically as unwillingly unemployed people. Armies of the unemployed, like Jacob Coxey's in 1894 or the bonus marchers of 1932, did not manifest themselves in the seventies, but significant numbers of tramps, more or less violent (or in any event in conflict with established authority and property owners), did begin to appear in the seventies—because it was during that decade that the economy for the first time was undergoing a depression that produced enough industrial unemployment to produce roving bands of the jobless.

Another kind of violence was distinctly modern: drawn battles between labor and capital, workers and established authority. A shock passed over the nation in the wake of the Great Railway Strike of 1877, the first nationwide labor battle, and indeed the first major occasion when, as later became habitual, the interests of capital and labor were regarded by each side and many other people as basically hostile rather than harmonious. When the strike of 1877 erupted at Pittsburgh, and state militia fired into a crowd, killing more than fifty people, the response of much of the press around the country was to approve. They said that though armed force was sometimes unfortunate in its effects, it was the only way to deal with threats to private property. Thus the gut reaction was to nail down even more tightly the tops of industrial powder kegs; and they blew off later at Homestead in 1892, at Pullman in 1894, and again and again down into the twentieth century.

Technological change was also, in itself, not new on the American scene, but certain kinds took place in the seventies which were critical to the development of the United States as an urban-industrial society. Some are so obviously important as to need no comment: Bell's telephone (1876) and Edison's phonograph (1877) and incandescent light (1879). But Edison also patented the stock ticker in 1870, Bissell patented the humble carpet sweeper in 1876, and others brought forth the arc light and the cash register in 1879. Clarence Scholes produced a workable typewriter in the early seventies, and later in the decade, after the depression eased, typewriters promoted significant changes in governmental and business office practices and hastened the employment of women in clerical jobs outside the home. Developments in refining, mining, metallurgy, and civil engineering allowed gold and silver to be brought to market far more quickly than ever before, and were one reason why the reopening of Nevada's Comstock Lode in 1873, bringing with it the prospect of floods of silver inundating the U.S. Mint, contributed to the fright of "sound money" advocates and to the attractiveness to reflationists of silver dollars rather than greenbacks. The introduction of the Bessemer-Kelly process in steel making, followed soon after by the use of the open hearth method, provoked an extremely sharp rise in the average size and total output of steel and iron companies. The average size of railroad firms rose markedly through developments in business practice and company organization, itself a kind of technology; entrepreneurs like Commodore Vanderbilt of the New York Central and J. Edgar Thomson of the Pennsylvania and others were creating transcontinentals, trunk lines, and the consolidation of appurtenances such as switching yards, round houses, and freight and passenger terminals.

The seventies produced another characteristic of an industrializing society: despite the depression, ratios between workers and

managers continued to increase in the direction of mass employment. In the 1860s, the East North Central states (Ohio, Indiana,
Illinois, Michigan, Wisconsin) saw a doubling or tripling of the
number of manufacturing establishments, and a similar rate of
increase in numbers of workers and in the amounts of capital
invested. In the 1870s, on the other hand, the number of
establishments actually declined, while invested capital and numbers of workers continued to rise. The average size of firms, and the
employee-to-employer ratio within firms, were growing. This
pattern was not simply a result of the depression, for it continued
into the relatively prosperous 1880s. The average number of
workers per manufacturing establishment was still only six people
in 1880, which basically fits the picture of an agrarian and
small-firm economy. Nonetheless, more and more people were
becoming involved in mass-employment situations, with dozens or
hundreds of workers in one shop or factory. In Indiana in 1880, the
state's 251 furniture makers employed, on the average, 11 workers;
the 4 box makers, 15; the 44 carriage builders, 41; the 120
foundries, 33; the 25 slaughterhouses, 72; the 12 iron and steel
makers, 167; the 4 cotton textile factories, 175; the 4 glassmakers,
200; the 3 makers of sewing machine cases, 333; and the 5 railroad
and streetcar shops, an average of 502. For an increasing number
of workers, then, a face-to-face relationship with the employer,
which is one measure of social and economic equality, no longer
existed. Individual employment was shifting toward collective
employment. But it would be many decades, in mass production
industries, before individual bargaining would be replaced by
collective bargaining. Partly as a result of the lack of unions and
collective bargaining, the average annual earnings of factory
workers in 1890 were $412 for men and $209 for women, figures
which barely kept up with increases in value of output. There is not
much mystery why a "labor question" or "labor problem" became
very evident and troublesome in American society.[24]

Another change occurring in the seventies was to a large extent
a product of the one just mentioned, and was catalyzed by the
depression. The self-images of farmers, workers, and manufacturers
was shifting. As we have seen, employee-employer ratios were
growing, agriculture was declining in relative strength in the labor

force and in its share of national income, workers (both on farms and elsewhere) felt with some justification that they were not getting their fair share of the new wealth they were helping to create. People who had capital (or who thought they were middle-class) reacted with discomfort to farmer-labor unrest, and with horror to episodes like the Pittsburgh railroad riot in 1877. For all of these reasons, an earlier sense of harmony among economic and social classes disappeared. A sense of a community of "producers," who included practically everybody who made some social or economic contribution, gave way to expressions of deep hostility between debtors and creditors, capitalists and workers, rich and poor. This development appeared very noticeably during the depression of the seventies, and it would continue for decades beyond. Undeniably the earlier harmony was more rhetorical than real, but the depression of the seventies revealed the hollowness of the producer ideal.

Thus American society, vigorous and homogeneous in so many ways, was undergoing major and unsettling changes. The Republic, so recently patched together after the appalling schism of Civil War, was entering the "Great Depression" of the late nineteenth century, affecting the industrialized countries of western Europe as well as North America. Industrialization and urbanization, those twin processes of radical social change, were already operating to corrode America's traditional agrarianism. The problems were great, and the lack of understanding of them and lack of tools with which to deal with them were greater. American society in the seventies possessed neither the ideological nor the institutional tools to cope with these changes. No apposite theory of large-scale enterprise, of decent labor-capital relations in mass employment settings, or of equitable wealth distribution, then existed. The prevailing attitude toward the functions of government was one of "positive negativism," the positive, structured relief that government activity to adjust social and economic imbalances should be minimal. Voluntary institutions were also ill-equipped to deal with social change. The political parties, despite the intense loyalties which they generated, were not able to absorb new programs or ideas easily; the Democratic party was even more averse to activism in government than the Republican. The churches were divided on many doctrinal and social issues, and on balance they reinforced prevailing ideas and thus helped resist rather than ease the understanding of social change. Public education was not a promising solution; elementary schooling was as yet not compulsory or even widespread in many areas, and secondary education was rare (only in 1874, in a court decision involving Kalamazoo, Michigan, had the law clearly stated that tax money could be spent on high schools, since such a tiny minority of the public used them).

The depression drew to a close in late 1878 and early 1879, gradually thawing into the recovery phase of a typical nineteenth-century business cycle. But the problems catalyzed and revealed by the depression were to recur again, twenty years older and tougher, in the depression of 1893–1897. By then the problems of the seventies were compounded by fears about the shifting sources of immigration, by the end of the frontier, by further urban and technological change and consequent social dislocations, and by more outbreaks of violence and disorder in every region of the country. The Centennial decade was thus a preview and a warning of an impending crisis in American culture. The warning was not heeded, but only temporized with. The 1870s, Janus-like, looked backward from the occasion of the Centennial over a history of a rural-oriented society proud of the development and survival of its republican virtue, and looked forward to a future fraught with radical social change which was scarcely understood or even recognized. As things happened through the 1880s and 1890s, the problems got worse before they got better.

2

Values and Institutions,
1878-1893

The years between the end of the depression of the seventies and the Panic of 1893 can be thought of, in briefest terms, as a time when social and economic changes already emergent in the seventies continued rapidly and pervasively in all parts of the country (except the still-lagging South), and also as a time when ideas and institutions failed to acknowledge or interpret such changes (with certain exceptions to be noted). In short, Americans were revising their social existence but remained unwilling to revise their intellectual existence. This incongruity grew more serious during this fifteen-year period; by the middle and late nineties, intensified by another major depression, the gap between the two kinds of existence produced a cultural crisis.

To understand how this predicament developed, it will be useful to look at patterns of American ideas and institutions between the two late-nineteenth-century depressions, and what happened to those ideas and institutions. In fact not that much did happen; the main point is that ideas and institutions functioned conservatively. The areas that need to be examined are, first, ideas about government, politics, and political economy; second, ideas and attitudes concerning social interaction and social structure; third, two major institutions—the churches and education—which theoretically ought to have midwifed ideological change but in general did not; fourth, the beginnings of the process by which the prevailing conservative attitudes of the Gilded Age were to be subverted.

First, government and the political order. As was stated earlier, the prevailing orthodoxy, most eloquently put by Liberal Republicans, genteel reformers, and mugwumps, was a positive belief in negativism. This negativism was differently expressed and acted upon by various groups and political parties across time, and there were significant exceptions made to it, but as a generalized ideal it was very widely held. Americans would readily agree, as they did at the time of the Centennial celebrations, that they were part of a republic, indivisible, with liberty and justice for all. But the indivisibility was cultural, symbolic, and almost transcendental. It certainly did not mean that Americans were interacting parts of a large community or collectivity. The government, as the Constitution said, was supposed to promote the general welfare, but the instances when it was to do so were rare and almost gentle. Critics and watchdogs of government, and they were many, possessed a chronic fear that government, especially federal, would promote the specific welfare rather than the general—through grants of land to the railroads, easy homestead terms, protective tariffs, or various forms of outright corruption at the state and local level. The effect of the criticism and watchdogging was that government really did not do much about either kind of welfare, general or specific. And in a society which had consisted mainly of farms and country villages inhabited by people accustomed to acting more or less self-sufficiently, an activist central government was just not necessary. There was not much that such a government could do for the average (i.e. rural) American, so it seemed; at any rate, whatever it could do would not be worth the risk that an expanded government would become despotic, like George III's did just before the American Revolution.

For practical reasons such as these, the ideal of laissez faire became orthodox in American thinking about government in the latter half of the nineteenth century. To be sure, there were many exceptions to the ideal, even with regard to a federal government. In 1871 that government consisted of 6,200 people, from President Grant to janitors, in Washington itself, about 37,000 postmasters scattered across the country, and a few thousand others. The ratio of federal civilian employees to the whole population was about 0.12 percent in 1871. (In 1971 it was about 1.25 percent, ten times the proportion.) In the 1870s and 1880s the federal government ran a postal service. It collected customs duties and some excise taxes and used the money to pay the interest on Civil War debts and to maintain a minuscule army and navy and bureaucracy. It supported lighthouses and other aids to navigation, and occasionally dredged rivers and harbors. It fought Indians and maintained trading posts, army bases, and travel routes in the West. It promoted the building of railroads, especially the transcontinentals, by making grants of land from the public domain. It provided tariff legislation to allow manufacturing to develop and, as the argument went, to insure that the workingman would enjoy secure employment. It continued to post troops in some states as late as 1877 for purposes of "Reconstruction." And of course it carried on its constitutional obligations such as conducting foreign affairs and coining money.

It was not wholly inactive. Indeed it grew rather substantially, faster than the general population, in the late nineteenth century: the 51,000 civilian government workers of 1871 expanded to 100,000 in 1881, 157,000 in 1891, and 239,000 in 1901. But throughout the period, half to two-thirds were local postmasters or post office workers, and even the "swollen" figure for 1901 included only 28,000 in Washington itself.[1] The laissez faire ideal could still be held to sincerely; the exceptions were not significant enough to make it hypocritical. And the ideal was held with tenacity, because it fit neatly with other realities and attitudes. As already mentioned, the rural character of the population, and the traditional fear of despotic central government (a key idea, after all, in the Declaration of Independence and the American Revolution), underpinned it. In addition, the prevailing conviction that natural laws existed, not just in physics or farming but in social and political affairs, bolstered the laissez faire concept for government: the basic idea was to let natural laws operate freely. Governments should stay out of the way and should confine their activities to removing hindrances to the operation of those laws, rather than to taking positive action. Americans were deep believers (though in a variety of ways in practice) in personal liberty, the right of a man (at least if white and over twenty-one) to go to heaven or hell in his own way, without governments telling him what to do, in the form of taxation, conscription, regulation of his business affairs, or whatever. The federal government was seldom any direct threat to personal liberty in the late nineteenth century, limited as it was by strict-constructionist interpretations of the Constitution and its Amendments. Most Americans were happy to keep it that way. An activist federal government was something which they neither needed nor wanted.

The term "government" then, before, and since conjured up something to be feared and watched, and meant to many minds the federal government rather than state and local government. The attitude toward state and local government was not so suspiciously anarchistic. The states and municipalities possessed a measure of police power and regulatory authority by long legal tradition and practice. They were considered closer to, and more directly responsible to, the people, and thus could be trusted to make such laws as were necessary to raise taxes, promote enterprise, root out criminality, provide for public education, take care of the indigent or insane, and maintain public works. The degree to which these functions were carried out, if at all, varied greatly from place to place and state to state, but in general the expectation existed that a certain amount of government activity had to take place, most of it at the state and local levels. At all levels, however, the ideal was for governments to leave people alone as far as possible, because the individual citizen could and should be left to his own devices. With very rare exceptions[2] it was considered abhorrent for governments either by executive or legislative action to intervene directly on behalf of specific groups within society.

Countercurrents to the prevailing negativism existed in American social philosophy, and would help justify certain incursions of federal and state governments into promotional or regulatory activity from the seventies into the nineties. One such countercurrent was the desirability of "progress," especially economic progress, or growth. This was expected to occur in any event through the working of the natural laws of political economy, but there was no harm, some people (frequently Republicans) thought, in abetting progress by devices such as protective tariffs or aid to internal improvements such as railroads. In the years immediately following the Civil War, the point of view that governments (including the federal government) could justifiably take an active role in promoting enterprise, or even in regulating social patterns to some extent, attracted many members of the Radical wing of the Republican party more than any other political faction. As the inheritors of the activism of Alexander Hamilton and Henry Clay, as members of the party which originated in the antislavery movement of the 1850s, these Republicans accepted, on some issues, a reformist role by government. Of all the major political groups in the country, they and their successors in the Republican party through the eighties and into the nineties were least attached to the strict theory of laissez faire. Liberal Republicans and the mugwumps of the eighties, and most Democrats as heirs of Jefferson and Jackson, were stricter negativists from ideology or demographic background or both.

To the fondness for progress as an underpinning for government action should be added the expectation of even-handedness, justice, and the "equal protection of the laws." In itself this notion presented no logical conflict with a dislike of government activism, but it occasionally (and increasingly) took the form of opposition to private monopoly. When this happened the results were forays by government into the area of regulation, the outstanding examples in the period being the Granger laws of 1870–1871 in Illinois and other upper Mississippi Valley states, to regulate railroads and grain elevators, and at the federal level the Interstate Commerce Act of 1887 and Sherman Anti-Trust Act of 1890. Support for regulation was sporadic, but when it did emerge, it came from elements within both the Democratic and Republican parties and represented the feelings, to a considerable extent, of businessmen who sought fair dealing in their practical competitive lives rather than fidelity to abstract laissez faire theory.[3]

Another exception to the prevailing negativism toward government activity came from those people who sought legislation to purify government itself, notably through civil service laws, and to cleanse and further homogenize American society. They included the kind of people who began or joined the Liberal Republican movement in 1872 partly in revulsion to the scandals within the Grant administration, partly from lack of enthusiasm toward Radical Reconstruction, and for other reasons; they were the most outspoken faction in favor of laissez faire economics. In the seventies and early eighties they backed civil service reform, rejoiced in the passage of the Pendleton Act in 1883, and were disappointed that it did not change the political world. Some of them constituted the "mugwumps" of 1884, Republicans who refused to support James G. Blaine's presidential candidacy, and were in general pleased with Grover Cleveland's exemplification, much more than any Republican president of the time, of the negative philosophy of government. But they also worried that American society was admitting too many foreigners and foreign ideas: they supported the restriction of immigration, including the Chinese Exclusion Act of 1882, the first general law to keep a specific national or racial group out of the country. At the state level such people, usually attached to the Republican party, sought legislation to restrict or prohibit the sale of alcoholic beverages on Sundays, or if possible other times, and legislation to restrict the role of nonpublic schools, particularly if the language of instruction was other than English. To be sure, there were significant differences between Eastern mugwumps and Midwestern moralists, but both shared a willingness to use government as an instrument of moral control, despite their attachment to a generally negativist philosophy of government.

As this discussion implies, there were probably as many interpretations of what has been loosely called the laissez faire attitude as there were factions within, and near to, the two major political parties. But few disagreed systematically with the general proposition that governments should function narrowly and minimally. Greenbackers and Greenback-Nationalists from the late seventies through the eighties, and the Alliancemen and Populists of the late eighties and early nineties, did develop a program involving an expanded role for the federal government, a program which many of them grounded on a thorough critique of the root assumptions of laissez faire political economy. But these people were exceptions. The prevailing orthodoxy as to the role of government, though of course applied differently by various groups at given times on given issues, was minimalist. The laws of nature, not the laws of men, would rule most effectively. That notion held without marked dissent (except from many Populists) through the eighties and into the nineties. It was not to change until enough people had undergone something different from the traditional rural experience and enough nongovernmental organizations of magnitude had come into being and had begun to threaten the social order, and until a group of social thinkers had begun to provide viable ideological alternatives. That would happen later, especially after the depression of the nineties. In the meantime, the ideas which most Americans held about government and political economy were traditional and resistant to change.

Ideas about social structure and social interaction also had a static quality during the decade and a half between the two depressions. Another ideological legacy of American society's rural past was a sense of the moral goodness deriving from the unity of the "producing classes." To produce something, especially something tangible like crops (or a horseshoe or an iron rail or a reaping machine), was good; it justified one's social existence; it was better than to consume. The principal written source for this view was Adam Smith's *Wealth of Nations*. That book, first published by the Scottish political economist in 1776, was widely regarded by Americans, Britons, and others with awe, because in their minds it had described the natural laws of political economy with the magisterial clarity and certainty that Isaac Newton had achieved in describing the natural laws of physics. Smith, and the nineteenth-century Americans who read him at first or (more often) second hand, took it as axiomatic that the productive function was vital to economic life. Smith opened the *Wealth of Nations* by saying that "the annual labour of every nation is the fund which originally supplies it with all the necessaries and conveniences of life which it annually consumes, and which consist always either in the immediate produce of that labour, or in what is purchased with that produce from other nations." [4] Obviously not every American farmer or factory worker read Adam Smith's book. But its ideas were famous, were regarded by editorialists, politicians, teachers, and preachers as the basic point of departure for understanding how economic life worked, or should work, were widely paraphrased, and of course were very much in accord with day-to-day realities for the mass of American workers, who were farmers or craftsmen in fairly small shops.

The economic necessity and moral superiority of "producers" was a widely accepted and well-rooted idea by the third quarter of the nineteenth century. Adam Smith was not its only source: other classical economists, the eighteenth-century physiocrats who argued that land and its cultivation were the source of wealth (thoughts echoed by Thomas Jefferson and other American writers), indeed, the many American sages who had long glorified rural life, contributed to its strength in Americans' minds. And as long as the great majority lived and worked on farms and in country villages, the notion squared with experience. As a consequence, the phrase "the harmony of the producing classes" recurred over and over again in the writing of the period. Not only were producers virtuous, but they functioned in harmony with each other. Until the depression of the seventies, an American commonly thought of himself as a "producer"; it was a normal, reasonably accurate, self-image. Textbooks in political economy defined the term very broadly, even more broadly than Adam Smith, to include farmers and mechanics and others who worked with their hands to produce tangible goods, and also professionals, merchants, scholars, or as a labor newspaper put it in 1872, anybody "who by physical or intellectual labor contributes to the substantial wealth of the nation."

During the depression of the seventies the meaning of the term "producer" became strained and less inclusive. Industrial workers began to experience more frequently the phenomenon of employment in larger factories or railroad companies; manufacturers, or some of them, realized that they no longer had as much in common with farmers and workers whom they formerly considered their fellow producers as they did with mine owners, bankers, and other capitalist magnates. The "producer" self-image, which carried the sense of participating in a harmonious economic society, was maintained (sometimes vehemently) by farmers, but began to lose its resonance among industrial workers and manufacturers. The return of relative prosperity after 1878 and before the Panic of 1893 reduced the speed with which the "harmony of the producing classes" idea was losing its grip; some very wealthy nonfarmers, such as Andrew Carnegie, continued to express it. But its correspondence with common experience was quietly eroding as the tides of occupational change and imbalanced wealth distribution continued to flow through the eighties. During the depression of the nineties the "producer" self-image seemed to fit farmers almost exclusively; by then it had lost its hold on industrial workers. A major consequence of that was the failure of William Jennings

Bryan to strike any substantial rhetorical spark among nonfarming laborers in the campaign of 1896. That failure had much to do with Bryan's failure to win the presidency.

Americans also assumed during the Gilded Age that social interaction properly involved acquisitiveness, the right and duty of a man to get ahead in the world as far and as fast as he could. They also assumed traditionally that extremes of wealth and poverty would not result. Why should they? In bygone decades they almost never had done so. It was also understood that, although the acquisition of wealth by many people was praiseworthy, the amassing of overweening, monopolistic wealth and power by a few was not. Up to a point in the history of American society, the two notions of acquisitiveness on the one hand, and of leveling, democratic antimonopoly sentiment on the other, generally squared with reality though they contained a potential for conflict. The potential began to become actual during the Gilded Age. The Grangers and their business allies had already complained around 1870 that railroad and grain elevator monopolies were infringing on their economic freedom. Businessmen complained through the eighties about the unfair competitive practices of other business-men and sought relief through antitrust laws and revisions of the tariff. After the onset of agricultural depression in the Midwest and South in the late eighties, farmers and their spokesmen demanded government action to regulate freight rates and ease the currency shortages and credit pressures which many of them assumed were foisted on them by the greed of railroad and banking monopolists. In their view, monopolies—unnatural combinations, run by manip-ulators of wealth rather than producers of it—threatened their economic well-being, even survival, and offended their sense of fair play. The trend toward business combination, popularly known as the trust movement, was recognized and detested by many agrarians and certain labor leaders in the late eighties. More general public alarm, however, was not to develop until after the depression of the nineties. In the meantime, during the interdepres-sion years, the prevailing attitude was respect and admiration for self-made men and belief in moral validation by the achievement of material success. The many novels of Horatio Alger, the most famous expressions of the work-hard-and-get-ahead ethic (though careful readers noted the large element played by luck in Alger's plots), were yet to come. But the idea that worldly success crowned honest effort had already been expressed countless times, from the writings and preachings of New England Puritans in the seventeenth century and, about a hundred years later, in Benjamin Franklin's *Poor Richard's Almanac*. McGuffey's *Eclectic Readers*, the primary moral and literary text of generations of American school children, were laced with the idea.[5] Perhaps not every American shared the notion of virtuous acquisitiveness, and undoubtedly many were disappointed as their lives drew on and worldly success eluded them despite their honest efforts. But it is safe to say, safer than is usually the case in discussing popular attitudes and ideas, that most Americans were familiar with the notion, absorbed it, and attempted to act on it.

American attitudes toward minorities were a revealing part of their ideology of social interaction. Here we are talking not about the attitudes of the minority group members themselves, but rather about the attitudes of the two-thirds to three-fourths of the population who were of British ethnic stock, who were at least nominally and traditionally Protestant (mostly evangelical), and who shared the common experience and life style of farms and country villages. For this majority, attitudes toward blacks, Indians, European immigrants, or Asian immigrants varied greatly, depending in part on which part of the country one is considering: the response to outgroups ranged from innocence and ignorance if no outgroups were around, to ostracism or even violent assault if the outgroup appeared to threaten tranquil order or community customs, to welcome acceptance if the outgroup seemed willing to accept majority values and had something to contribute economically or intellectually. Not all natives were nativists, even latently so. Some were. Even some immigrants joined nativist organizations. The key point, however, is that one's views of minority groups usually depended on how strongly one felt a part of, or alienated from, the prevailing social order, whether that social order seemed in some way threatened, and whether a minority group or groups appeared to be to blame for the threat. In an ascending scale of nervousness, the native-born, British-stock American majority (and more-or-less assimilated immigrants too) had opinions about European immigrants, Asian immigrants, Indians, and blacks.[6]

European immigrants were accepted most readily when they most resembled the resident majority. English, Scottish, and Scots-Irish (and Canadians of the same stock) were readily accepted and quickly assimilated, as they had been in the seventeenth and eighteenth centuries; culturally, they were "the same kind of people" as the native white majority. They fit in easily, with their British ethnicity, their evangelical Protestant religious identification, their skills and predilection for farming or craftsmanship or mining, and their possession of the Anglo-American language.

The cultural similarity of British immigrants to the already present American population allowed the British to escape being stereotyped, for the most part. Such stereotypes of the British immigrant as did exist were mild and favorable. For other minority groups, however, stereotypical views usually involved negative, even potentially hostile, elements. They also involved the presupposition that the minority group was innately inferior to a greater or lesser degree, and that it possessed qualities which were at best endearing, entertaining, or quaint, and at worst antisocial. Such stereotypes could persist in the face of personal acquaintance to the contrary (the "some-of-my-best-friends-are-Jews" attitude) and functioned to hinder the assimilation of stereotyped groups into the cultural mainstream. Racial and ethnic stereotypes were, by definition, unoriginal and unimaginative ways of classifying unfamiliar people, but they were also unoriginal in that the same content of the stereotypes was applied to unrelated groups. The stereotypical image of the Irish in American popular literature and presumably in popular mythology contained features also applied to blacks, to Spaniards, to Latin-Americans, to French, to Italians, and later with some variation to East European Jews. These features were opposites of those which the native white stock liked to think they possessed themselves. (Stereotypes of course reveal less about the groups being stereotyped than about those doing the stereotyping.) Americans were supposed to be given to hard work and frugality; the Irish, blacks, Italians, and so forth tended to be lazy and spendthrift. The minority group, whichever it was, was quaintly but unproductively fond of music and dancing; the native white stock wished it had time for such things, but after all life was more serious. The minority group was romantic, even sexy; the native white American possessed self-control. The Irishman or black abused alcohol; the native white American was temperate, even an abstainer. The Irishman or black was often an accomplice in political corruption; the native understood purity in democratic government. The antinomies could be extended.

For some immigrant groups the stereotyping was basically positive. References to Swedes or Norwegians were sometimes prefaced with adjectives such as "industrious," "sober-minded," "hard-working." Germans were also usually "hard-working" or "sturdy," sometimes "freedom-loving," as in the case of Carl Schurz and other free-thinkers who emigrated after having been on the losing side in the Revolution of 1848; sometimes, especially in the case of Catholic Germans, they were simply "beer-drinking."

Religion was a major determinant of whether a group was *prima facie* desirable or not: Catholicism had never been warmly regarded in America, a society whose cultural origins were so closely attached to the experience and tradition of the Protestant Reformation in England. The anti-Catholic strain grew in strength when, beginning in the late 1840s, the small body of American Catholics of well-assimilated, often upper-class English stock were inundated with hundreds of thousands of poverty-stricken Irish peasants who happened to be their co-religionists. In the age of "no Irish need apply," the 1850s and a while afterward, anti-Irish and anti-Catholic sentiment fused. The Catholic church in the United States, as many church historians have pointed out, became culturally Irish (though in certain Midwestern areas such as Wisconsin, after the heavy German immigration of the 1870s and 1880s, culturally German). The defensive reaction of certain important Irish-American bishops to anti-Catholic sentiment only accentuated disharmony.

Jewishness was also of little help if one sought social assimilation. Problems were not so severe as with Catholics, partly because of the difference in numbers; the peak years of Jewish immigration to the United States did not arrive until after the 1890s and even then involved many fewer people. The Jewish presence in

America prior to the depression of the 1890s consisted chiefly of a few congregations of Sephardim, dating back to the late eighteenth century, groups of German Reform Jews living chiefly in the larger cities, and an occasional merchant or peddler in small towns around the country. American attitudes toward Jews were ambivalent, in that, on the one hand Jews were understood to be the lineal descendants of the Chosen People described in that Bible with which Americans were so familiar, which was good, but on the other hand they were held responsible by some Christians for the death of Jesus and were suspected of the kinds of faults, especially involving economics, that they had been blamed for since the Middle Ages.

More will be said about the interface of Jews and Catholics with the dominant native white majority in late nineteenth-century America, and it is worth repeating that by no means were all members of that majority nativists, anti-Catholics, or anti-Semites. Stereotypes commonly existed, however, and the acceptance of ethnic minorities was slower if they were non-Protestant.

Asian immigrants carried a further distinctiveness. Different in religion, in language, in dress and social customs, and comprising the lowest economic level in California, where most of them lived, they were most definitely an outgroup. Although the term "race" was often used in the late nineteenth century to refer to what would now be called "nationality" or "ethnic group," such as the "Italian race" or "Jewish race," it was understood that the Chinese (the Japanese were yet to arrive in significant numbers) were racially more distant from the native stock than European immigrants were. The stereotype of the Chinese—the pig-tailed, impoverished, obsequious Chinaman—was for the most part unfavorable. A positive element did exist for some, based upon a more or less vague understanding that Chinese civilization was ancient and that it had produced important contributions to world literature, science, technology, and architecture. Presumably the Chinese workers who emigrated to the West Coast of the United States from the 1850s to the early 1880s possessed some trace of these virtues, according to the stereotype. But the positive element was not sufficient to prevent Congress from passing the Chinese Exclusion Act of 1882, forbidding the entry of any more Chinese workers, skilled or unskilled, and providing "that hereafter no State court or court of the United States shall admit Chinese to citizenship." Ethnic or national or racial group, or whatever, it made no difference; the Chinese were to be permanently excluded from political and legal rights. At least the European immigrants did not suffer that indignity.[7]

Attitudes toward American Indians also included a few positive features scattered among many negative ones. A degree of regard for the Indians as creatures of God, living in a state of nature, ready to be evangelized, had existed in American thought ever since the Massachusetts Puritan, John Eliot, translated the Bible into an Indian language and condemned enslavement attempts in the first years of the Bay colony. The novels of James Fenimore Cooper, the histories of Francis Parkman, Henry Wadsworth Longfellow's *Hiawatha*, and many less elegant literary products, described the Indians of the Northeast and Midwest in occasionally flattering terms. The "noble Red Man" was a journalistic cliché, and Fourth of July celebrations, as we have seen, included pageants of Columbus meeting with the Indians, or the signing of a treaty with Powhatan, or perhaps a battle scene with Tecumseh, or some such historical encounter, as if by cultural knee-jerk. Also, the majority culture had learned a healthy respect for, and indeed fear of, Indians after 250 years of armed conflict. The Fourth of July pageants of around 1880 were much less likely to include Sitting Bull or Geronimo, perhaps because they were not yet dead and therefore "noble." The attitude and interest of the dominant majority were in the exotic and aboriginal qualities of Indian cultures; there was never any slight expectation of meeting them on equal terms. The majority culture would meet the Indians, through the instrumentality of government, with policies which would help them accommodate to the majority. But despite all humane intentions the results and the policies were to decimate the Indians culturally and physically.[8]

Attitudes toward the black minority have been rehearsed so often in recent years as to need no extended discussion here. But a few points are worth noting. First, given the fact that ninety percent of the black population lived in Southern states during the final quarter of the nineteenth century, conscious consideration of black Americans as a cultural minority was much more evident in the South than elsewhere, and Southern attitudes tended to become national attitudes. Outside the South, the black minority could for the most part be forgotten. Even the remnant of the pre-Civil War abolitionists lost their enthusiasm for the "black cause" during the waning years of Reconstruction and were almost never heard from during the 1880s; the reason, in part, was that for many of them, the "black cause" meant the abolition of slavery and not the extension of full social equality or civil rights.[9] The embryonic women's rights movement, many of whose prewar leaders had been abolitionists as well as proponents of women's suffrage, seldom included much enthusiasm for black rights in the seventies or eighties. Why, asked white Northern suffragettes, should black men vote but not white women? Both notions were good, they felt, but one right should accompany the other.

In the North, legal, social, and educational discrimination against blacks remained during the post-Civil War years, less intensely than in the South if only because black-white contact was much less frequent. Social action reflects social thought, however, and such social action for blacks as existed in the Northeast and Midwest reflects the prevalence of the stereotype of the Negro as racially inferior, culturally quaint but childlike ("they love to sing and dance"), and economically unproductive.

In the South, the "black problem" was more immediate. The Redeemer governments which followed congressional and military Reconstruction in state after state during the 1870s reinstituted major portions of the Black Codes passed during the abortive presidential Reconstruction period just after the end of the war. In statutes concerning labor relations, juries, property holding and debt, marriages, and finally voting, the "strange career of Jim Crow" had already well begun by 1880 and proceeded apace after the U.S. Supreme Court struck down the Civil Rights Act of 1875 in its decisions of 1883.[10] The white South perceived its black minority as economically useful in many ways, but also as an extremely serious potential threat to social order. Slave rebellions had been the *bête noire*, literally, in antebellum days, and the same fear persisted of black popular uprisings of any kind, or a return of the "black rule" that was fabled to have existed during military

Reconstruction. Such things were not an immediate threat in the eighties, but when the possibility did arise in the early nineties of blacks achieving political power, in combination with poorer whites in the Populist movement, the repressive machinery moved into high gear. The idea was that blacks were all right, even nice, but they had to be kept in line.

Majority cultural attitudes toward the black minority lacked the kind of positive features present in the stereotypes of most immigrants, even the Chinese. If a Negro was "good" in some way, it was not as a result of his own racial attributes, which supposedly precluded such a thing, but because he had been to some extent a pupil and beneficiary of white paternalistic efforts to improve him or because he had some white blood. Paternalism, or an assumption of low achievement, was manifested both by well-meaning whites, Northern and Southern, at the Lake Mohonk conference of 1890 on Negro improvement, which urged support for industrial education, i.e. manual training, and by the foremost black leader of the time, Booker T. Washington, in his efforts at Tuskegee Institute beginning in 1881 and in his accommodationist manifesto, the Atlanta Compromise speech of 1895.

Blacks were to be admired in the instances that, and to the degree that, they had learned the ways of white culture and were descended from white people. Nonwhite peoples—Asians, but especially blacks—were assumed to be innately and hopelessly inferior. Although education and moral exhortation could make them useful to the general society, and to a degree self-respecting, there was no way by which they could be brought up to, or evolve toward, the level of white society. This attitude rested not only on what might be called "normal" race prejudice stemming from political conflict or economic competition or even fears of violence against the social order. It was immensely strong in the minds of Gilded Age Americans because it was also supported by the best and most respectable social science of the time. Anthropologists almost to a man (Franz Boas of Columbia was the leading exception, and his main efforts came after 1900) asserted the inferiority of non-Caucasians after studying such things as the size of skulls and brain capacity, comparative incidence of disease and life expectancies, and ethnology. They concluded that evolution did not mean progress in the case of the Negro. Instead, the natural laws of evolution would find the Negro "slowly succumbing to the rigors of competition" and eventually becoming extinct. The new science of anthropology thus provided what seemed to be a reasoned, empirical footing for racism.[11]

Evolution as a fundamental idea for understanding social interaction was an attractive one for Gilded Age Americans and was not limited to discussions about racial superiority or inferiority. In various forms the term antedated Charles Darwin's publication of *The Origin of Species* in 1859, but in that extremely influential book, evolution was identified and explained as the basic law according to which the biological and geological world functioned. Differing radically from the conception of a universe whose moving parts interacted like a vast machine but whose principles of operation remained statically unchanging over time— the Newtonian model of the universe—the Darwinian conception presented a universe which was slowly but always in flux. The world was not just *there*, it developed and proceeded. How? By change, over a period of millions of years, from minute and uncomplicated organisms to increasingly elaborate and intelligent ones. Darwin called the process of change "Natural Selection: or the Survival of the Fittest." [12] The latter term had already been employed by another Englishman, Herbert Spencer, to refer to changes in human population. Indeed the whole notion of evolution as a developmental process, particularly in biology and geology but also in human affairs, had had partial expression many times in the first half of the nineteenth century in England and Europe.[13] While Darwin's books were capturing the minds of natural scientists and infuriating theologians from 1859 onward, Spencer, through his books and articles published in the sixties and seventies, was achieving widespread popularity in Britain and America for his application of evolution to human society. Darwin's and Spencer's authoritativeness reinforced each other (as happened in the case of Newton and Adam Smith, even more discrete authorities), and many readers and opinion-leaders in the United States could not resist making the illogical but seductive jump from admitting the explanatory force of evolution in biology to applying it to social relations and political economy.

In the sixties and seventies, "social Darwinism"—meaning the application of the ideas of natural selection, the struggle for existence, and survival of the fittest to the analysis of society—was understood within the context of the still very powerful belief in natural laws. As explained earlier, the natural law idea had been exemplified and made widely acceptable by Isaac Newton's explanation of physics and Adam Smith's of political economy, and it involved a fundamentally static, machinelike operation of either. To this, the concept of evolution was logically opposite. In these first decades of social Darwinism's popularity, however, which for most people included the 1880s and part of the 1890s, evolution was assimilated into the mechanistic world view: Newton explained the laws of physics, Adam Smith and his successors the laws of political economy, Darwin biology and geology, Spencer sociology. The greatest American exponent of social Darwinism, William Graham Sumner, was one of many who understood evolution mechanistically. Evolution, including natural selection and the struggle for existence, was a law of nature and as such was foolish to tamper with. When in 1883 Sumner posed a key question in his book entitled *What Social Classes Owe to Each Other*, his answer was, basically nothing. Some people were inherently better than others; those who had wealth had won it in the struggle for existence; to use government or philanthropy to aid those without wealth was useless; to interfere by means of legislation with the natural process of social evolution (even through protective tariffs) was socially pernicious. Sumnerian social Darwinism had, obviously, a conservative impact.

The evolutionary model could logically be understood in a very different way. If change was pervasive in biological and human affairs, then man's *nature* was also subject to change. Natural laws, and the kinds of social relationships and struggles which Sumner talked about, were subject to the same developmental process as anything else. Perhaps the direction of that development could even be controlled. This view began to be expressed by another pioneer sociologist, Lester Frank Ward, in the early eighties, and others would join him later. Ward and Sumner argued their respective positions through the decade. In those days, however,

Sumner's conservative version of social Darwinism had the better of it, in the opinion of his many readers.[14]

In various ways, then, Americans' ideas and attitudes toward government and toward social interaction in the period from the depression of the seventies to the depression of the nineties justify the description, "conservative," because of their resistance to change. Except where the idea of progress, the antimonopoly spirit, or the need to purify government intervened, the usual attitude toward governments was minimalist. The ideal, observed or breached, was laissez faire. Social interaction was understood in terms of traditional notions congruent with farm and country-village life: the unity of producers, the validity of wealth-seeking, the assimilation of minorities where possible and their exclusion or repression if not, and the pervasiveness of natural laws, among which the evolutionary concept was at that time included.

Social institutions which might have engendered changes in popular ideas did exist, of course, during the interdepression years. Churches and schools might presumably have conveyed new ways of looking at social realities, and in some respects they began to. In a few major Protestant denominations, notably the Episcopalian and Congregationalist, a minority of urban-based clergy were already awake by the early eighties to problems of poverty and the increasingly obvious and dangerous tension between laborers and capitalists. Convinced that urbanism and industrialism were beginning to threaten social order, and imbued with a theological outlook that included liberal views such as the moral perfectibility (or at least improvability) of earthly society, they urged the churches to lead in the improvement of labor conditions and the education and uplift of the urban poor by means of institutional churches and settlement houses. A few churchmen advocated "Christian socialism," a radical realignment of society based on Christian charity and justice and the immanence of God. But they were a minority within a minority: the term "socialism" ran too abrasively against the grain of secular acquisitiveness as well as Protestant individualism. Still, when George D. Herron and other ministers began to publicize the idea of the "kingdom of God on earth" in the early nineties, they made some converts and laid the groundwork for the Social Gospel movement which became a fixture in most major Protestant denominations by about 1910.

Through the eighties and into the nineties, however, "social Christianity" in the sense of a liberal movement to regenerate the whole of society through Christian ideals, and thus to solve the emergent problems of poverty and labor conflict, meant much less to most American Protestants than more traditional concerns. To them, the taproot of religion was Scripture and not the Church; the salvation of the individual soul had much more meaning than the saving of the soul of an abstract collectivity called society. Seminary professors, ministers, and the faithful were inclined instead to argue about eschatology, the branch of theology which studies how the world will end, than about how the secular world should be made a Christian society. Formal ethics at that time discussed the ways in which individuals should behave in order to gain salvation, rather than ways in which the "kingdom of God" would be brought about. For those within the Calvinist tradition, such as Presbyterians and Baptists, the salvation of the world would take place in God's good time anyway; the main question for eschatology was whether it would be before Christ's literal second coming, or afterward. The former position, called postmillennial (or millennialist), was maintained by members of various evangelical denominations (a variety of Methodists, Baptists, Presbyterians and others) through the eighties, and gradually weakened by the turn of the century. By then, biblical criticism and the impact of evolutionary natural science undercut the literal interpretation of Scripture on which postmillennialism essentially depended. The latter view, called premillennial (or millenarian), also cut across denominational lines but was especially prominent among Presbyterians and Baptists. It too underwent a crisis and a thinning-out of adherents around the turn of the century, as a result of the dying off of older spokesmen and problems with biblical literalism, but the tradition was reinvigorated in the second and third decades of the twentieth century and became the basis, as Ernest Sandeen has shown, of the Fundamentalist movement.[15] Neither the millennialists nor the millenarians, however, were exercised about reform of the secular world. In the eighties and early nineties, their traditional questions far outweighed any tentative steps toward what was to become the Social Gospel. During the interdepression years, Protestant discussions about social ethics centered on matters such as how people ought to behave on the Sabbath, whether they should drink alcoholic beverages, whether Scripture should be read in schools (there was general agreement among them, but not among Catholics, that it should), and whether civil governments ought to pass laws regulating personal behavior in those areas. Protestants by no means agreed on the last point. Even within American Lutheranism certain synods supported total abstinence from alcohol and others did not. Methodists, Baptists, and other evangelicals made up the backbone of prohibitionist strength, though not all of them favored legislation on the subject. The evangelical churches, however, were numerically the largest denominations and supplied the chief support for Sabbatarian, temperance, and other moral legislation. They provided the main body of people who identified their own moral viewpoint with what ought to have been, in their minds, that of the whole country.[16]

In general, then, the Protestant churches in the eighties were not supportive of secular reform except when members of the larger evangelical denominations sought legislation to preserve and encourage personal morality. Their membership was overwhelmingly Anglo-Saxon, native-born, rural or small-town, and theologically in the Arminian (Methodist) or Calvinist traditions. They were seldom in daily contact with the most rapidly changing aspects of secular society and did not, at that time, spearhead changes in prevailing ideas or economic relationships. The Catholics did not do so either, but for different reasons: as a church whose members in the eighties were to a large extent working-class immigrants or children of immigrants, and whose cultural roots while deep in Ireland and Latin Europe were shallow in the United States, American Catholicism looked mostly inward at its own internal stresses. With the exception of Archbishop John Ireland of St. Paul and a few articulate native-born converts like Isaac Hecker and Orestes Brownson, Catholic leaders spent most of their energies on institutional survival in a society which most of them felt was at best neutral and more often hostile except for the constitutional guarantee of religious freedom. They worried about

whether labor organizations such as the Knights of Labor were
secret societies like the Freemasons or were legitimate for Catholics
to join; they argued about the proper relation of the American
Catholic church to the civil government, to the culture, and to
Rome; they struggled for ecclesiastical advantage among themselves along German and Irish ethnic lines; their bishops at
Baltimore in 1884 mandated the building of parochial schools
wherever possible. They denounced atheism, liberalism, modern-
ism, and socialism; they (especially the Germans but also many
Irish) fought attempts by evangelicals to restrict their "personal
liberty" through Sabbatarian and temperance laws; they even
created a body of fiction which amounted to an imitation of the
second-to-fifth rate genteel romanticism of non-Catholic authors of
the time, but whose content and aim was to inculcate morality and
fidelity to the church—fiction, as a recent study has shown, with "a
parochial purpose" and almost devoid of literary merit.[17] From this
religious group, although for different reasons than was the case
with evangelical Protestants, ideological change applicable to social
and economic change was not likely to come. And it did not.

Education paralleled organized religion in being a social institution with enormous potential for instigating ideological change, but
which in most respects functioned instead as a reinforcer of
traditional attitudes. Change did take place in American education
during the interdepression years: numbers of schools, teachers, and
pupils outran population increase; some states passed compulsory
attendance laws; teacher certification was begun or tightened up in
a number of places; the seeds of what would become in the next
generation the progressive education movement were being sown
by William Torrey Harris of St. Louis, G. Stanley Hall, Francis W.
Parker, and other pedagogical theorists. In higher education, the
beginnings of graduate and research training, intertwined with the
development of professional social sciences, constituted changes
which would have vast consequences in fairly short order. But not
yet. For the most part, educational changes in the 1878–1893
period were either tentative or relatively superficial. The function
and content of education generally remained conservative.

The principle of local, nonprofessional control of the public
schools was well established, and while it insured that the voters of

a ward, township, or county controlled, through school boards and superintendents, the curriculum and practices of the schools their taxes paid for, it meant also that the schools were not likely to become hotbeds of intellectual inquiry. Instead the main aims were the inculcation of patriotism and moral rectitude and a sufficient degree of basic literacy and numeracy to allow a person to function in the largely agrarian society. Even these modest aims represented a victory for the ideas of mid-century educational reformers like Horace Mann; the very notion of universal public elementary schooling had just recently taken hold, and even in the 1880s only about two-thirds of the country's children and teenagers were enrolled, and those enrolled showed up for school about eighty or eighty-five days a year, on the average. The purposes of universal public education were generally understood and accepted, however. As William T. Harris put it in 1871, "Common schools increased opportunity; they taught morality and citizenship; they encouraged a talented leadership; they maintained social mobility; they promoted popular responsiveness to social evolution." [18] A hundred years later most Americans would agree with these aims. But the kind of morality and citizenship, and the training requirements for leadership and mobility, were very different then. The elementary curriculum included reading, spelling, grammar, arithmetic, geography, United States history, and sometimes civics, hygiene, natural science, and bookkeeping. The emphasis was practical and moral, and the morality was that of William H. and Alexander McGuffey, the authors of those ubiquitous readers. New Englanders, or Midwestern authors with New England (and Puritan) cultural roots, wrote most of the textbooks in use, and the morality which they taught was that of a generalized Protestant Christianity. As Henry Steele Commager has summed it up, "It was a middle-class, conventional, and equalitarian morality. . . . Industry, sobriety, thrift, propriety, modesty, punctuality, conformity—these were the essential virtues, and those who practiced them were sure of success." [19] The innate virtue and providential destiny of the United States—the republican virtue discussed earlier—also saturated the curriculum. Reform movements except for temperance made few appearances; the negative role of government and the admirability of self-reliant, self-made men, however, did receive stress. United States history courses served a dual conservative role: they glorified the republican past, and they set forth rural, country-village society as a norm in opposition to urban-industrial values and developments. When kindergartens were introduced in certain city schools, they became devices for the socialization of immigrant children into the majority culture and language. The elementary schools, in short, did the job that the local communities which controlled them intended; they prepared people to live and function according to the moral values of the past, and present, society of their day. They were much less effective in preparing people to live in the quite different future.[20]

The same could be said of many of the country's several hundred colleges and universities. A very large proportion were basically the educational arms of religious denominations, mostly Protestant and some Catholic, whose job it was to provide a liberal education (consisting chiefly of general history, literature, classical languages, and theology) and to train ministers. Study of the social sciences meant a reading of textbooks of political economy by New Englanders such as Francis Wayland or Simon Newcomb, who were steadfast exponents of classical orthodoxy; the result was a predilection for laissez faire and the gold standard among most educated Americans. The natural sciences were ignored or taught nonexperimentally. Even in a very good college, such as Oberlin, the emphasis was on the building of "Christian character"; the church-related liberal-arts college extended, for an elite of about three percent of the college-age population, the function of primary and secondary schools, but within a specific denominational context. A new type of higher educational institution, the land-grant college, had begun to emerge from the late sixties on, to provide training in "agriculture and the mechanic arts" (later, engineering); these were to become centers of "utilitarian education for the producing classes," according to the founders of one of them, the Illinois Industrial University, in 1867.[21] The land grant colleges represented a significant break with the classic liberal-arts pattern, but only in the practicality of their curriculum and their public sources of funding, not in the pattern of moral values which were to be inculcated. The large state universities of the Midwest and Pacific states were almost entirely a thing of the distant future:

Indiana University, for example, though chartered back in 1820, remained little more than a classical liberal-arts college, beset by denominational squabbles despite its public provenance, until the biologist David Starr Jordan became president in 1885 and began to lead the institution toward the twentieth century. Very few state universities remotely resembled their modern shapes, despite the introduction of Greek letter societies, intercollegiate athletics, and female students in the seventies and eighties. The University of Michigan, the largest university in the country with 2,700 students in 1892, had taken a radical step when it abolished compulsory chapel attendance in 1872 (but chapel services, personally led by President James B. Angell, continued for many years; in those days the separation of church and state seldom extended to higher education). [22]

The most strikingly new and ultimately devastating development in higher education was the founding of universities solely or chiefly dedicated to postgraduate training and research, and symbiotically with them, the emergence of the social sciences, especially sociology and economics. The fundamental purpose of these institutions and disciplines, unlike almost anything else in the whole structure of education in America at that time, was not dedication to good morals and good citizenship. It was, at least in principle, the pursuit of practical and abstract knowledge, as in the university seminars of Germany in which so many young Americans were being trained. With the founding of Johns Hopkins in 1876, followed by Clark in 1887, Chicago in 1890, and Stanford in 1891, together with the invigoration of graduate-level work at older institutions such as Harvard, Yale, Michigan, and Wisconsin, milieux existed for the empirical, value-free study not just of natural science but of society itself. The new emphasis, on German empiricism and historicism rather than on the perpetuation of the moral convictions of evangelical Christianity, on seeking what was unknown rather than transmitting what was assumed to be true, was shortly to have radical consequences for American value patterns and the ways in which American society would cope with the social and economic change suffusing it. Specifically, the new graduate schools, and the work of the bright young social scientists within them, were going to mean nothing less than the erosion of the fixation on natural law which was so fundamental a bulwark of ideological immobility. Not that these young men were amoral or un-Christian: far from it. Indeed they often undertook their social analyses and announced reform programs out of a missionary zeal, rooted in their own evangelical and rural origins, to create a more moral society. Most were leaders or allied with leaders of the early Social Gospel movement. But their methods, tools, and philosophy of knowledge were basically different from, and subversive of, the rationalistic approach of political economists and educators before them.

Most prominent among this group of intellectuals in the eighties were the economists Richard T. Ely and Simon N. Patten, the sociologist Lester Frank Ward, and the educationists William T. Harris and G. Stanley Hall. To them should be added the philosopher Charles Sanders Peirce, the founder of pragmatism and possibly the most profound intellect which America produced in the late nineteenth and early twentieth centuries. Graduate students and friends of theirs, such as Washington Gladden, John R. Commons, E. H. Bemis, Edward A. Ross, Albion Small, and Thorstein Veblen, shared their basic premises and themselves contributed in the nineties and after 1900 to the building of an intellectually valid foundation for social change. The common elements and radical contributions of Ely, Patten, Ward, Peirce, and others in the eighties were many, but above all the following. First, as students of the German philosopher G. W. F. Hegel and the German historical school of political economy, they accepted the historicist idea that all things are subject to change over time; everything exists and develops within the matrix of history. Even human nature—in fact human nature preeminently—changes with the passage of time. Their acceptance of that idea allowed them to see the radical implications of Darwinian evolution; evolution and historicism reinforced each other by agreeing that nature, biological or human, was constantly in process of development—and not static, as in the Newtonian and classical-economic paradigm. Second, they accepted the view that people should be considered not as isolated individuals but as part of a general social whole, and indeed that individuals were more shaped by the community of which they were a part than they were shapers of it. Hegel helped them here too, but so did Charles Sanders Peirce, who had maintained as early as 1868 that individual perceptions were solely derived from the individual's social and physical environment, not from innate natural patterns.[23] Peirce's assertion in 1877 and 1878 of the fundamental axiom of pragmatism, that the meaning of any thought or proposition lay in its consequences, also helped to assert the logical and psychological primacy of societies rather than individuals.

Third, the economists among this group, such as Ely, believed and proclaimed that the premises of classical political economy, whether of Adam Smith and his successors or of John Stuart Mill and the British Utilitarians, were arrived at more by rational deduction than by empirical observation and analysis, and as a result failed to serve as either a description or a prediction of how economics worked. Contrary to what was so often maintained in America's lecture halls and textbooks, Richard Ely asserted, in the words of his biographer, that "Economic behavior cannot be explained by rigid laws like chemistry and physics. . . . Christian moral responsibility should be emphasized rather than the search for mechanistic laws." [24] Fourth, the group agreed that, given the importance of society as the shaper of individuals, and given the basic truth of historical evolution rather than static natural laws, it becomes possible and necessary for people to shape their environment in socially beneficial ways. This idea was most effectively expressed by Lester Ward who, with William Graham Sumner, of all people, later founded the American Sociological Association. In *Dynamic Sociology* (1883) and other writings, Ward insisted on the need for conscious, rational efforts to improve society. Fifth, there was general agreement (though differently emphasized) that the instrument of rational social evolution would have to be government. With that, these thinkers helped break down the negative concept of government so widely held by Americans at that time. And the collective burden of their ideas was to contradict a whole series of dearly held attitudes: the laissez faire philosophy of government, the principle of the harmony of the producing classes, the individualistic ethic of the acquisitive self-made man, and the axiom of a static natural law.

They were able to get away with maintaining these very

subversive notions in large part because they couched them in nonthreatening, familiar language—and only then with difficulty. Peirce was unable to hold any significant academic appointment during his life; Sumner carried on an acrimonious public debate with Ward; Ely's job at Johns Hopkins was threatened by the enmity of Simon Newcomb, a leading orthodox political economist; and several of the group or their students were the victims of dismissals or the danger of dismissals from their academic posts through the nineties and past 1900. Nonetheless, the fact that most of them denounced socialism and social revolution, were usually tepid with regard to labor unions, and maintained that they sought changes of society in a more Christian direction, saved them from academic and ideological oblivion. Ely, for example, claimed contact with leading churchmen, both Catholic and Protestant, and believed in the eighties that "to avert a violent revolution and to restore the practice of brotherhood required dramatic and imaginative action by the better educated, the clergyman, and the responsible employer." [25] Few could take exception to that.

During the eighties the prevailing conservative ideology of Americans wore a smooth and seemingly impenetrable surface. Occasionally a rash appeared on that surface, as in the form of sporadic doubts that society was entirely sound. For a few, the malaise seemed cancerous, and as the decade wore on the uneasiness grew. One kind of answer to social problems appeared in the form of utopian tracts calling for, or predicting, revolutionary changes in order for society to survive the urbanizing and industrializing corrosions within it. Popular utopias or panaceas such as Henry George's *Progress and Poverty*, Edward Bellamy's *Looking Backward 2000–1887*, and William Dean Howells' *A Traveler from Altruria*, all products of the eighties, sold hundreds of thousands of copies and in the cases of George and Bellamy generated reform clubs of nervous middle-class people from New York and New England across the country to California. Ultimately, however, it would not be George or Bellamy or Howells whose ideas would provide the intellectual underpinning for the avoidance of social revolution, but rather the subversive academics like Ward and Ely, though their ideas were little noted in the eighties except as whipping boys for the likes of William Graham Sumner.[26]

3

Life and Labor,
1878-1893

During the decade and a half between the depression of the seventies and the depression of the nineties, American society merited the description of "conservative" with regard to its prevailing ideology and institutions. It was scarcely conservative, however, in its demographic and economic aspects. There, changes took place which were rendering the old value system obsolete. Within that value system there was little place for large economic units, large cities, social conflict, or gross disparities in wealth, income, or living patterns. But these phenomena were emerging with increasing insistence. Changes were already taking place during the 1870s in the rural–country-village pattern by then traditional in the United States, and some of the main changes, as described in Chapter one, were the cessation of farming as the majority occupation, the emergence of a number of cities of metropolitan size, depression-induced problems of law and order, new technology, and the introduction of mass employment situations. A national transportation network was well under way, permitting among other things a labor conflict of national scope in 1877. Debate raged in the federal Congress for three years, 1876 into 1878, over currency legislation, a focal issue for conflict among social, economic, and sectional groups.

In retrospect, the seventies appear to have contained the first confrontation of American society with its industrial and urban future. Americans might have learned much more from the confrontation than they did. As it happened, they learned little from it, in large part because their traditional and prevailing ideology provided them with almost no bases for doing so. And for the next fifteen years, that ideology continued to prevail, while at the same time the changes emergent in the seventies spread further, and still new kinds of demographic and economic ferment appeared. By 1893 the actualities of American society, and the processes of change which pervaded it, differed even more than they did in 1878 from the visions of the traditional, rural-derived ideology. The result was a crisis in thought and action beginning with the depression of 1893–1896 and continuing for several years thereafter.

The social changes of the interdepression years can be grouped under three large headings: demographic shifts, including mobility patterns and changes in the shape and structure of population; labor and occupational changes; and macroeconomic developments, including the continued strengthening of the manufacturing sector and above all the visible emergence of large-scale enterprise, or "big business," as a force in social and economic life. In short, the American population was increasingly caught up in urban-situated occupations, professions, and businesses, while the trend toward large, complex units accelerated: in all, a process which might be called, were the word not so clumsy, "complexification."

What was the demographic character of American society during the interdepression years, and what demographic changes were taking place? It is never easy to generalize accurately about large populations, especially when they are spread across a large land mass, but census records and other data afford some rational description according to several major topic headings: first, population density and the rural-urban mix; second, the age structure; third, changes in the relation of foreign-born and foreign-stock Americans to the native white population; fourth, population structure and mobility, which differed among the various geographic sections of the country (including the black population); and fifth, recent studies of localities which indicate a surprising degree of mobility of people from place to place. These five areas comprise the demographic substrate of economic changes which occurred during the interdepression years. Together with those economic changes (which will be discussed shortly), they constituted the practically irreversible movement of American society toward its twentieth-century pattern of urban-industrial life.

The total population grew from about 48 million at the end of the depression of the seventies to about 67 million at the time of the Panic of 1893, a 40 percent increase in fifteen years. If the same rate of increase had taken place since 1960, the population in 1975 would have been over 250 million, or nearly 40 million more than it actually was. This increase was unusually rapid and large by virtually any standard, and was substantially higher than the decade-by-decade increases reflected in the federal censuses of 1870, 1880, 1890, and 1900, which do not show the cycles of depression and prosperity, heavy or light immigration, and high or low birth and death rates, which happened within each decade. The interdepression years were by definition a period of relative prosperity, and thus they provided an economically favorable context for increases in both the native and foreign-born populations. Immigration was heavy: each year from 1880 through 1893, except for the recession years of 1885–1886, brought more foreigners into the United States than at any time in the past except 1854 and 1873. The attractiveness of the United States was not the only cause. Conditions elsewhere, especially in certain parts of Europe, contributed strongly. Among the native-born, the crude birth rate declined somewhat during the 1880s while the death rate stabilized, but nonetheless the natural increase among the native-born (especially white) population was substantial. Overall, the population density of the United States rose from about 16 per square mile to about 22, and by 1900, when the density was over 25, it had reached a level of about half of what it was at the 1970 census.

The remarkable population increase in the United States between the depressions of the seventies and the nineties occurred in various ways, sometimes only vaguely related, such as the sudden expansion of very large cities like New York and Chicago, and the rapid settlement of the Great Plains states by commercial farmers. As nearly always happened in the United States, however, urban population increased faster than rural population.[1] Rural population increased by almost five million during the 1880s, but urban population by eight million, with the result that the proportion of rural residents, shifting from about 72 percent in 1880 to less than 65 percent in 1890, dropped more rapidly than in any other ten-year period between censuses in American history. Almost certainly the shift was even more striking for the interdepression years as a whole, or would be if census figures were available to permit comparisons between 1878–1893 and other periods of the same length. The rural-to-urban trend, however, was very unevenly felt in different parts of the country—a fact which would increasingly mean differences in the daily life-styles and experiences of people living in one part of the country or another, and which would consequently help to produce wide variances in receptivity to ideological change. In plainer words, certain parts of the country were beginning to regard urban (and industrial) life as normal, while others hardly experienced it at all and thus saw little practical reason to revise traditional ways of thinking. Among the four regions of the country as defined by the Census Bureau (Northeast, North Central, South, and West), the Northeast and the South were as different as two separate countries in terms of their rural-urban distributions, and the rates at which those distributions were changing. In 1870, 53.8 percent of the population of the Northeast was rural, but only 40.3 percent in 1890, while in the South, the rural population in 1870 was an overwhelming 87.9 percent of the whole in 1870, and had diminished only very slightly, to 83.7 percent in 1890 (the proportion was about the same, by the way, for both white and black Southerners). In 1890, about 40 percent of Northeasterners lived in cities of 100,000 or more, a proportion which had doubled since 1870, while in the South, in both years, just over 5 percent lived in cities of that size—specifically, in New Orleans, since it was the sole example of a Southern metropolis.

Rural dwellers still comprised the majority in the North Central and Western regions in 1890 and would continue to do so for some time, but within those regions, especially the five East North Central states, urbanism was becoming the norm as it was in the Northeast. To make the same point in another way: twenty-two cities had achieved metropolitan size (100,000 or more) in the censuses of 1880, 1890, and 1900. Of them, only two (Denver by 1890 and Los Angeles by 1900) were Western, and only one (Memphis, 1900) was Southern. Nine of the others were in the Northeast, ten in the North Central states. Through the 1880s, then, the United States contained a substantial area in the Northeast and eastern Midwest in which the urban life experience was becoming common, even the norm, and another area, geographically larger, in which farms and country villages continued to predominate. No other country in the world, not even China or India, contained as many cities of more than a million or more than a hundred thousand as the United States did in 1890, but several European countries (England, Scotland, Germany, Belgium, and the Netherlands) had populations considerably more urban-dwelling on the average. The skewed distribution of rural and urban population in the United States was becoming more pronounced during the interdepression years and would continue to do so. Inevitably, the disparity was to induce political and ideological tensions.

Changes in the age structure of the population between 1878 and 1893 were not as pronounced or far-reaching as changes in rural-urban distribution, but a few are worth pointing out. In the first place, the median age began to increase in the seventies more rapidly than before, and continued upward into the nineties. For whites, it rose from 20.4 years in 1870 to 22.5 years in 1890, an increase of about 10 percent. Median age of nonwhites remained nearly steady, at about 18.5 years. The rise during the 1880s was greatest for white males—about 1.5 years. The most important cause was very probably foreign immigration, or more precisely the high proportion of males among the arriving immigrants. Birth rates among the native white population declined somewhat, which helped raise the median age, but the factor was in all likelihood less important than the nature of immigration. Infant mortality[2] remained steadily high through the period, higher than during the years before 1870 or after 1910, and death rates changed very little during the 1880s: these two factors did not play much of a role in changing the age structure at that time. It is clear, however, that in general the population's median age increased at a faster clip than in the depression years before and after, and would do so again during the years of mass immigration between the end of the depression of the nineties and the onset of World War I.

In any event, the youngest age cohort, those under five years old, shrank as a proportion of total population (and would do so most of the time until the present), as yet not because the size of the average family was shrinking, but because of increases in the numbers of those who were childless or nearly so, or who were unattached to any family at all. We do not know how many of the latter kind of people there actually were, but apparently there were more than ever before—another indicator of urbanism and the intensified velocity of population movement that went with it. The next youngest age cohort, children and adolescents from five to nineteen, remained proportionately almost stable at just about one-third of the whole population during the 1880s; nor was there much change in the proportion of people in their twenties. The increases occurred among older people, especially those in their thirties and early forties, the roughly one-fifth of the population who were in their most productive years. The population was turning over more quickly than it would in the late twentieth century, in the sense that people lived shorter lives but were born or died at faster rates. But despite the rapid turnover, during the interdepression years a proportionately large number of people were in the age groups which could contribute significantly to economic growth. Conversely, the very young and the very old—those cohorts which draw on resources rather than add to them—were fewer than in the periods just before and just after. Thus the age structure was peculiarly favorable to the expansion of the economy.

The interdepression years brought another shift in population structure, one already mentioned: historically unprecedented immigration from abroad. Total numbers of immigrants had fallen to about 138,500 in 1878, the lowest level since the Irish potato-famine emigration began in 1845 (except for two years just after the Panic of 1857 and the two years at the beginning of the Civil War). The number rose slightly in 1878–1879, and then from mid-1879 through mid-1893 rose as high as 789,000 in 1882 and achieved an annual average of 520,000 and a total of more than seven and a quarter million before the depression struck. Nearly all were Europeans or Canadians: although the peak years of Chinese immigration were the mid-seventies and the early eighties, the total of incoming Chinese for the ten years from 1873 through 1882 was only about 160,000.

In both numbers and proportion, the foreign-born population increased rapidly from 1846 to the onset of the Civil War. Those were the heaviest years of immigration in American history relative to the population already in the country. Foreign-born population rose a little more during the 1860s, and then fell proportionately behind the natural increase of residents during the depression of the seventies. It fell behind again during the depression of the nineties. During the interdepression years, however, enough immigrants arrived to raise the proportion from about 13 to 15 percent. Meanwhile the foreign-born already living in the United States increased and multiplied, and the "ethnic" population—foreign-born themselves plus native-born Americans with one or two immigrant parents—rose approximately from 29 percent to 33 percent of the whole population between 1878 and 1893. Many of these were English, Scottish, Welsh, or Canadian, and their children, and therefore of the same British stock as the "native Americans." For them assimilation was easy. Still, Irish and Germans outnumbered them and together comprised 57 percent of the foreign-born in 1880 and 50 percent in 1890.

By the latter year, however, the foreign-born population included over one million Scandinavians, 147,000 Poles (triple the number in 1880), 183,000 Italians (four times the number in 1880), over 300,000 from Austria-Hungary, and over 300,000 French Canadians. The source of immigration was beginning to change once more. It had done so in the fifteen years preceding the Civil War, when the "old, old immigration" of Protestant British gave way in numbers to the Irish and Germans, who together with the Norwegians, Swedes, and Danes arriving in the seventies and eighties made up the so-called "old immigration." It was beginning to happen again, and although the combined numbers of "new immigrants," those from southern and eastern Europe, would not surpass the combined numbers of Irish, British, Germans, and Scandinavians until after the depression of the 1890s, the ethnic variety was already unprecedented by 1893. The native-stock majority had had great difficulty in coming to terms with the "old immigration," or at least its non-British part, and had by no means fully done so by the eighties. They were to have even more difficulty with the second wave of ethnically unfamiliar immigrants.

To the native-stock majority, especially those who were observant as well as concerned about preserving the traditional fabric of American culture, one of the most disturbing aspects of the influx of immigrants between 1878 and 1893 was their propensity for living in cities. Substantial numbers of the "old immigrants" who arrived during the seventies and eighties—British, Irish, Germans, Scandinavians and smaller groups such as Swiss, Bohemians, north Italians, or German-Russian Mennonites—joined the mass movement of native-stock Americans who were taking up land and beginning commercial farming in the Great Plains states or on the Pacific coast. These people were playing the American game of trying to get ahead by honest work and possibly good luck. Other immigrants, however, and they seemed to include nearly all of the Poles, Italians, east Europeans, and other "new" immigrants, were gathering in the larger cities. The suspicions of the native-stock majority about immigrants were reinforced by a rural people's suspicions about the evils of cities, especially large ones. In the Northeast and North Central regions, the proportion of native-born of native stock decreased steadily from rural areas to small cities to large cities to metropolises; the proportion of foreign-born and their children increased in a steady inverse ratio. In 1890, over 70 percent of the rural population in the Northeast were native-born of native stock, but that group comprised less than 27 percent of the population of New York and Philadelphia, both well over a million by then. In the North Central states in 1890, 62 percent of the rural people, but only one out of five Chicagoans, were native-born. One could almost guess the proportion of immigrants and their children in a city if one knew its size: as a general rule, the smaller the city the more native-stock its people; the larger it was, the more it was almost sure to have a foreign-born, foreign-stock majority.

American historians of immigration have most often stressed the attractions of the United States when they have sought to explain the causes of the immigration, and undoubtedly the factors tending to pull immigrants from Europe to the United States were very important in determining the size as well as the sources, age, and sex of the immigrant inflow. "Pull" factors included the availability of good farm land in the upper Mississippi Valley and Great Plains states during the seventies and eighties, the need for manual workers to create the network of railroads, the chief "growth industry" from the end of the Civil War until 1893; the existence in the seventies and the eighties of railroads in the trans-Mississippi

West, affording immigrants and natives a way to get to potential farm land (some of it sold to immigrants whom the land-poor railroads actively recruited), and also affording a way to get wheat and corn to markets; the expansion of factory jobs in industries such as steel, and indeed the creation of hundreds of thousands of urban-located jobs requiring little previous training. All of these factors drew Europeans to the United States, so much so that the large majority of British, Irish, and Scandinavians who emigrated at all went to the United States.

While "pull" factors were important, however, it has to be realized that "push" factors were even more important in many cases. Things happened in Europe from time to time which made emigration possible and desirable. The ongoing process of industrialization and railroad-building was also taking place in Britain, Germany, and Scandinavia, and it operated together with improved agricultural technology to create surpluses of people who in former times would have made a living as farmers in Europe. Instead it seemed more opportune to take up farming, or some other occupation, in the United States. Emigration also coincided with times of relative prosperity in Europe: people could leave only when they had some excess of wherewithal, perhaps through sale of real or personal property, to afford the costs of steamship passage and resettlement. But the most important element was a periodic excess of population in the fifteen-to-thirty age group. As the economic demographer Brinley Thomas has pointed out in a remarkable study,[3] emigration to the United States from Britain, Ireland, Scandinavia, Germany, and later Italy, was heaviest fifteen to thirty years after times of abnormally high birth rates in those countries. When periods of prosperity coincided with periods of unusually large numbers of people in the most mobile and manually productive age group, heavy emigration took place. Conditions in the United States operated as limiting or accelerating factors, but not as decisive ones; even during the depression of the nineties immigration never dropped below a quarter million a year. European conditions would also play a critical role in the changes in the numbers and sources of immigration during the mass wave from 1897 to World War I.

The fact that 60 to 70 percent of immigrants were male helped cause the unexpectedly high ratio of males to females in the general population in the late nineteenth century. This was particularly true in the West. Mining camps and cattle ranges were chiefly male enclaves, and frontier areas in general tended to attract young, unattached males, either native or foreign-born, more than families or single women (although many people did migrate as family units to Great Plains farming areas). Only in the Northeast among native-born whites, and in the South among blacks, was there a slight excess of females over males in 1890. To some extent that reflected migration of native white and black males out of the Northeast and South respectively to the Midwest or West. It also resulted from the tendency of white or black females to live a few years longer than males, as is usually the case; also, males were often involved in occupations such as mining, construction, factory work, or railroading, then unusually prone to industrial accidents and job-related diseases.[4]

Sectional differences existed with regard to other population characteristics as well as sex ratios. Among the four census regions, the South was unique for several reasons: it not only lacked any cities of metropolitan size except New Orleans, but also contained a much more heavily rural population in general, as was noted earlier. It contained few of the nation's foreign-born or foreign stock; only about one out of fifty Southerners were immigrants as of 1890. With the exception of a few cities, and parts of Texas which were more typically Great Plains than "Southern," immigrants were not attracted to the South. None of the reasons which brought them to the Northeast and Midwest held true there: no agricultural frontier, no industrial jobs, almost no previously established immigrant communities (except in Texas), a less hospitable attitude toward religious out-groups (except in parts of Louisiana), less chance of making an upward social and economic climb. The South did not need an influx of able-bodied workers for farm or factory. It already had them, for one-third of the Southern population were Negroes. While the other three census divisions were 1 or 2 percent black and 40 to 48 percent foreign-born or foreign stock in 1890, Southern ratios were virtually the reverse. Ninety percent of the American black population was Southern, and about 85 percent of the Southern black population was rural—one percentage point more than the regional average for both blacks and whites.

Black mobility of the kind that was to become so prevalent in the twentieth century, i.e., the exodus out of the rural South to Northeastern and Midwestern cities, was minimal during the years from the end of Reconstruction to about 1915. Roughly ten thousand blacks per year left the South during the eighties and somewhat more than that in the early nineties, but compared to the whole, or to the numbers who would migrate later, this migration was scarcely noticeable and was more than made up for in the South by natural increase. Of those who did leave, a number went west, like the Exodusters who despaired of any economic progress in northern Louisiana and in 1879 trekked out to western Kansas to farm, or like the unattached black males who made up perhaps one-fourth of the cowboys in Texas and the southwestern territories.[5] More often, however, when a black male (or less often, a black family) moved about from place to place, the movement was within the South rather than out of it. During the Reconstruction years immediately following the end of slavery a considerable amount of this kind of mobility took place. Under the Bourbon regimes of the 1880s, however, less of it happened; the sharecropping and crop lien systems afflicting both black and poor white Southern farmers served to tie people to one plot of land, and in addition the white supremacist Bourbon governments were not eager to have a substantial number of unattached blacks moving about from place to place.

Other factors inhibited black mobility. One was the lack of a place to go, in the social sense. Upward occupational mobility for blacks was harder to achieve, and occurred less often, than for native whites or for the few foreign-born in the region.[6] Another was residential segregation, although it was much less rigid than it would later become, especially in the North, and was probably only slightly more pronounced for blacks in the South than for immigrants in the Northeast and Midwest. Family and work patterns, however, militated against movement from place to place. Black families on Southern farms (or in Midwestern cities) were, as a historian recently wrote, "basically a two-parent, male-headed family that showed little evidence of retaining structural characteristics of the slave family," and were by no means the matriarchal units, a youngish female surrounded by several children, so often thought in recent years to have been typical.[7] The black population was not only Southern but usually family-organized and strongly attached to a particular piece of land much like the peasants of Poland or southern Italy who would soon emigrate to the United States. One final reason limited the mobility of blacks in the late nineteenth century: their lives were too short. One demographer observed in 1965 that no country in the world then had a population so young, because of a high fertility rate, or a life expectancy so short, as the American black population had before 1900. Some major changes would soon take place, however, as consequences of the economic and political upheaval of the 1890s.[8]

In the Midwest, the demographic story was the dual one of rapid urban growth in the eastern part of it and rapid farm settlement, for a time, in the western part. Except for the northern counties of Wisconsin and Michigan, rural settlement of the East North Central states was virtually completed by the time of the Civil War. Yet that census division enjoyed one of the highest growth rates of any division during the eighties because of the expansion of industrial cities, following the pacemaker, Chicago, whose half million more than doubled in that decade. West of the Mississippi a different kind of Middle West existed, growing in numbers more rapidly than any other part of the country. Kansas, Nebraska, and Minnesota increased by factors of 1 1/2 to 3 during the seventies and into the late eighties, each adding several hundred thousand people per decade, and the Dakotas, which became states in 1889, experienced their most rapid expansion during the eighties and into the nineties. Frontier days lasted briefly and then passed into legend as the long cattle drives and their attendant cow towns in Kansas folded up after the Panic of 1873, and as the destruction of the buffalo and the ravages of the U.S. Cavalry ended competition from Indians for land during the middle and late seventies. Erstwhile cow towns like Abilene, Wichita, and Dodge City transformed themselves into middle-class communities whose sobriety was broken only by the scramble for financially promising town lots. Speculators and developers platted towns and cities all over the prairie, envisaging quick profits along with a town-farm pattern hoped soon to be as dense as Ohio's, but which was never to be. The town development boom became almost frantic in Kansas and Nebraska in 1885–1887, but deflated within a few weeks after crop failures, then low prices, occurred in 1887 and thereafter. The depression of the nineties began early, in 1888, for farmers and others in the Great Plains and the South. The flow of migrants, so strong during the seventies and much of the eighties, hesitated, then stopped, then reversed. About as many people left Kansas in the decade following 1887 as arrived there in the seven or eight years before that. As economic difficulties engulfed the area, political tensions increased. In the western half of the Midwest, the years after 1887 carried a foretaste of the depression that would strike the industrialized parts of the country after 1893.

One further aspect of the demographic substrate needs to be considered before taking a look at economic developments in the interdepression period: the high rate of mobility from place to place of certain segments of society. As already indicated, some spatial mobility occurred among the black population. A great deal took place to produce the rapid population growth of the West North Central states and the Mountain and Pacific West; and immigration from Europe proceeded apace. In addition to all of that, a remarkable amount of movement occurred among the urban working-class population of the Northeast and Midwest. A recent study of the population of Boston during the eighties concludes that in- and outmigration in that city was almost incredible. Boston had a population of 363,000 according to the census of 1880, and 448,000 according to the census of 1890. The increase of 85,000 is accounted for in part by natural increase—the excess of births over deaths in the population already there in 1880. That takes care of 20,000, with the other 65,000 accounted for by net immigration. But the net figure is only the residue from a much vaster movement in and movement out. The authors found that "nearly 800,000 people moved into Boston between 1880 and 1890 to produce the net migration increase of 65,179," and most of that 800,000 moved out again. More than twice the number of people moved in and out of Boston during the eighties than the total resident population in 1880. The study also suggests that about half the population of the city changed residence in any given year, a rate of mobility about two and a half times greater than in the post-World War II period; that those who moved were much more apt to be unskilled or semiskilled workers and their families, rather than skilled workers or people in middle-class or professional positions; that mobility rates for the foreign-born, especially the Irish, were higher than for the native whites, whose rates were in turn higher than for blacks, although black mobility was also considerable. In cities other than Boston, mobility may have been less, and persistence greater, as indeed was the case in Indianapolis. Movement was nonetheless very frequent by late twentieth-century standards.[9]

Adding this mass of urban working-class people to the numbers of European immigrants, to the potentially mobile Southern black population, and to the economically marginal agricultural workers who lived in and out of the Great Plains states at the same time, produces an impression of a very unstable, mobile society during the interdepression years especially at the lower or lower-middle-class strata. These people were mobile, however, only in the geographic sense, and not in terms of occupation, status, education, or property-holding. They could move from one working-class area to another, perhaps within the same city or perhaps several hundred miles away, but their ties to local community structure remained weak. The assimilation of these people into a stable social order was to become an acute problem during the depression of the nineties, and became a major, conscious concern of social theorists and reformers during the two decades thereafter.

The changes just described in the demographic character of Americans between 1878 and 1893 necessarily involved changes in occupations, conditions of work, and adaptation (or lack of it) to increasingly large-scale industrialism. Of those considered to be gainfully employed workers, the great majority were "blue collar" —farm workers, factory workers, miners, railroad hands, domestic servants, construction workers. Managers, professionals, merchants, bankers, even clerical workers were in the minority. The largest single occupational group remained, of course, farmers. They comprised about half of the labor force at the close of the depression of the seventies, a time when farm settlement, especially in the Great Plains, expanded quickly, and they continued to increase in numbers during the interdepression years until the late eighties. But despite the addition of about 1.4 million farmers during the eighties, their numbers grew at less than half the rate of the labor force in general. Compared to other groups they were slowing down, and by 1893 they made up only about 40 percent of the gainfully employed. In several other occupations, although none of them was even half as large as farming, the numbers of workers were increasing much more rapidly than the general average. The number of miners, as a result of steady demand for coal and iron, expanded by more than 50 percent in the seventies and again in the eighties and in the nineties. Construction, a sector of the economy which grew at rates far below the national average during the depression decades of the seventies and the nineties, flourished during the eighties, and numbers of construction workers grew at more than twice the rate of the labor force in general. Workers involved in railroading and other aspects of transportation and public utilities increased faster, proportionately, than any other group during the eighties; their numbers rose about 78 percent (the total work force increased about 37 percent). People involved in trade and finance, the major "white collar" activities, also expanded in numbers well above the average during the eighties. Most importantly in terms of numbers of people, manufacturing workers increased by about 50 percent, to nearly five million, and in 1890 constituted one-fifth of the gainfully employed.

Women entered the work force during the interdepression years in substantially greater numbers than before. By 1890 more than one out of six workers were female, and the four million working women in that year represented an increase of more than 50 percent during the eighties. Some worked on farms and some as domestic servants, but the principal growth during the eighties took place in clerical and other white-collar jobs. The great majority were white, single, and young. In those same years, child laborers—workers under sixteen years old—increased in absolute numbers but remained at just over six percent of the total work force. In general, then, the years from 1878 through 1893 were a time when the ranks of the gainfully employed expanded considerably, as did the whole population, but more than four out of five of the new jobs were in urban-located sectors of the economy rather than in farming and other extractive industries.

The material rewards for all this labor increased substantially during the interdepression years for a great many nonfarm workers and also for many farmers. Daily and annual earnings changed very little during the seventies, but began to rise after the end of the depression in late 1878. During the fifteen years until the depression of the nineties, income of nonfarm workers rose, especially for clerical workers and those in public utilities. Construction workers did especially well, and were making about $2.75 for a ten-hour day in 1890. Since the interdepression years were part of the long-term deflationary period which lasted from 1873 to 1897, more dollar income meant more buying power; rises in wages meant rises in real income, since inflation was not present to eat away at the value of the dollar in terms of food or housing or other necessities as has usually been the case in the twentieth century. At the same time, however, it should be pointed out that workers were not being rewarded lavishly. Increases in wages during the eighties did not quite keep pace with increases in productivity: the value of the things which workers produced increased slightly faster than the wages those workers received. Such was the case for wage earners in manufacturing, the largest single group of nonfarm workers.

For a number of others the situation was less happy. Wages in the lowest-paying major industry were only 40 percent of those in the highest, and women were paid half to two-thirds as much as males. Just before the depression of the nineties began, the average annual income for all workers, including farmers, was in the neighborhood of $450—more in dollars than in 1878, more in terms of buying power, but a little less as a share of the new wealth the workers helped produce. Those who received the average figure worked about a sixty hour week, in six ten-hour days, to earn enough for the necessities of life but often not enough to amass capital for such purposes as buying a home, especially at the mortgage terms then prevailing, or providing for emergencies such as sickness, the injury or death of the principal wage earner in a family, the death of another member of a family (infant mortality was especially frequent), or retirement. Such protections and aids as workmen's compensation, sickness and accident insurance, social security, pension plans, and consumer credit were yet to be invented. Until they were, workers got along as best they could, which was not very well, with voluntary-membership associations such as burial societies, benevolent and protective associations, and private and usually badly funded insurance cooperatives. Even for better-paid workers such as clericals or those in the building trades or in public services like gas and electric companies and street railways, life was precarious, working hours were long, and dollar compensation insufficient to justify the prevailing idea that hard work could fulfill dreams of capitalist accumulation.[10] During the relatively prosperous interdepression years, when actual and real income was rising for many, when demand for workers was generally high, when promising farmland was available for settlement and farm products commanded a good market (as they did before 1888), the blue-collar mass could afford to overlook the precarious aspects of their situation at least part of the time. But they were increasingly subject to forces far beyond their control. Depression was to strike again with the harsh impersonality that characterized it four times previously in the nineteenth century, and it had already begun to wreak its inevitable damage on many Southern and Western farmers before the eighties were out. Even in prosperous years, both farm and nonfarm workers were increasingly experiencing the dehumanizing conditions of steam-age industrialization: for the manufacturing workers, rigid production schedules, the spreading pattern of mass employment with hundreds of workers in a single plant or firm, and diminishing control over wage rates, hours of work, and amenities; for farmers, having to sell their produce in distant markets where prices were set quite beyond their control, yet having to buy the land and implements necessary for production also at rates they could do virtually nothing about.

Increasingly, both workers and managers were being caught up in an economic situation involving rapid increases in output, gains in real wages which did not quite keep up with the value of output or of invested capital, and changes in the structure of the economy in the direction of complexity and interrelatedness. As a productive machine, the American economy made enormous advances between 1878 and 1893. Manufacturing output rose 247 percent in those years, with especially large jumps occurring in 1880, 1886, and 1892. Only in 1884 and 1885 was there a particularly significant or widespread recession; for the most part, and for most sectors of the economy and sections of the country, prosperity prevailed. The value of capital invested in many industries more than doubled during the 1880s—for example, food processing, paper-making, iron and steel, and farm and factory machinery. Of the large industries, only textiles grew more slowly than the average; as a long-established form of enterprise which was not undergoing major technological changes at the time, it did not attract new capital investment as did smaller but technologically exciting or high-demand industries such as printing and publishing, rail equipment making, or oil refining. Real growth proceeded at rates of 3 and 4 percent per year except for the recession years of 1884–1885, much of it coming from the manufacturing sector, and specifically from industries which made producer durables—goods such as rails, machinery, fertilizers, or bricks and lumber which did not go directly to ultimate consumers but rather were used in the production of some other goods or services.

The strongest trends in the economy through the eighties and the years just before and after were those typical of a certain stage of the development of all industrializing capitalist societies before and since. In the United States as elsewhere, these trends included a high rate of savings and reinvestment in new productive capacity (manufacturing, railroads); a strong emphasis on production for the purpose of generating further production, rather than production for a mass consumer market—that is, an emphasis on "heavy industry"; and a greater concern for the output of workers than for the conditions and rewards of their labor. If a greater proportion of the new wealth being produced in manufacturing and other sectors had been passed on to workers in the form of higher wages, rather than being retained for further capital investment or as profits for owners, economic growth would undoubtedly have taken place at slower rates. But quite possibly the social dislocations and sheer human misery which were a byproduct of this kind of industrialization would have been substantially less. In effect, and without realizing it, Americans were gambling that by maintaining a high rate of savings and reinvestment, and deferring rewards to the mass of population, they would at some point in the future arrive at a happy economic result; the risk in the gamble was that social evils would become so intense as to ignite into a social revolution and destroy the whole system.

Besides manufacturing, transportation was a key growth sector during the interdepression years. The brief prosperity that existed from just after the Civil War until the Panic of 1873 rested on railroad building. When depression ended at the close of the 1870s, railroad building resumed, and the miles of track more than doubled to well beyond two hundred thousand miles by 1893. By that time the railroads were not so uniquely important as the thrusting force behind industrialization as they had been before 1873 and during the early 1880s. Other industries, some of them built up as a result of very heavy demand from the railroads for their products, and other factors for change such as technology and new management techniques, were playing important roles. Nonetheless, as the railroad network became an increasingly complex web linking raw materials to factories to consumers and making it possible (and often necessary) to sell goods on distant markets, it continued to perform critical functions in the industrializing process. Railroads continued to require iron and steel in their construction and maintenance, coal in their operation, capital for their expansion, and human labor for all of those purposes. They were by no means always profitable, or large, or well-run. Railroad expansion in the eighties and early nineties was accompanied by continuous efforts to reduce competition (on one major occasion, by government action: the Interstate Commerce Act of 1887), to streamline management, and to increase profits. Yet they continued to grow, and as they did they provided American industrialization with an essential underpinning.

Economic historians have argued at length about the relative importance of railroads, producer-durables output, productivity gains, rates of savings and investment, new technology, and managerial innovation as factors in the process of industrialization. The argument will continue, because all these factors were present in the United States in the interdepression years of 1878–1893, all played some role, and all were interdependent. Technology was crucial, and innovation took place in thousands of ways, some obvious, some not. It is inconceivable, for example, how railroad building and everything dependent on structural steel could have happened without the Bessemer-Kelly and, later, the open-hearth processes which permitted the making of quality steel in large quantity; or how newspapers and magazines could have become common and inexpensive (and later, instruments of social and political reform) without such inventions of the eighties as the linotype and high-speed presses; or how electricity for factories, homes, and streets could have been carried to them without the invention of large dynamos, the transformer, and durable wires and filaments which were the outcome of sophisticated metallurgy. Examples could be multiplied indefinitely. Technology was essential. So also, however, were managerial innovations—so much so that Alfred D. Chandler has said that, while the creation of the railroad network, the rise of urban markets, and new technology were present and basic, "*the* major innovation in the American economy between the 1880s and the turn of the century was the creation of the great corporations in American industry." [11]

Large firms dealing on a regional or national market were virtually unknown at the close of the depression of the seventies, except for some railroad companies. By 1893 they were the dominant form of business enterprise in a number of manufacturing industries and to a considerable extent in transportation. Hundreds of railroad companies operated during the 1880s, but many were short, local affairs, and the bulk of track and traffic was coming to be the property of a small number of trunk-line companies such as the Pennsylvania, the Erie, the Boston and Maine, the New York Central, the Baltimore & Ohio, and the transcontinentals. The Pennsylvania and the B & O had put together trunk lines from East Coast cities to Chicago and St. Louis in the late 1850s, and the Vanderbilts, Commodore Cornelius and his son William H., gained control of the New York Central and made it into a New York-Chicago trunk line in the late sixties and the seventies. For them and for other entrepreneurs the process was usually one of consolidating smaller companies into the larger firm, a process which involved standardization of gauges and equipment, rapid utilization of technological innovations, and continuous expenditure on a large scale. Simultaneous growth of urban population, farm produce, manufacturing output, and demand for railroad facilities all favored railroad expansion, and expand they did, all through the eighties and especially in the five years after the resumption of prosperity in 1879. The expansion was also competitive; as one of the Vanderbilts remarked, five railroads came into New York but there was only enough business for two (he meant, if business were conducted efficiently and profitably). It was clearly evident that cutthroat competition was not profitable, and it was also evident that larger firms could mobilize capital with the help of investment bankers like J. Pierpont Morgan, take advantage of new technology, and function profitably with more effectiveness than small firms could. The natural dynamics of the railroad business led toward large companies controlling the transportation facilities of a considerable geographical area. Morgan, whose aim was to reduce competition and maximize profits through what he called "rationalizing" the transportation system, played a critical role in negotiating the mergers of a number of railroad companies (and, especially after 1893, mergers in other industries as well). One of the results was indeed "rationalization"; another was the creation of intricate, practically indissoluble linkages between finance and transportation, or "Wall Street" and the railroads.

The trend toward large firms was also present in manufacturing. Here again the pressures toward bigness included the desire to reduce cutthroat competition, thus not only maximizing profits but reducing risks which threatened steady output; the desire to employ new technologies, which could be expensive; and the hope of taking advantage of growing urban markets. The interplay of these forces fostered the appearance of large, national-market manufacturing firms first of all in consumer-goods industries, as Chandler points out. The Swifts in meatpacking, Duke's formation of the American Tobacco Company in 1890, Standard Oil as a producer of kerosene for homes, and a number of other entrepreneurs and firms were created or reorganized between 1880 and 1893 to combine large shares of the output in their particular industries in maximally efficient manufacturing plants, and then to sell their products through a regionally or nationally integrated marketing network. Combinations in producer-durables industries, such as steel and chemicals, began noticeably in the late eighties, but the most spectacular mergers in heavy manufacturing took place after the depression of the nineties. By 1893, however, the word "trust" was in general use as shorthand for a large firm producing a significant share (or as in the case of Standard Oil nearly a total share) of the output of a given industry, often controlling its raw materials sources, often monopolizing patents for essential technology, and as a rule operating its own marketing network. In manufacturing combinations, capital for mergers was much more often generated internally rather than borrowed or mobilized by investment bankers, as was the case with the railroads.

"Big business" was thus a reality by 1893. In 1879 the application of the trusteeship concept to company organization was only a gleam in a lawyer's eye. More was heard of it after the formation by John D. Rockefeller and his associates of the Standard Oil Trust in 1882. The limited-liability corporation as a form of business organization had existed for decades, but in the 1878–1893 period it was applied much more frequently than before to manufacturing and marketing concerns and to facilitate the creation of large companies with million-dollar or multi-million-dollar capitalization. The existence by 1878 of general incorporation laws obviating specific charters by state legislatures in the states where most of the nation's business was done hastened the trend toward incorporation and bigness. Along with all of this, of course, came an increase in the average number of workers per firm, especially in railroads and manufacturing.[12]

In agriculture, the main trends were in important respects the opposite of what was taking place in manufacturing and transportation. Anything but a merger movement occurred. On the contrary, agriculture continued to include an increasing number of small, discrete production units. Except in total output, which was high in either historical or comparative terms, agriculture was a sector with many problems. Its position relative to the "growth sectors" such as manufacturing, trade, finance, and transportation was unfavorable: although 40 to nearly 50 percent of the country's gainfully employed were engaged in farming throughout the 1878–1893 period, agriculture as a sector generated only about one-sixth of national income, a share during the eighties less than that generated by manufacturing and no greater than that deriving from trade. It is not easy to make accurate generalizations about farming and farmers because inter- and intra-regional differences in crops, methods, and returns were so great—for example the position of New York dairy farmers, cotton growers in the South, Indiana corn-hog producers, and Nebraska wheat raisers, differed substantially. But a few remarks can legitimately contrast agriculture with other sectors and show why farmers, or many of them, were the first large group to encounter social and economic crisis.

In the first place one should note that the number of farms and farmers, and the total output of crops and livestock, rose considerably through the period. So did productivity per farmer, thanks to mechanization, fertilizers, hybrids and other new crop strains, and more accessible transport for crops. But so also did tenancy and mortgages. Moreover, the value of the gross output of the country's farms rose only 4 percent during the eighties in current dollars, and although this disappointing result was mitigated in part by dollar deflation, the returns from farming compared unfavorably with other types of enterprise. A large part of the trouble was the great expansion of commercial farming into new areas, especially the West North Central and West South Central states, in the seventies and the eighties, an expansion which amounted to an overexpansion for the individuals involved. This overexpansion accentuated the uncoordinated character of production in a sector composed of several million independent units, and it encouraged farmers to produce more and thus compete intensively with each other, just at a time when other sectors of the economy were rapidly coordinating and centralizing. The railroads, which had done so much to make agricultural expansion possible, served also to put the Midwestern and Southern farmer into competition with staple-crop producers all over the world. Proceeds received by Southern cotton producers, for example, depended on what happened in India and other distant places which had become part of the same world market; wheat prices depended on what happened on the Liverpool commodities exchange. For well-established farmers, such as those in the older Middle West, conditions even after 1887 allowed for survival if not prosperity. In the Southeast, which was not only more than four-fifths rural but also concentrated its energies in staples including tobacco, sugar, and above all cotton, miseries accumulated throughout the period. Cotton sold for well over ten cents a pound in 1879 and 1881, but its price fluctuated downward to a low of seven cents in 1893 and would fall further during the nineties. Sharecropping, the crop lien system of credit, and tenancy, all spread, to the distress of small farmers; a historian wrote recently that in Louisiana, twenty dollars was an unusually good cash return for a sharecropper or field hand in a year. For such people there was no practical hope of homesteading or otherwise owning land.[13]

In the western part of the Midwest, the area of heavy recent settlement, farming operations were very often marginal. The Homestead Act of 1862, considered in the hopes of its authors and in historical legend the route toward a West of happy small farmers, proved not to be that. Only a small fraction of the newly settled farms in the trans-Missouri states were homesteads, and of those, many failed to last for the five years required to attain ownership; the failure rate in Nebraska was 43 percent.[14] Money and credit were briefly abundant in the early and mid-eighties, but with the onset of crop and livestock failures in 1887, shortages became endemic. While the money supply expanded in the Northeast and in cities elsewhere, mobile money was very scarce in the South and West. Railroad freight rates decreased somewhat during the eighties and early nineties, but did not do so in coordination with crop price fluctuations, and in a bad price year such as 1889 freight became an excessively high proportion of a farmer's fixed cost, especially so for farmers in central Kansas or Nebraska, whose great distance from ultimate markets caused their total freight bill to be very high despite diminishing rates per mile. It is quite possible that the owner-operated family farm, that entrancing vision of how American society should ideally be organized, had ceased to be a viable economic enterprise as early as the late 1880s. It is certain that the family farm was an economic prison for thousands in the South and Midwest in the late eighties and early nineties. Agriculture was already becoming a problem sector, caught on the one hand by its increasing number of independent units producing ever-increasing amounts, and on the other by increasingly interlocking market forces on a national and international scale.

Workers in the nonfarm sectors also had problems, some similar to those of farmers and some different. Both groups experienced increases in wages or income, a greater reward for their efforts as "producers." But in both instances the rewards were not sufficiently high to permit, as a regular occurrence, the acquisition of much personal or real property, and were not equivalent to productivity gains. Like the farmers, industrial workers also had difficulty in coordinating their efforts to effect collective bargaining in order to gain some measure of control over the enlarging market forces in whose context they had to operate. The desirability of organization among workers had long been recognized and in certain instances, especially among skilled artisans, had been achieved from time to time. In the 1878–1893 period the most prominent attempt to unionize workers on a mass basis was the Order of the Knights of Labor, headed through most of the period by the Irish immigrant Terence V. Powderly. The Knights were regarded by their leaders and members as an instrumentality for achieving that legendary aim, "the union of all the producing classes," and as such was open to "producers" of various kinds, including not only factory operatives but railroad workers, farmers, miners, even tradespeople, the skilled and unskilled, natives and immigrants. In being so inclusive, the Order prevented itself from coming to grips with specific problems in specific sectors and thus revealed the growing inapplicability of the widely-held "producer" ideology to contemporary economic trends. Despite this and other structural flaws, the Knights did enjoy a rise in membership in the early eighties, and after momentary successes in 1885 in lobbying for federal legislation to prohibit importation of contract labor and in striking against several major railroads, its numbers soared to over 700,000. From that high point the Order declined and expired. Failure to enroll any more than a fraction of industrial workers, much less all "producers"; public revulsion over the Haymarket Riot in Chicago in May, 1886, following a strike of 25,000 packinghouse workers which the Knights were supposed to have led (though Powderly insisted they did not); and the lack of success of subsequent strikes and boycotts, all led to its demise. Neither management, nor courts, nor churches, nor middle-class opinion (including many farmers) were cognizant of the realities of industrial life, or ready for industrial unions. The floating mass of people moving in and out of America's large cities were not to be easily organized by anyone, and despite the brief heyday of the Knights of Labor, were not organized. Skilled workers achieved some success, and the American Federation of Labor began a relatively healthy infancy in the late eighties, in large part because of the policies of its leader, Samuel Gompers, who avoided the rhetoric of producerism and apparent threats to the whole capitalist system. And it did not ask for too much.

The mass of workers, meanwhile, remained outside trade unions. Without the benefit of organization, they had to pass through the difficult process of adaptation to large-scale industrialism. Each year from 1886 through 1893 brought from one to two thousand strikes, usually over wages and hours problems, some as famous as the Haymarket affair of 1886 in Chicago or the strike of Carnegie's Homestead steel mill in Pittsburgh in 1892, but most of them limited and local, in either case harsh. For the people involved, who usually, whether native-born or foreign-born, had been raised in preindustrial, rural situations, the industrial-urban context forced on them radical changes in work habits, a substitution of the regularities of machines for the gentler regularities of nature, a confrontation with corporate systems rather than with people of basically equivalent power and status, and a fear that they were becoming part of some impotent proletarian mass instead of free men and women. The apparently inexorable process of industrialization was forcing on millions of people a set of realities which clashed at all critical points with their social patterns, their ideological conceptions of what society should be like, and their future material prospects.[15]

In sum, the American economy underwent transformations of irreversible kinds during the interdepression years of 1878 to 1893. It had increased its share of world iron and steel output from one-sixth to one-third, becoming the world leader by the early nineties; it outranked all other countries in steam and electrical power used, in railroad operations, and in other major indicators of industrialism. But the demographic and economic processes which

all of this change entailed also brought intense stresses which were
to be felt not only in social, economic, and political relations, but in
values and ideology. Traditional value systems would have to be
revised if they were not first demolished. The reckoning could be
postponed as long as prosperity lasted. But the cyclical disaster of
depression arrived again in 1893, and as depression had catalyzed
group and value conflicts from previously unobserved socioeco-
nomic changes, it would do so again in the nineties, when the
chances of ignoring the serious problems of urban-industrial reality
were much reduced.

4

Depression and Social Crisis, 1893–1901

The depression of 1893–1897 was the fifth episode of its kind to afflict the American economy in the nineteenth century, and the second under industrial conditions which were more or less advanced. Like the depression of the seventies before it and that of the 1930s after it, it served to intensify disharmonies; in this case the cleavages in society which had developed since 1878. Unlike the depression of the 1930s, it was not met by a head-on political and legislative attack just at the point when economic indicators descended to their lowest levels. Instead, as was the case in the late seventies, the depression ended when "things worked themselves out" and "nature took its course." No coordinated set of remedies, in fact hardly any responses at all, were applied. To the contrary, the end of the depression apparently came about in part by the resounding defeat at the polls of those who sought massive legislative remedies (or what passed for massive remedies at the time), the Populists and Democrats who supported William Jennings Bryan in the election of 1896. The Bryan movement was significant for a number of reasons, one of which was that it convinced much of the public for several more years that legislative attacks on economic and social problems were unnecessary and undesirable. The call of Bryan's version of reform was strong enough to convince many that it was the only version; and that version the people voted down.

As a consequence of that vote, and some other factors, the experience of the depression of the nineties did not generate the sober reevaluation of social goals and political practices that American society had already begun to need badly before 1893. Instead, by adding further evidences of disharmony and division, the depression (in political context) only made things worse. The sense of an impending social crisis, even social revolution, did not

end with the appearance of economic recovery, but continued to
gain strength until after the turn of the century. The narrative of
this gloomy process takes several parts: first a look at political
structures and issues from the late eighties into the nineties,
including a discussion of the Farmers' Alliance and Populist
protest which arose in response to the agricultural depression that
began in late 1887; then a description of the economic and social
dimensions of the Panic of 1893 and the subsequent depression
itself; a note on some evidences of intelligent response to socioeco-
nomic problems—in some quarters a recognition that the problems
existed; the culmination of agrarian politics from 1893 through
1896; and the continuation of social crisis and disruptive economic
trends through the rest of the nineties.

Prior to the agricultural depression of the late eighties, prevailing negative attitudes about the role of state and national
government and the lack of a sense of urgency about the legislative
solution of common economic and social problems did much to
confine political response to local and cultural issues. In the
absence of economic crisis, economic issues were not central to
elections. In the absence of charismatic national leaders and
well-structured, continuing party machinery at the national level,
political issues of national scope were few and feeble. Although
civil service reform and levels of tariff protection received much
discussion from editorialists and mugwumps during the eighties,
there is little indication that either issue—and they were the main
ones in "national" politics during the decade—was of burning
importance for the mass of the voters. Instead, politics revolved
around matters of style, temperament, ethnic and cultural values,
and either their reform (usually by Republicans) or preservation
(usually by Democrats). Politics also meant the withholding or
conferring of more or less petty economic advantages through state
or more often county or ward organizations of the political parties.
The parties, as voluntary institutions within society, were poorly
equipped by structure or tradition to effect far-reaching policies,
either conservative or radical, at the national level. But they were
decidedly able to mobilize or suppress support for legislation or
administrative action involving moral behavior, and to maintain
loyal support at the local level from voters by means of the kind of

favors and functions associated with "political machines." The term "political machine" carried an entirely negative connotation among mugwumps in the eighties and nineties, and again among the more vocal Populists and progressives in the nineties and after the turn of the century. Thanks to several generations of progressive and liberal-oriented lessons in civics and political science, the connotation still holds. But a negative attitude toward "machines" or, to use a more proper and less loaded term, party organizations, is difficult to maintain if one also maintains that the more participation in government there is, the better democracy is served: levels of voter turnout in elections have never been higher than in the 1880s and 1890s. The "machines" did a better job of getting people to vote than reformers did. Mugwumps and progressives railed against party organizations, aside from theoretical reasons, because they could not control them. Despite reformers' criticisms, the parties, at the state and especially the local levels, obviously served a great many other people, as evidenced by record-high voter participation and intense party loyalty.

The political process then as at other times came down to the old question of who gets what, when, and how; or, to put it a bit differently, who wanted what, when, and how. In the America of the eighties and early nineties, a society in which large organizations were a novelty in business or urban government, and in other areas of life practically unknown, politics was expected to provide, as far as economic matters went, advantages or equities (one man's fair treatment being another man's spoils) with regard to taxes, licenses, fire and police protection of life, limb, and property, and other day-to-day concerns of county and city government. Stockholders and managers of larger companies might wish government, state or federal, to provide tariff protection or land grants or to prevent restraint of trade, but aside from that minority interest it was not widely believed that governments should intervene in market forces.

What else did people want from politics? To judge from the election returns of the late eighties and early nineties, the majority wanted governments to leave them alone in cultural matters, while a minority perceived government as a device for insuring public morality of an evangelical kind. Recent research on the social bases

of politics in the Midwest and Northeast has revealed that the
major determinants of voting behavior and the outstanding issues
in that place and time were cultural, and that public response to
those cultural issues depended not on wealth, occupation, or
income but on ethnic and religious affiliations.[1] Through the
eighties and until elections in 1888, 1889, and 1890, the salient
features of politics in the Midwest and Northeast were high voter
turnouts and very even balance between the Democratic and
Republican parties in all elections, and especially in presidential
years. In 1888 third-party voting was higher than it had been in
eight years in certain states, particularly those already experiencing
agricultural depression. In those cases the third-party appeals were
basically economic. In 1889 and 1890, however, the Republican
party suffered defections in states of the older Middle West and the
Northeast, and in those cases the basic reasons were cultural rather
than economic. In several states, legislation was introduced or
urged, and sometimes passed, restricting the sale of liquor on
Sundays or other times, prohibiting doing business on Sundays,
and regulating the relation of public and parochial schools. In
1889, the Bennett law in Wisconsin and the Edwards law in Illinois
decreed that elementary education was to be compulsory and
instruction was to be carried out in the English language. These
were straightforward enough measures to bring about a higher
literacy level and to restrict child labor. They were interpreted as
attacks on parochial schools, Lutheran or Catholic; in many cases
the interpretation was accurate. Temperance, Sabbatarianism, and
education were the three main cultural issues, with antigambling
laws a fourth in some areas. On all of them the Republican party
became identified with the activist, and to many voters the
repressive, position. The Republican party still showed outcroppings of its moralist roots of thirty years before, and voters of
immigrant stock, especially Catholic and non-British immigrants,
had reason to view it with suspicion. Republican leaders and,
sometimes, platforms called for the enactment of moralistic laws.
Northern Democrats, on the other hand, were by long experience
and philosophy the more negativist of the two groups, and it suited
their temperament as well as their political strategy to regard
themselves as the party of "personal liberty" and to encourage the

identification of the G.O.P. with repressive cultural laws. In 1889 and 1890 they successfully did so in many states, with the result that the Republicans lost seventy-eight seats and the Democrats gained seventy-six in the U.S. House of Representatives. Not only was the turnover the largest up to that time, but it appeared to mean the end of the two-party balance in national elections (which had begun in 1874) and the beginning of Democratic dominance. Elections in 1891 and 1892 appeared to reinforce the trend. Shrewd Republican leaders who by then had realized the great damage their party was suffering from its identification with temperance people, suffragists, Sabbatarians, and other cultural moralists, tried to dissociate the party from moralistic positions. But many former Republican voters (German Lutherans notably, but some others as well) either stayed home or switched to the Democrats. The majority of the voters had rejected moralism in politics, or at least middle-class, native-stock evangelical moralism. Morality was fine, political moralism was not; the majority of voters evidently felt it was a matter for preachers, not politicians.

The trend toward the Democratic party was to be short-lived. Though demographic currents were running in favor of urban and foreign-stock elements who leaned Democratic on cultural grounds, and though the party had successfully taken the winning position in opposing moralistic laws, it also opposed almost every other kind of legislative action and would soon be perceived by voters as failing to cope with pressing economic problems. Ethnocultural issues and attachments would continue to affect voting behavior and party composition through the nineties and in fact well past the middle of the twentieth century, but in the depression years of the nineties they were to be sufficiently superseded by urgent economic matters to put the Democrats at a long-term disadvantage.

In the solidly Democratic South, ethnocultural issues did not arise; there were few ethnics in that region. But the politics of race substituted quite adequately as a cultural preoccupation. The Bourbon Democrats who controlled Southern state governments through the eighties had had little to fear from black voters. Not only was disfranchisement usually unnecessary, but it could have been harmful to Bourbon interests. Black voters were useful to the

Bourbons for stabilizing and securing "establishment" regimes in some cases.

Southern politics changed radically in 1889 and 1890 with the onset of agricultural depression and the emergence of political responses to depression in forms hostile to Bourbon supremacy. Farmers' Alliance and then Populist candidates bitterly criticized the prevailing Democratic organizations and began to pose a real threat at the polls, and in the process of building anti-Bourbon coalitions in various states they actively sought the help of the Colored Farmer's Alliances and black voters generally. Their success as well as their motivation differed from state to state and even from county to county, but the generalization holds broadly that the Alliancemen and Populists did succeed, momentarily at least, in building an interracial, cross-class coalition on economic issues. Nothing could have been more frightening to white Democratic leadership. The responses of that leadership were several. In Louisiana, for example, Bourbon Democrats practiced vote fraud and other forms of electoral manipulation either to retain black votes in the Democratic column or to keep blacks from voting, whichever tactic was more practical. There and in other deep-South states the movement toward disfranchisement laws quickly accelerated, and everywhere across the South, blacks effectively lost the ballot by legislation or constitutional amendment in the late nineties and the first five or six years of the 1900s.

A separate but ultimately related development took place during the nineties: the emergence of a progressive element within the Democratic party, hostile to Populism, supportive of disfranchisement, but different in leadership and aims from the Bourbons. In Alabama, Populism and progressivism "were contemporary rather than sequential," according to Sheldon Hackney; progressivism "was a substantially different reaction by a separate set of men to the same enemy Populism faced—the dominant industrial wing of the Democratic party." Texas politics presented a similar situation in the elections of 1890 and 1892 of James S. Hogg, a non-Populist, proto-progressive Democrat, to the governorship.[2]

In the early nineties, however, any movement resembling progressivism had far to travel before it would become full-blown. The overwhelmingly rural South was experiencing agrarian protest at the hands of its Alliancemen and Populists, but the protesters were to enjoy neither electoral nor ideological victory. White supremacy, so axiomatic in Southern culture and politics, was too strong to permit the Populist interracial coalition to last. When the South confronted the social and economic problems generated by urbanism and industrialism, it would do so, as it began to do in the nineties, in its own way.

Elsewhere in the country, "reform" was not unknown in the eighties and early nineties. The publicists, preachers, and professors often termed "mugwumps" viewed social and economic problems through class and cultural lenses, and with a hostility to political party organizations either Republican or Democratic. The term "mugwump" applies most specifically to Northeastern Republicans who refused to support their party's candidate, James G. Blaine, in the 1884 presidential election, on the ground that Blaine had been involved in some shady deals and lacked appropriate moral rectitude. But the term had broader meaning. Through the eighties and nineties mugwumpery referred to a set of mind in which the natural-law, social Darwinist, native-American-morality ideology was a preoccupation. The most vocal exemplar of mugwumpery was Edwin L. Godkin, editor of the leading genteel periodical, *The Nation.* The readership of *The Nation,* and people who were mugwumps, were probably almost coterminous groups. With Godkin, who was himself an Anglo-Irish immigrant, the outstanding mugwumps were centered in New York and New England, were of old-stock upper-class and upper-middle-class families, and considered themselves (and managed to convince many others) that they were "the best people," the civic, church, and class leaders of their communities. Mugwumpery was manifest also in women's clubs, church organizations, civic leagues, and liberal-arts colleges all over the Midwest. Geographically diverse but ideologically similar, the mugwumps were reformers of an essentially conservative kind, and were united as much by their social class as for their ideas. They provided much of the impetus for civil service reform, not only prior to the Pendleton Act of 1883 but for years afterward, because they believed that the "merit system" would not only strike at the patronage power of party organizations, which to them was the festering matrix of corruption, but would also cost less in taxes. In their own towns and cities they perceived and condemned links between politicians and the most immoral and degraded elements, the purveyors of vice, gambling, liquor, and prostitution, and believed that any weakening of the politicians' power automatically meant a blow against social evils. It also meant very often a measure of control over the taxes which they, as the leading property owners, had to pay. Convinced that political machines depended on immigrants and others of the working class for their power, the mugwumps favored immigration restriction, opposed unions, and usually supported temperance and sabbatarian legislation. They were dissatisfied, as were many other groups including farmers and workers themselves, with many of the turns that American society was taking, but their response to the problems of the day was the basically negative one of promoting moral uplift and economy in government. This platform was to prove inadequate for meeting the social and economic problems of industrialization and business concentration, especially during the depression.

Political activity in the years just preceding the depression of the nineties thus centered largely on cultural, racial, and class issues. Although voter participation and public concern with politics was high, elections and political discussion turned much more on matters affecting morality, religion, ethnicity, and race than on economic issues. One major exception to this pattern existed before 1893, an exception already noted but which needs further discussion: the political response to economic problems which took place in the agricultural areas of the Midwest and South after depression struck there in the late eighties. The Farmer's Alliances and their offspring, the People's party, discussed these problems as broad ones involving basic changes in the national economy, whch they certainly were, and sought to build an effective political coalition without regard to cultural, ethnic, or racial divisions. In both their rhetoric and their politicking they fell far short of their aims; their analysis was inaccurate in many ways, and their coalition-building subject to the same stresses from cultural and racial divisions that plagued the Republicans and Democrats. Still, the Populist response was compelling to hundreds of thousands of people for several years.

Populism in the South, from Virginia to Georgia to Texas, was a political response to low crop prices, especially for cotton, and the increasing necessity for many farmers to cross the thin but vital line from mortgaged ownership to tenancy and sharecropping. Populism in Kansas, Nebraska, and other parts of the western Midwest, was a political response to low wheat and corn prices, near-constant costs of production (especially freight rates and mortgage interest), and scarcity of money and credit. The mass voting strength of the party came from farmers who were most vulnerable to these problems because their capitalization was low and their assets consisted almost entirely of the land and implements with which they themselves worked. For the most part, they were not a landless rural proletariat but rather a rural, capitalist lower-middle class. The Populist party's managers sought to build a voting coalition which would be as large as they could make it, and they were willing, on pragmatic as well as ideological grounds, to use any materials available. Thus in the South, Populism included, whenever possible, blacks as well as whites; in the Midwest it included (or sought to include) people from all ethnic groups. As a new party, it was at least as susceptible as the old parties to fragmentation on cultural issues such as prohibition and women's suffrage, or race hatred. Its opponents—entrenched Democrats in the South and entrenched Republicans in the Midwest—were often successful in driving cultural or racial wedges into its fragile coalition. When the Populists did not allow themselves to be distracted by ethnic and racial divisiveness, however, they espoused a political program which concentrated on alleviating specific agrarian problems, summarized by the three words, money, land, and transportation.

The rhetoric in which their editorialists, pamphleteers, and speechmakers couched their demands was borrowed heavily from that of the greenbackers and free-silverites of the middle and late 1870s. The primacy of producers (and the need for a union of the producing classes, especially with the Knights of Labor) was a constantly recurring idea. Like the greenbackers before them, they had a sense of American nationalism which led them not to a nativist rejection of foreign groups or ideas but rather to a condemnation of the plutocrats, international bankers, and big

businessmen whom they were convinced were taking the government and the country away from "the people." They parted
company with mugwumps and Cleveland Democrats and other
respectable contemporaries on the critical question of what governments ought to do; for them the government was the servant of the
people, indeed as some of them said, the government *was* the
people. They believed, then, in governmental activism, with the activism to be paid for by taxes on corporations and wealthy individuals, not on land and the instruments of production. As the
Populist governor of Kansas said in 1893, "The survival of the
fittest is the government of brutes and reptiles, and such philosophy
must give place to a government which recognizes human brotherhood." [3] Spencer and Sumner were not Populist prophets; neither
were Marx or Bakunin.

Two of the Populists' greatest contributions were, first, their
attempt to create a politics of economic issues cutting across ethnic
and racial lines, a politics functioning on behalf of "the people,"
and second, their advocacy of a much more positive role to be
taken by government. In these ways they provided the progressive
reformers of the following decades with useful precedents. Their
program of national reform, however, as a comprehensive attack
on the economic problems that had developed by the early nineties,
missed the mark. Populism's producerite rhetoric no longer resonated among industrial workers; it failed to win consistent and
convincing victories at the polls for a host of reasons connected to
state and local political contexts; its analysis of national problems
was based on a thorough knowledge of farm problems but also on
considerable ignorance of urban and industrial conditions of the
time; and, finally, it was in many ways too exclusively agrarian in
membership and ideas in a society which was fast losing its historic
agrarian character. Nonetheless it differed very greatly from the
rest of politics in the years just before the depression of the nineties,
and, depression-based as it was, it provided something of a preview of the political responses to problems which concerned many
other Americans from the Panic of 1893 through the turn of the
century.

The Panic of 1893 differed from that of 1873 at its outset in a
way which reflected the proliferation of large enterprises during the

interdepression years. The failure of one large firm, Jay Cooke & Co., had touched off the Panic of 1873. In 1893 the Panic followed the failure of a number of important companies almost simultaneously. Business conditions (except in agriculture) had favored expansion through the early nineties, and economic activity reached an all-time peak in January, 1893. In the following weeks, seasonal slack degenerated into a crisis of business confidence. The Reading Railroad, one of the major lines in the Northeast, declared bankruptcy on February 20, and while that in itself was not sufficient cause for panic, it severely shook investors and was taken as a warning that the prosperity of the past several years might be ending. Two months later, in late April, the news circulated that the federal government's gold reserves had dipped below one hundred million dollars, a "magic number" which had been generally assumed for many years by businessmen and economists to be the minimum amount to insure the redeemability of paper currency and payments on government securities. The reasons why the one hundred million was a magic number, why it was the conventional wisdom that the money and credit system would be in grave danger of collapse if the figure was not exceeded, are part of the complex mythology of the gold standard. The hundred million was an idyll of the marketplace with a powerful hold on men's minds. The reasons why the Treasury balance declined below one hundred million in gold are simpler to state. The McKinley tariff of 1890 was designed to produce less revenue than before, and it did; meanwhile the Harrison administration, which had entered office in 1889 with a substantial Treasury surplus built up during Cleveland's first term, succeeded in spending most of it, particularly on veterans' pensions and on warships, during the "billion dollar Congress" of 1889–1891. Furthermore, the Sherman Silver Purchase Act of 1890 increased the Treasury's silver purchases in order to keep up with domestic production and thus subsidize mine owners. But the silver provided backing for paper currency much of which was redeemable, illogically enough, in gold. Any waning of public confidence in the Treasury's ability to redeem such paper currency increased withdrawals of gold from the Treasury and made monetary stringency more likely. Cleveland returned to the White House in March, 1893, after the four-year Republican interlude with the Treasury gold reserve about to slide below the "magic number" regarded as safe, and with money and revenue laws on the books which insured that the problem would get worse before it got better.

Get worse it quickly did. In May and June, panic struck the stock and investment markets. Stock prices fell markedly, and bank and business failures multiplied. Nearly five hundred banks closed their doors during 1893, especially smaller banks in the South and West; the failure rate was about one of every nineteen banks in the country. Other businesses failed too, about twice as many as in 1873, many of them substantial manufacturing and commercial firms. Railroad bankruptcies multiplied: after the Reading folded in February, over 150 railroad companies followed suit, including all but one of the transcontinentals. From panic in the early summer in manufacturing, transportation, trade, and finance, and with the large agricultural sector already depressed long since, the national economy settled into a full-scale depression.

The winter of 1893–1894 was perhaps the worst in the country's history as an industrialized society. The rate of unemployment at the time has been variously estimated, but a recent analysis (by Charles Hoffmann) puts unemployment during that winter at more than 20 percent of the gainfully employed in manufacturing areas. The depression scene was unusually grim. Millions of people were jobless and without resources. Bank failures had wiped out savings. Welfare relief was minimal. Municipalities could not collect taxes needed to maintain essential services, much less provide significant aid to the poor. The story is told that one of the most notorious ward bosses of the time, Chicago's "Hinky Dink" Kenna, provided food for more than eight thousand impoverished and jobless men in one week during the winter of 1893–1894 at his saloon on Clark Street near Van Buren. For a night's rest the destitute slept in City Hall itself.[4] Kenna and other politicians refused any payment for these services. The assumption was simply that those who were helped would remember who helped them, come voting time. The politicians may not have been respectable in any middle-class sense, and the police graft, prostitution, and gambling that went on in Kenna's ward caused a stench in the nostrils of the mugwump-ish. But they provided the only source of relief for thousands of people from hunger and Chicago's winter cold. Baffled mugwumps wondered why political machines prospered and "clean government" proved a perennial mirage. The answer was simply that the machines solved, to some extent, problems of poverty and unemployment that the mugwumps did not even recognize as problems.

President Cleveland called Congress into special session during the summer of 1893 to repeal the Sherman Silver Purchase Act. Repeal, it was expected, would restore confidence in the monetary system (the confidence of Eastern businessmen and investors, at any rate) and halt the flow of gold from the Treasury. After long weeks of debate, the most heated discussion of the money question since the free-silver debates of 1876–1878, Congress did as Cleveland asked. By the end of October, silver purchases were no more; and neither, as a result, was any semblance of unity in Cleveland's Democratic party. The repeal, moreover, had very little impact except to contract the currency further. Notes were still presented at the Treasury for redemption in gold, the gold reserve continued to dwindle, and the problem of confidence remained. Tariff and other government revenues did not increase, and without revenue the Treasury reserve was not replenished. Business confidence remained in a slump. The depth of the depression was reached by the middle of 1894.

By then the disruption of the economy had begun to generate severe social and labor unrest. The late spring brought the pitiable episode of the march on Washington by the "army of the unemployed" led by a Populist small manufacturer, Jacob S. Coxey of Massilon, Ohio. It was the first protest march on the capital in American history, and one of the least successful. As was generally the case with Populist protest, it was nonviolent; but it also got little result except publicity and consequent further hardening of attitudes on both sides. In May and June, violence threatened to erupt in Colorado, as miners at Cripple Creek went on strike and the local sheriff, functioning as the military arm of the mineowners, lined up forces for a pitched battle. It was avoided only when the Populist governor, Davis Waite, interposed the state's national guard. During those same months and into July, workers at George M. Pullman's Palace Car Company near Chicago struck in protest at layoffs and severe wage cuts (while prices and rents in company-owned stores and homes remained stable). The recently formed American Railway Union, led by Eugene V. Debs, brought relief to the Pullman workers and organized a boycott of Pullman cars and sympathetic railroads from the Midwest to the Pacific. President Cleveland sent in federal troops to break the strike, despite the protests of John Peter Altgeld, the Democratic governor of Illinois. The Pullman strike was broken, Debs went to jail, and on his release several months later he began his rise to prominence as the leader of the American Socialist party. The Democratic party was further split along class and sectional lines, and the depression continued.

From the low point of June, 1894, some economic recovery took place over the next eighteen months. Several attempts by President Cleveland and the Treasury in 1893 and 1894 to raise the gold reserve through the public sale of bonds failed, but in early 1895 the monetary situation at the Treasury began to stabilize. Cleveland called upon the investment banking houses of Morgan and Belmont to act as agents for a private sale of government bonds, half to be sold in Europe. This was done, at a substantial undisclosed profit to the bankers, and the Treasury's leakage was reversed. By early 1896 that aspect of the depression was over. But others continued: bank failures, unemployment, and monetary contraction all increased once more beginning in the winter of 1895–1896, and a second phase of the depression, nearly as bad as the first, continued until general recovery finally began in the late summer of 1897. Even in 1899, as Hoffmann states, unemployment still lingered at 8 percent, and industrial output did not return to capacity levels until 1901.[5] Lack of business confidence played a role in the second phase of the depression as in the first, and again the specific problem was lack of confidence with regard to the monetary system. While the monetary crisis of the first phase was resolved not by the repeal of the Silver Purchase Act but by the private arrangements made between President Cleveland and J. Pierpont Morgan, the crisis of the second phase was resolved by the most public confrontation possible: the national election of 1896.

In 1894 the social and economic turmoil in American life deeply affected the course of politics. Populism gained strength in the

West and South, despite factional problems in several states and the cleverness with which opposing political-party organizations attacked it. Republicans in the Midwest, while making strenuous efforts to divorce their party from the stigmata of culturally divisive issues such as prohibition, woman suffrage, and Sabbatarianism, tried with some success to ridicule the Populists as cranks and calamity howlers, and also to exploit latent cultural antagonisms among them; in Kansas the Republican leadership installed a Republican counteragent in the temporary chairmanship of the Populist state convention, who saw to it that the suffrage and prohibition questions surfaced sufficiently to prevent fusion with the Democrats. Democrats in the South carried on equally devoted and sometimes physically violent efforts to quell the Populist threat, and in some areas legislatures began disfranchising of Negroes and poor whites. Within the next dozen years they carried that campaign to success. In the Midwest the Populists threatened the dominant party, the G.O.P., most directly through fusion with the Democrats; in the South the threat of fusion was not so much between Populists and the minority Republicans, though that sometimes happened, but rather through the socially much more dangerous fusion of blacks and whites along economic lines. In both areas, the dominant party waited until Populism was mortally weakened, as it was after the 1896 election, and then passed laws prohibiting fusion (two parties running the same candidate for an office) and the much more vicious disfranchisement laws in the South.

In 1894–1896, however, Populism was still very much alive. At the same time, Grover Cleveland's every act had served to split the Democratic party along sectional lines. Many Midwestern Democrats, like many Republicans in the region, had been in favor of monetary reflation either in the form of greenback issues or unlimited silver coinage ever since the seventies. The rhetoric of producerism, taking in the nineties a directly antibanker, anticorporation, antimonopoly form, resonated loudly among them; in the states of the Great Plains, where Populism was strongest, they had little to lose politically or ideologically by fusion with the Populists. Cleveland had infuriated them by demanding the repeal of the Sherman Silver Purchase Act, then by supplying federal troops to break the Pullman strike, then by turning a deaf ear to Coxey's Army and other protest marchers, and finally by his secret deal with the Morgan-Belmont bond syndicate. The more business-minded, monetarily deflationist Eastern leadership of the Democratic party was not altogether delighted with Cleveland's actions but were thoroughly out of sympathy with the Westerners, and Cleveland's steadfastness hardened their attitudes.

In the election campaign of 1894 the Republicans capitalized on Cleveland's unpopularity. They gave the impression that they had a positive program, especially a better tariff policy to deal with the depression, in contrast to Cleveland's negativism, and they avoided wherever possible and necessary their former identification with cultural issues.[6] The results of the election were disastrous for the Democrats, who lost 113 House seats. They were deeply disappointing for the People's party, which gained 40 percent more votes than in 1892 but lost a few House seats. And for the G.O.P., which gained 117 House seats and control of the Senate, 1894 was exceptionally gratifying. Republicans were delighted, and eagerly awaited their chance at the presidency in 1896. They would have been even happier had they known that their victory in 1894 represented the beginning of an electoral shift toward Republican majority status which would last almost without interruption for thirty-five years.

Social and economic tension persisted, however, and its political ramifications intensified over the next two years. Victory in 1894 was not yet victory in 1896, and when the Democrats, seconded by the Populists, nominated the charismatic and indefatigable William Jennings Bryan for president, and when Bryan based his campaign on Populistic rhetoric and the issue of unlimited silver coinage, many Republicans, businessmen, and Easterners thought they were looking down the gun barrels of socialism and anarchy. Their fears at what a Bryan victory would bring bordered on paranoia. To their own minds, the Republicans stood for stability and economic recovery, the Democrats and Populists for revolution and bankruptcy. When Bryan lost and Populism immediately began its permanent decline, they not only rejoiced at the immediate outcome but determined that by one means or another—even possibly including action at the state and national levels to deal with some of the problems which the Bryan coalition raised and represented—that social stability as they saw it would not be threatened again. As it happened, stability would not be seriously jeopardized in the future by the silver issue. But for the more basic problems for which unlimited silver coinage was just a surrogate, they had few coordinated answers as yet.

Bryan's defeat and McKinley's victory were clearly marked along sectional lines. They were much less clearly distinguishable along class lines, since the union of the producing classes, however defined, failed to materialize for Bryan. The depression, like that of the seventies, had an unequal impact on different groups and areas at different times. As stated earlier, industrial unemployment was heaviest during the winter of 1893–1894, and although it remained high through the next three to four years, and although the Pullman and Cripple Creek episodes were only two among over six thousand work stoppages from 1893 through 1897, the depression affected workers to quite varying degrees. Certainly the churning mass of mobile unskilled workers, farm and nonfarm, suffered most severely and were the least able to organize for effective protest. Workers in certain occupations actually made gains during the depression years: average annual wages for clerical employees of manufacturing and railroad concerns rose from $885 in 1892 to just over $1,000 in 1898, those for workers in gas and electric companies rose from $625 to about $700 in those same years, those for schoolteachers from $270 to about $300, while annual wages for railroad and streetcar workers remained roughly stable at about $510–560. These were the lucky few, a minority of the total work force. The much more numerous farmers, coal miners, production workers in manufacturing, and construction workers suffered declines in annual wages and in days and hours worked. The average soft-coal miner made $270 in 1897, the average farm laborer $224. The agricultural depression was worst in 1894, when the corn crop failed and the price of wheat dropped to forty-nine cents a bushel, and in some areas such as rural Wisconsin depression was so severe that farm workers migrated to towns and cities in the faint hope of finding employment, contrary to the usual tendency to remain on farms where some food, at least, could be had.

Farmers, miners, and industrial workers thus suffered grievously during the depression of the nineties, while those in a better position to defend themselves, because they happened to have highly desired skills or some capital, were much less affected. Stock prices declined 32 percent, by Hoffmann's estimate, wholesale prices 16 percent, wage income 10 percent, but bond prices only 2 percent: it helped to be a capitalist or at any rate a clever one. While railroads were badly hit by depression, steel manufacturing was not. The hundreds of bankruptcies and receiverships among railroad companies were reflected in swiftly reduced demand for, and production of, locomotives and freight cars in 1894, but after that terrible year production rose almost without setback, and in 1898 had about reached predepression levels. Steel output continued to rise even in 1894, fell back in 1896 from 6.1 to 5.2 million tons, then climbed again until in 1898 it was almost twice that of any predepression year. The balance of international trade was generally favorable, and money markets, though tight until 1897, were not so contracted as to prevent an increase in the total volume of money, from $5.8 billion in 1893 to about $7 billion in 1898. As was the case during the depression of the seventies, those least able to weather the storm took the brunt of it. For the fortunate few in an entrenched position in manufacturing or finance, the depression provided opportunities for consolidations, mergers, and monopolization.

The depression began to ease in the latter half of 1897, and the economy moved again, as it had in 1879–1882, into a recovery phase characterized by tentative, then rapid, expansion. In this instance recovery also involved a resumption of the trend toward ever larger firms, the trend already evident in the late eighties and early nineties. The easing of the economic crisis of 1893–1897 did not mean an easing of the social crisis which was developing prior to it and which worsened during it. On the contrary. The social and economic distance between capitalists and workers, between rich and poor, continued to widen rapidly, and the distance between nineteenth-century social and economic ideology and the realities of life became unbridgeable. These gaps were already present by 1893. The depression, wreaking its selective damage, made class divisions and the inadequacy of preindustrial ideology more visible and distressing. The shape which recovery took intensified these divisions further, accelerated the trend toward bigness and monopoly, and continued to reduce the degree of control which the individual could apply to his social and economic environment.

Recovery began for millions of small reasons and a few general ones. Agriculture came out of its long depression as the world market began to work in its favor: unusually large American harvests of cotton, corn, and wheat coincided, for once, with short or moderate harvests in other parts of the world, and dollar returns to farmers (especially wheat farmers) climbed upward. By the late nineties, too, the more marginal producers had long since been pushed off the land, as frequently happened in the Midwest, or into tenancy, as happened in the South. At the expense of the economic survival of many farmers, agriculture was becoming a healthier sector. In manufacturing, demand for producer durables resumed, and the index of manufacturing production rose almost 50 percent from 1896 to 1899. Wholesale prices rose almost one-fourth between 1896 and 1900. Another factor, the psychological one, played a major role in the recovery of manufacturing, transportation, and finance: the restoration of business confidence after the election of 1896. Fears abounded among investors and the Eastern business community as to what would have happened to capital values if Bryan had been elected and had actually brought about his announced aim of unlimited coinage of silver. Orthodox financial theory claimed that the reintroduction of the silver standard could be safely done, if at all, only after the major trading nations of the world had agreed by treaty to a stable ratio between gold and silver—the theory known as international bimetallism—or else gold would be driven from circulation, property values completely deranged, the country bankrupted in international trade, factories and farms shut down far more securely than even in 1894. While it is most unlikely that the consequences of silver coinage would have been anything like as dire, since for one thing the supply of it was finite and demand would have tended to stabilize its value, many people believed that the results would have been catastrophic. Bryan's defeat was an enormous relief to them. Although the idea that free silver was no longer a threat was a self-serving Republican argument, it nonetheless had a real effect in restoring business confidence. Confidence in the economic future is an intangible often resting on faulty judgment, but then as in other times it was as helpful to recovery as the absence of it had been productive of panic and depression in 1893 and 1894.

A final reason for recovery was most ironic in view of the fears about Bryan's plans for reflation through silver. The hostility to silver was predicated on the theory that only gold provided a stable measure of value and standard for the payment of debts. In the late nineties, gold itself came into much more abundant supply as large deposits were discovered in Canada and Alaska, as the Yukon gold rush went on, and as the cyanide refining process made extraction possible from mediocre ores. The quantity of the fundamental monetary substance expanded substantially, permitting an expansion of other forms of money based upon it. The result was a reflation of prices of all commodities, agricultural and manufactured, and a reflation of wages. Nearly all of the major nations of the world regarded the gold standard as the cornerstone of monetary policy, and as a result maintained demand for the limited amount available. This worldwide demand kept the price of gold high in relation to everything else. With the increase in supply resulting from the Alaska finds, the price of gold relative to commodities dropped; that is, general price inflation occurred. The "Great Depression" of 1873–1897 was over. Long-term deflation, which the Greenbackers had tried to attack in the seventies and early eighties by advocating more paper currency, and which the Populists and Bryanite Democrats tried to end through silver, stopped because of a sudden and unforeseen expansion of the world's gold stock. Inflation replaced deflation as the long-term monetary trend and, except during the 1930s, has been with us ever since. The Bryanites' demands for monetary relief indeed took place, and quickly, but by a means opposite to that which they had proposed.

The recovery phase of 1897–1901 thus meant rapid pickups in activity in agriculture, manufacturing, transportation, and trade, underpinned by a restoration of business confidence and by currency reflation based on expansion of the gold stock. Recovery also brought intense and rapid changes in the structure of business organization. The brief period from the end of the depression of the nineties to just past the turn of the twentieth century was the heyday of the merger movement in American business history.

Incorporation, the trust device, and the creation of monopolies or near-monopolies in a number of manufacturing industries was, as indicated before, well under way before the Panic of 1893. During the depression, combinations continued to form, particularly in railroading. The great investment banking firms, notably J. Pierpont Morgan's and the Rockefeller-affiliated Kuhn, Loeb & Co., sorted through the wreckage of bankrupt railroads from 1894 onward, refinanced them, and "rationalized" their operations, incidentally taking profits and substantial stock control with them in the process. Morgan put together the Southern Railway in 1895 from the pieces of the Richmond Terminal, Danville, and other lines, and by the end of the depression had been instrumental in reorganizing the Reading, the Erie, the Baltimore & Ohio, and several other major companies. The process continued during the recovery period, especially in 1899 and 1900, and by 1906, as a leading railroad historian has put it, "nearly two-thirds of the nation's rail mileage of 225,000 miles was in the control of seven groups." [7] During the recovery phase, new trusts were formed in addition to the existing monopolies in petroleum, sugar, tobacco, and other businesses. These new mergers took place in heavy industries such as copper, shipbuilding, chemicals, rubber, and electrical equipment. The most spectacular combination was created in 1901 in iron and steel, the most basic heavy industry. Morgan brought about the merger of a number of companies which he already controlled with the immense holdings of Andrew Carnegie, who wanted to retire. The result was the United States Steel Corporation. Capitalized at $1.4 billion, and as such the first billion-dollar company, U.S. Steel controlled 60 percent of the steel productive capacity of the country, together with much of the ore, transportation, and marketing devices it needed. By 1904, according to the best available figures, 318 trusts with capital of $7.25 billion dollars controlled 40 percent of American manufacturing.[8] The biggest combinations in manufacturing, railroading, and finance had been created in the recovery period of 1897–1901. The contrast in the structure of American business enterprise between 1901 and 1879, or even 1893, was immense. So were the social and ideological problems thus engendered.

It would be very misleading to assume that the depression and recovery period of the nineties produced no popular responses to the remarkable economic changes taking place except Populism and the Bryan movement. In certain ways, the nineties saw more thoughtful responses developed than in predepression days; the trouble was that those responses were insufficient to meet social and economic changes, fundamentally because they lacked an ideological framework adequate to those changes. Nonetheless they should be noted for their own sake and as building blocks for more extensive responses after 1901. The reform of taxation at state and local levels had been discussed prior to the depression, but mostly in terms of efficiency of collection, lowering of rates and frugality in expenditure, and tinkering with types of taxes to replace the increasingly obsolete general property tax. Those who tried to think innovatively about taxes realized that corporations could and should be a major source of revenue, but were uncertain about how to proceed. In a number of Eastern and Midwestern states during the depression, frugality and low rates appeared less of a desideratum than the desperate need for government money for welfare and public works. Efficiency remained a goal, but parsimony was often replaced by a willingness to experiment with new forms of taxes particularly upon corporations, including utilities and railroads. The tax reform movement spread in states such as New York, New Jersey, Wisconsin, and Michigan during the recovery phase.[9] When public utilities tried through court fights or disobedience of ordinances to resist taxation, and when many of them maintained high rates for gas, water, or transportation during the depression, local governments, backed by angry citizens, began to consider ways to make the utilities municipally owned. Private franchises remained the rule until after the turn of the century, but the beginnings of "gas and water socialism" appeared in the nineties. Some states began more stringent regulation of railroads in intrastate commerce, especially where agricultural distress made it a popular political issue, as in Texas when James Hogg was governor in the early nineties. Elsewhere, despite the farm depression, railroad-controlled Republicans or ineffectual Populists made little impact on railroad rates or practices during the depression and recovery periods. Nonetheless the revitalization of the Interstate Commerce Commission, and stronger state railroad boards, became the subject of widespread discussion and in a few cases, action. Most legislation concerning industrial practices such as hours and wages, the recognition of unions, and child and women labor, was also to wait a few more years, but the first laws requiring safety devices to protect railroad or manufacturing workers, and to compensate workers or their survivors involved in the appalling number of industrial accidents, began to appear in the nineties. Wisconsin's Bennett Law of 1889, which had such momentarily disastrous effects on Republican fortunes when German Lutherans condemned it as an attack on parochial schools, was intended in large part to reduce child labor. In several Midwestern states, new laws tightened the lending practices and capitalization requirements of banks.

These and other efforts to deal with problems arising from social and economic change proceeded during the depression and recovery more rapidly than before, as poverty and unemployment became too obvious to ignore in many areas, and as increasing numbers of citizens were willing to modify or at least suspend their commitment to laissez faire ideology in order to do something about the immediate, tangible needs of others around them. The facts of the depression made strict adherence to social Darwinism very difficult. As yet, with the exception of utopians such as Edward Bellamy, socialists such as Daniel De Leon or Eugene Debs, or a number of Populist leaders, legislative remedies were uncoordinated, piecemeal affairs rather than structured programs, and reform campaigns usually sought to replace the corrupt and corrupted with "better men," rather than to recognize that labor and farmer problems and the emergence of monopolies required much more than that. But many more people were willing to support some government activism and to begin to rethink their presuppositions about society. The Social Gospel movement, at most embryonic before the depression, made considerable gains, and the adoption of reformist programs by clergymen in major denominations and leading pulpits gave social reform a respectability it had lacked among middle-class people. Muckraking journalism, which would become a powerful arouser of social conscience and protest in the next decade, had its precursor in Henry Demarest Lloyd's 1894 book, *Wealth Against Commonwealth*, a long and documented exposé of the ruthless business practices of the Standard Oil Company. Many who would not listen to Populists or Socialists (though Lloyd was deeply involved in both movements his class affiliation was genteel) found the indictment convincing.

Thus the culture crisis of the nineties was not wholly devoid of the seeds of its own solution. The trouble was that by the end of the recovery period, by the turn of the century, the gaps between ideology and reality, between social and economic classes, between the dynamics of large-scale capitalism and the knowledge and will to make it serve the many instead of the few, were so great as to convince many observers that American society had no future except social revolution. Trusts were appearing everywhere; the size of corporations seemed limitless. Foreign immigration resumed during the recovery period in larger waves than ever, and from increasingly strange sources, further fragmenting the one-time ethnic homogeneity of Americans. In the South, Jim Crow had about reached adulthood, lynchings occurred almost daily, and the absorption of the black minority became less likely than ever. Big cities proliferated, labor conflict seemed endemic, socialism and anarchism gained adherents. The acquisition of an overseas empire as an unintended consequence of the Spanish-American War momentarily distracted attention from domestic social problems but had almost no immediate impact on them. By 1901 the United States had achieved an economic position in the world greater than that of Britain, France, and Germany combined. But many were wondering what it profited America to gain the world but lose its social soul.

5

Values and Institutions, 1901–1916

The years between the turn of the new century and America's entry into the First World War to make the world safe for democracy have traditionally been labeled "the progressive era." Although the term "progressivism" and its derivatives are fraught with analytical difficulties, because there were so many different kinds of progressives and shadings of progressivism, it is still a useful catch-all. For one thing, it indicates something historically true, that an unusual amount of conscious effort to come to grips with social and economic problems manifested itself during the period, an unusual amount of mind-changing and attempts to assert and apply new ideas in law, politics, and institutions, compared to the periods before and after it. Some writers have gone so far as to suggest that most of the typical modes of thought and ways of acting toward urban-industrial society which Americans adopted during the next sixty years of the twentieth century were basically laid out in the progressive period: an exaggeration, I think, but one containing a large measure of truth.

For another thing, the term "progressivism" cannot be ignored or abolished, if for no other reason than that it was in contemporaneous use. The progressives chose to call themselves progressives, and not collectivists or socialists or millenarians or even liberals. Those terms would have fit some or even many of them, in one sense or another, but the label which they commonly preferred and widely used was that which denoted a faith in the attainability of progress, and which reflected their absorption of Darwinian evolution (in L. F. Ward's version rather than William Graham Sumner's), and of essentially moderate rather than radical change. They were reformers, not revolutionaries. But these terms, like "progressivism," have many meanings; they convey more the flavor than the substance of the problem. In this chapter and the two that follow it, we need to look at the substance of social change during the period dubbed "progressive" by its inhabitants and people since. How did progressives perceive, and attempt to cope with, the social crisis generated by the friction between ideas and realities in the late nineteenth century? Did they do so through the development of a rational, systematic critique, or by frantically stuffing laws, sermons, and manifestoes into the worst leaks in the social dike and by that patchwork manage to prevent a flood of radicalism? How was it that so many different people—one is tempted to say practically anybody alive then—could claim to be progressive at least at some point and on some issue?

The groundwork for answering these and related questions about social change in the first decade and a half of this century lies in (1) a consideration of changes in social ideology, (2) the development of new theories of social order and the common elements in those theories, (3) how new ideology was transmitted (or failed to be transmitted) from articulate elites to broader populations, and (4) how social institutions functioned as agents of measured change—rather than as inhibitors of it as had generally been the case in the late nineteenth century. So far it has been asserted, and not yet proved, that social ideology and social theories did change during the progressive period. Such changes differed in content and depth among the various groups taking part in progressivism. Agrarian ideology, for example, as expressed by the Populists, did not change much; its exponents simply dwindled in number, became unattractively shrill, and lost most of whatever political effectiveness they had, except in limited areas and times. Ideologies of labor leaders and organizations underwent some changes during the progressive years, and when they were sufficiently accommodationist, as in the cases of the American Federation of Labor or the United Mine Workers, they received a more attentive hearing than before; but again this was not the area of most striking change. Immigrant subcultures and urban political organizations, although at times cooperating with other groups to achieve limited gains particularly in the area of social welfare, for the most part continued to assimilate at what seemed to be glacier-like speed and were neither the subjects nor the agents of rapid ideological change.

All of those groups played some part in progressivism. But the essential element, allowing for progressivism to take place then, and not some other time, and in the way that it did, lay elsewhere. The critical transformation took place among the native-stock white middle class, first among clergy, lawyers, academics, and other professionals, and then among those who listened to their sermons, read their books and editorials, and supported them in politics. Farmers and industrial workers did not need to be told that the society in which they lived had problems. They bore the brunt of them. It was rather among those people and institutions who had resisted change in the late nineteenth century that perceptions of social problems had to develop, and did. As they perceived that problems existed and were severe enough to threaten social order, they accepted the notion that rational, humanly contrived attacks on problems were possible. Many of them by no means gave up on the goals of the mugwumpish, middle-class reformers of the eighties and nineties, and indeed the progressive era brought success in areas like prohibition and the weakening of political party organizations, goals which the mugwumps in the native-stock white middle class had conspicuously failed to achieve in 1890. The road from mugwumpery to progressivism was often short. But in order to travel it, and thus to arrive at a position which permitted not only the accomplishment of certain important mugwump aims, but also a broad-scale reduction of social tensions, it was necessary to clear away some stubborn ideological hurdles. The success with which Americans absorbed large-scale business organizations and ethnically and culturally diverse peoples into their social thinking and attitudes during the progressive period depended on the working out, by a fairly small elite of academics and intellectuals, of a critique of the new urban-industrial order which comprehended and accepted its broad outlines yet preserved as many traditional social values as possible. The critique had to be realistic, but it also had to be nonradical. It had to come from respectable middle-class sources, which Populism and socialism lacked, in order to serve a wide spectrum of the growing white-collar middle class. The new social theories and critiques which appeared at that time possessed these qualities, and thus functioned suitably as an intellectual framework for many Americans who in the nineties increasingly knew that social problems had to be solved but did not know how to do so with ideological legitimacy.

The beginnings of this intellectual framework had been wrought by thinkers as diverse as C. S. Peirce, Lester Frank Ward, and the young Richard T. Ely back in the eighties.[1] Its development slowed during the depression of the nineties, when Ely and a number of other outspoken reformer-social scientists lost, or nearly lost, their professorial positions because they seemed to be giving aid and comfort to Populists and socialists.[2] After 1900, however, a few dozen economists, sociologists, political scientists, and historians were providing new perspectives on social structure and new evidence, scientifically arrived at by empirical research, of social problems; and their models, evidence, and proposed solutions were reaching an increasingly wide and attentive audience. Most of them not only wrote technical treatises but lectured, wrote textbooks, advised government agencies, and were frequently quoted in the press. They transmitted their ideas in several ways, functioning as publicists as well as theoreticians, as appliers of theory as well as the first generation of academic social scientists in American universities. Ely played a role for economics in America almost as important as that played by Lester Frank Ward for sociology, and approaching that played by William James in psychology and philosophy. For all of these people, the role was a triple one: to establish their disciplines as research and teaching areas within the universities; to write and publish treatises which became the points of departure for exploration in their fields; and to see to it that the insights of the new social sciences which they were developing were applied in the most immediate ways possible to produce the amelioration of social problems such as maldistribution of wealth, concentration of power in business monopolies, diminishing control of state and local government by "the people," the repression of labor, and the erosion of Christian ideals in society.

Ely was an excellent example of the pioneer whose youthful ideals and zeal had a tremendously stimulating effect on others, and indeed on the whole field of economics, and who became gradually less of a crusader, more of a pure academic, and ultimately a social conservative. During the progressive era itself his main output consisted of technical work in land economics, valuable for what it tried to do but not of great social impact. As his biographer states, he continued to inspire students and reformers but less from new pronouncements than on the basis of what he had done in the eighties and early nineties; they "often found his contemporary views not advanced far beyond the general public." [3] By that time, however (roughly 1901–1910, the heyday of La Follette progressivism in Ely's Wisconsin), Ely had made several contributions aside from his strictly academic work. He had been a leading founder, with Simon Patten and others, of the American Economic Association in 1885, the intent and effect of which was to shake up the rationalistic, classically dominated field of political economy. He had done as much as any of the sizable group of young Americans who had studied at German universities to introduce the German historicist approach to economics developed by Wilhelm Röscher and others into American thought, thus transplanting to America the relativism and empiricism so destructive of the old classical certainties. As major professor or advisor, he conveyed his historicism and his devotion to Christian morality in economic life to a procession of graduate students who were to become a virtual who's who of academically based reformers in the progressive period. [4] His textbook on political economy, first published in 1889, went through many subsequent editions and had an incalculable effect in undermining the nineteenth-century political economy centering upon static natural laws, laissez faire, and producerite harmony. For these orthodoxies Ely, historicist and reformer that he was, substituted the views that political economy like everything else was subject to historical change, that the goal of society was Christian brotherhood, that the means of reaching that goal was the empirical, scientific search for economic facts and relationships, and that it was permissible to employ not only exhortation but government power to effect changes.

As has often been the case with academic reformers, Ely's positions on the concrete issues of the day, either in the nineties or during the progressive era, were often almost conventional; as a seminal thinker, however, as someone who reconsidered the very roots of political economy and outspokenly proclaimed his theories, Ely was radical indeed. As the great English economist John Maynard Keynes said some decades later, we are all slaves to the ideas of some dead economist. Richard Ely, that product of rural-evangelical western New York in Civil War days and of German universities, who spent most of his active life as an economics professor at Wisconsin, did much to insure that twentieth-century Americans became emancipated from slavery to Adam Smith, Ricardo, John Stuart Mill, and their American popularizers and simplifiers like Francis Wayland and Simon Newcomb. Of all the many areas of social theory, political economy had the most direct impact on law and politics, and in the days of classical orthodoxy before progressivism, that impact was powerfully conservative. Ely and some other professors, much less well known to the general public than their presidents and senators, far surpassed those household words in creating the ideological framework which legitimized institutional and legal change. Their efforts, supported and complemented by the efforts of sociologists, historians, theologians, philosophers, political scientists, and educators, probably constitute the best example in American history of academics having a really significant impact on social change.

We dwell on Ely at some length not because he was unique but because he was something of a paradigm, combining as he did the qualities of theoretician, pioneer, teacher, propagandizer, Christian evolutionist, Social Gospeler, and old-stock middle-class man. Other academics shared some if not all of these traits. In economics, significant contributions also came in differing ways from E. R. A. Seligman, Wesley C. Mitchell, John R. Commons, and Thorstein Veblen. Seligman and Mitchell were not so much crusaders as promoters of empiricism and providers of expertise. Seligman was a founder of the American Economic Association in 1885 and during the progressive period published books on currency, the income tax, and farm problems which laid forth the facts and assumed that remedies were possible. Mitchell's *Gold, Prices, and Wages under the Greenback Standard*, published in 1908, was not only suggestive of whole new research fields on income distribution and monetary theory, but also set new methodological standards for the discussion of money and credit. His statistical empiricism was incomparably and irretrievably more "modern" than the competing propaganda of a J. Laurence Laughlin or "Coin" Harvey over the gold standard and bimetallism which generated so much heat and so little light in the years just before the 1896 campaign. Commons, an Ely student who also went on to a brilliant career as an economist at Wisconsin, was famed for his multi-volume history of labor unions in America, and also ranged into political science with a book on proportional representation in 1907 and his *Races and Immigrants in America* of 1908 (to be remarked on in a moment). Veblen, whose academic career was much more checkered than these other men, was also less obviously an empiricist; his most famous work, *The Theory of the Leisure Class*, was an iconoclastic essay deeply critical of the prevailing capitalist system, employing terms like "pecuniary emulation" and "conspicuous consumption" to deflate the claims of the *nouveaux riches* to high status. But his deep belief in the progressive evolution of society was shared with the other new economists, and he had an impact on them during the progressive era, and on the general public later. Not as socially respectable as most progressive academics, a second-generation working-class Norwegian, he stood somewhat apart from the mainstream native-stock reformers and was, as Henry May put it, "the first major American social thinker to come from the wrong side of the tracks." [5] Along with the others, however (and the people discussed here were not the only reformer economists), he contributed to the growing impression that political economy could change along historicist, evolutionary, empiricist, and socially activist lines.

Related developments took place among sociologists. As in economics, the people who were developing theory were also, often, zealous advocates and appliers of ideas, and in sociology the combination was especially common; professional social work did not split off clearly from research-oriented sociology until after World War I. The most influential figures had learned well the lessons of Lester Frank Ward's *Dynamic Sociology*, that the social environment could and should be controlled and directed. Edward A. Ross and John R. Commons at Wisconsin, and Albion W. Small at Chicago, were the most prominent of the new group. Small's environmentalism, his efforts to organize empirical research concerning the realities of urban life (the city of Chicago being at the

same time specimen and laboratory), his close cooperation with
settlement house leaders, and his vision of social change in terms of
Christian morality, earned him a place in the history of the Social
Gospel movement as well as in the history of education and ideas.
Ross, an outspoken giant of a man, insisted on his right to go
outside the ivory tower (a term which scarcely fit the University of
Wisconsin in the days of Governor La Follette and President Van
Hise anyway) and to preach the reform message from Chautauqua
and other lecture platforms. He was proud of the tens of thousands
whom he counted as former students, and in his autobiography he
boasted that "with such a clientele I can walk up to the Chicago
Tribune and kick it in the jaw." [6] Ross's most widely read book was
a 1907 tract called *Sin and Society*, which was studded with blasts
at business barons who sit at the center of "a spider-web of
fiduciary relations" and rob and poison the people, and get away
with it because "there is nothing like distance to disinfect dividends"; the main point of the book was that sin, in its most vicious
forms, no longer meant individual peccadilloes but social crime.
His most thoughtful book, however, was *Social Control* (1901),
which argued that social evolution had passed the point when
individual energies could be allowed to manifest themselves in a
helter-skelter way, since that was rapidly producing a situation
where violent social revolution was imminent. Instead individuals
must give way to society's collective well-being by submitting to
controls. Ross's impact in this and other works was to provide a
corrosive, one which seemed realistic and yet which reaffirmed
middle-class evangelical ideals, to the traditional ideal of unfet-
tered individualism.[7]

Commons has been mentioned already as an economist, but he
is worth considering for a moment for his social ideas, as expressed
in his *Races and Immigrants* book. Commons was as familiar as any
progressive with employer manipulation, poverty, ethnic division,
and dehumanizing working conditions among miners and factory
workers, and he strongly favored unionization as a protection and
solution. But his attitude toward foreign-born workers was at best
ambiguous: while the brotherhood of unionism was a "discovery
and a revelation" to feuding ethnics, he suggested that the diversity
of immigration had been so great as to prevent assimilation and

industrial peace. His suspicions about the new immigration on grounds of labor competition were reinforced by the racist ideas which he shared with nearly every other educated person of the day. If class struggles persist, he said, "the reasons will be found in the immigration of races and classes incompetent to share in our democratic opportunities"—incompetent by reason of heredity. The only chance of satisfactory assimilation lay in "conscious improvement through education and social environment," especially the learning of English. Commons shared with other social progressives a belief in evolution, but not the strict Darwinian variety; for him, environment might change heredity. At least there was a chance with the immigrants, the "strongest, healthiest and most energetic and adventurous" of Europe's working class. With blacks it was most unlikely: "The very qualities of intelligence and manliness which are essential for citizenship in a democracy were systematically expunged from the negro [sic] race through two hundred years of slavery." [8] It will be noted that if this was the thinking of one of the most well-meaning, high-minded, intelligent, and educated of the progressives who were deeply concerned with social problems, then (1) the progressives differed in important respects from liberals of the 1960s and 1970s, and (2) the less high-minded of them were likely to operate more unthinkingly from white, middle-class, native-stock, evangelical premises. Professor Commons nonetheless was an outstanding reformer by the lights of his time.

Sociology and economics were not the only academic disciplines which were undergoing intellectual definition and pathbreaking theoretical change, and also contributing very directly to reformist activism. Nor were the people mentioned here the only sociologists and economists making such contributions. Political scientists and historians also contributed to the general ferment. J. Allen Smith's *Spirit of American Government* (1907) and Charles A. Beard's *An Economic Interpretation of the Constitution* (1913) ruthlessly but entertainingly insisted that the founding fathers were not the demigods of popular legend but had had their personal financial axes to grind when they wrote the Constitution. Beard's economic interpretation was of little help to many progressives who sought to Americanize the children of immigrants by the inculcation of patriotic legends in public school history classes, but it did amount to a historicist interpretation of historical events, and as such it better prepared lawyers, jurists, and politicians to view constitutional law as a field in which static rationalism was not the only approach. Justice Oliver Wendell Holmes, Jr., Louis D. Brandeis, and other legal scholars played a more direct role in historicizing constitutional law than Beard did; but Beard's impact was not slight.

One could go on and on discussing personalities and theories in the social sciences. But the main points of change should already be evident: the progressive academics in a multitude of fields employed empiricism, evolutionary relativism, and often iconoclasm to break down the intellectual certitudes of the late nineteenth century. They recognized that real dysfunctions in social and economic life existed, and they sought to do something about it, both through their personal practical efforts, and even more importantly by providing Americans, especially literate middle-class Americans, with new intellectual tools which bore the stamp of respectability. For nearly all of these progressive academics were of the native-stock majority, nearly all had their personal and ideological origins in farms and small towns in the third quarter of the nineteenth century, and nearly all were but a step removed from the mugwumpery of the eighties and nineties. They were not regarded as social renegades, like the Populists; not as utopians, like Bellamy or Henry George; not as a reactionary elite, like the mugwumps. The novelty of their contributions was great, but they also provided and manifested substantial links with the intellectual past. Again, progressivism was reformist, not revolutionary.

Although formal philosophy seems at almost any historical time and place to bear little direct relevance to social change, developments in philosophy did take place during the progressive period which bore more or less directly on events, not least by providing, as the new social sciences were doing, a quality of legitimacy to change itself. Pragmatism, universally regarded as the most important American contribution to the history of philosophy, had begun with C. S. Peirce's work in the 1870s. Despite Peirce's misanthropy he produced the seeds of a social theory, and it flowered during the progressive era at the hands of William James and John Dewey. When people read James or Dewey, or heard them speak, or as often happened picked up their ideas at second hand, they encountered an invitation to discard rationalistic dogmas, to seek social change, to embrace the evolutionary outlook toward the world and the people and institutions in it. At the same time, they were assured, religion, morality, and the ethical welfare of society should continue to be upheld. James was perfectly right when he said in 1907, in his most famous discussion of pragmatism, that it "represents a perfectly familiar attitude in philosophy, the empiricist attitude, but it represents it . . . both in a more radical and in a less objectionable form than it has ever yet assumed. A pragmatist . . . turns towards concreteness and adequacy, towards facts, towards action and towards power." The crux of the matter, any matter, was results. James restated and extended Peirce's logic of the "pragmatic test" in terms blunt enough to be understood by anybody, and to be criticized by some for that bluntness: "Pragmatism . . . asks its usual question. 'Grant an idea or belief to be true,' it says, 'what concrete difference will its being true make in any one's actual life? How will the truth be realized? What experiences will be different from those which would obtain if the belief were false? What, in short, is the truth's cash-value in experiential terms?' . . . The truth of an idea is not a stagnant property inherent in it. Truth *happens* to an idea. It *becomes* true, is *made* true by events. Its verity *is* in fact an event, a process; the process namely of its verifying itself, its veri-*fication.*" James seemed to be saying that an idea was true if it got good results. Theology is true primarily, James said, as a result "of being good for so much," of achieving some palpable good. In so saying, he provided an underpinning not for the erosion of religion, which Darwinism was doing to many believers, nor for unbridled individual accumulation, which is the result a Sumner might have come to from such a base, but rather for the Social Gospel movement with its emphasis on "life and work," applied ethics, instead of "faith and order," theology and church organization. Progressives wanted to hear that pragmatism, or something, "means the empiricist temper regnant and the rationalist temper sincerely given up"; they were anxious to do just that, but needed an impeccably respectable authority like William James to tell them they could.[9]

Dewey was also helpful. He shared the pragmatic outlook but stressed even more than James the need and possibility for consciously guided evolution toward social good. The means were to be any instruments which worked usefully; his philosophy, though closely akin to pragmatism, thus bore the name "instrumentalism." Dewey insisted that "the fatal decrees of iron necessity, called natural law," were nothing more than "an animistic survival. . . . No, nature is not an unchangeable order, unwinding itself majestically from the reel of law under the control of deified forces. It is an indefinite congeries of changes." Dewey specified that the natural law thinking he was referring to came from medieval theology through Newton, then through the classical economists and the utilitarians, "to make its last stand in Spencer's philosophy of the fixed environment and the static goal." What to do? Know and act; use the mind to effect change. What resulted? "Knowledge of the process and conditions of physical and social change by experimental science and genetic history has one result with a double name: increase of control and increase of responsibility; increase of power to direct natural change, and increase of responsibility for its equitable direction toward fuller good."

Pragmatism and instrumentalism underwent severe criticism from philosophers and others because they were so exclusively a description of means without reference to ends, as if one could follow a recipe without knowing what one was trying to make. In the sentence just quoted, for example, nothing indicates *whose* control is meant, nor whose responsibility, nor whose power, nor what is equitable, nor what is "fuller good." Dewey apparently felt, and many of those who read him or heard about his ideas undoubtedly felt, that these things were generally understood.[10] Progressives understood him to be talking about *their* control, responsibility, and power, and social equity and human good as they in their native-stock middle-class respectable way comprehended those things. Instrumentalism, with its lack of defined goals, could have served as a method to take society in any number of directions, beneficent or frightening. As it happened the people in the best position to employ it did so, with the consequence that the middle-class, evangelically derived ethic was reinforced.

The progressives were an articulate lot, and many of them, as well as others whose claim to the label of "progressive" was dubious, tried their hand at setting forth plans and programs which embodied the instrumentalist notion that people acting collectively could change society for the better. The National Civic Federation, a group of several thousand "enlightened and responsible" business leaders, tried to work with labor leaders such as John Mitchell of the United Mine Workers and Samuel Gompers of the A. F. of L., and with academics and sympathetic politicians, to help solve the "trust problem" and the "labor problem," to improve city government, and to secure the acceptance of the large corporation as a fixture of American life.[11] Such disparate individuals as King Gillette, founder of Gillette razor company, the inventor-engineer Charles Steinmetz, and the young Reinhold Niebuhr have been described by a recent historian as seeking to make "collectivism," meaning an acceptance of large economic organizations, the architectural plan for the good society of the future.[12] Frederick Winslow Taylor's device was human engineering through "scientific management." Church leaders continued to stress "uplift," frequently (though not always) the uplift of society through institutional change and not simply individual uplift through redemption, right belief, and respectable behavior. Other progressives seemed to think that little more was needed to cure society's ills than to prohibit the distribution and sale of alcoholic beverages. There were nearly as many instrumentalist programs as there were progressives.

Among them all, two or three stand out because of their secular character, their thoughtfulness, and their wide audience. One was organized socialism, which as a radical movement stood on the extreme left wing, or sometimes outside the left wing, of progressivism; but it shared many concerns and ideas with midstream reform. The Socialist party and its leader, Eugene V. Debs, won nearly a million votes in the election of 1912. For a third and then-radical party, it did reasonably well in other elections during the progressive period. The Socialists were not as radical as they theoretically might have been; they did not ask, for example, for ownership by the workers of all of the means of production nor for the extirpation of the capitalist class. They were not Marxists, even non-violent ones. But they did lay at the door of the capitalist system and the plutocrats whom they said ran it the leading ills of society, such as the high cost of living, unemployment, "the increasing burden of armaments, the poverty, slums, child labor, most of the insanity, crime and prostitution, and much of the disease that afflicts mankind," and maldistribution of the wealth being produced in the country. Many of their specific measures, including conservation, wage and hour laws, insurance against industrial accidents, the graduated income tax, woman suffrage, and abolition of the Electoral College, were also supported by progressives in other political parties. In their 1912 platform the Socialists called themselves "the party of the present day revolution which makes the transition from economic individualism to socialism, from wage slavery to free co-operation, from capitalist oligarchy to industrial democracy." Had the Socialists been anywhere near as numerous as the Populists, they might have been feared even more. As it was, their ideas and platforms were frightening enough to the middle class.

Another social blueprint based on instrumentalist and evolutionary concepts was the one set forth by Herbert Croly in his 1909 book, *The Promise of American Life*. Many progressives, Theodore Roosevelt among them, plowed through Croly's tract of nearly five hundred pages, discovering a capsule history of the United States and an assertion of what had to be done in the future if the national ideals of a moral democracy, economic opportunity, and individual advancement were to continue. Croly maintained that those things constituted "the promise of American life." By the early twentieth century, he said, social and economic evils threatened to snuff it out. In order to revive and maintain the national promise, "the sense of a serious national purpose" was required: Americans had to take conscious action. The substance of our national Promise has consisted . . . of an improving popular economic condition, guaranteed by democratic political institutions, and resulting in moral and social amelioration. These manifold benefits were obtained merely by liberating the enlightened self-interest of the

American people. Now, however, the Promise "is to be fulfilled—not merely by a maximum amount of economic freedom, but by a certain measure of discipline; not merely by the abundant satisfaction of individual desires, but by a large measure of individual subordination and self-denial. . . . I am far from believing that this concentration of economic power is wholly an undesirable thing. . . . Efficient regulation there must be." Croly described at length the regulations he had in mind. He closed by putting the onus of change on enlightened individual leadership: "If a noble and civilized democracy is to subsist, the common citizen must be something of a saint and something of a hero." But in the meantime he had argued that government should be the instrument of economic regulation and of the achievement of national purpose, and he asserted throughout that conscious action, by people acting in concert, could improve the social environment and achieve stated goals. For Croly and his readers that was what progressivism was all about: collective action, use of available instruments, uplift of individuals and society, and the "sincere and enthusiastic imitation of heroes and saints"—possibly like their own political hero and saint, Theodore Roosevelt.[13]

Croly and the Socialists stood at ideological extremes of the reform movement, and many others in between them provided their own blueprints for change—social scientists, churchmen, journalists. The young Walter Lippmann wrote in 1914 that "we can no longer treat life as something that has trickled down to us. We have to deal with it deliberately, devise its social organization, alter its tools, formulate its method, educate and control it. In endless ways we put intention where custom has reigned." [14] Lippmann said it for all of them—despite their great variety of ideas, occupation, degree of religious affiliation, entrancement with science and technology, political allegiance, or other differences. The nub of the problem, the place where the progressives made signal contributions in the area of ideological and attitudinal change, was in the creation of a new framework of mind, a new world view, which allowed not only themselves but masses of other Americans to come to grips realistically with the world around them rather than through long-fossilized nineteenth-century frameworks.

Specifically, the new world view replaced that of the late nineteenth century in the following three ways.

The natural-law concept was severely modified in certain critical areas and was replaced by the pragmatic-instrumentalist mode of approaching reality. Social truths were no longer to be discovered, but to be invented. This change took place in several areas of social science and social theory, among them political economy and sociology. In those two fields, a change of outlook was especially important because of their immediacy to the "literate public" and to judges and legislators. At the outset, the erosion of belief in immutable natural laws of economic and social behavior antedated the philosophical work of James and Dewey, but that work reinforced the trend toward thinking in historicist, evolutionary ways. The original subversive in the story of the overthrow of the reign of natural-law thinking was more likely the metaphysician Hegel (perhaps Keynes should have said that we are all slaves in the hands of some dead philosopher) rather than the biologist Darwin or other evolutionists. But Darwin certainly helped, especially after evolution came to mean more than just a natural law explaining how some things got to where they were and then stopped evolving, and instead began to be grasped as an ongoing process in which the present was but one point on a continuum proceeding indefinitely into the future. The radical implications of Darwinism and other expressions of evolution were not understood by William Graham Sumner or by Herbert Spencer who, ironically in retrospect, called his book *Social Statics*. The implications were grasped by Lester Ward, who called his book *Dynamic Sociology*, and by Ely and the progressive economists.

The upshot of this was, for the progressive intellectuals and their followers, that it would no longer be satisfactory to evaluate the merit of, say, financial legislation or wage-price-profit policy by setting the new proposal up against "natural law" to see if it fit, and if not rejecting it; it would no longer do for judges to evaluate the constitutionality of laws simply by juxtaposing them to a Constitution considered fixed and ahistorical, and then discarding the laws if the match was poor, as the Supreme Court did with the Civil Rights Law in 1883, and as many other judges did when they denied the right of labor to organize and bargain collectively, time after time, on the ground that such efforts violated freedom of contract. Admittedly, legal conservatism of this kind by no means disappeared abruptly after the publication of a few books by evolutionist, instrumentalist, progressive intellectuals. Indeed it continued to manifest itself among a majority of U.S. Supreme Court justices until 1937 and occasionally later than that. But it began to be rejected, even as early as 1881, when the future Justice Oliver Wendell Holmes said in *The Common Law* that "the life of the law has not been logic: it has been experience"; when Holmes, on the Supreme bench in 1905, declared that "The Fourteenth Amendment does not enact Mr. Herbert Spencer's Social Statics";[15] when future Justice Louis D. Brandeis persuaded the Court in 1908 that empirical fact rather than abstract legal principle should decide whether an Oregon law rightly limited women to a ten-hour day (the "Brandeis brief" in *Muller* v. *Oregon*); when Charles A. Beard's *Economic Interpretation of the Constitution* in 1913 reduced the popular conception of the Philadelphia Convention of 1787 from the empyrean level of Greek drama to practical, everyday historical reality. The natural-law concept did not die a sudden death in 1901 in economics, sociology, jurisprudence, or even in history—Edward P. Cheyney's presidential address to the American Historical Association sought to enumerate the principal laws of historical development, and that was in 1923. Indeed, the concept continued to grip many Americans, particularly those to whom social reform was not urgent, well beyond the First World War. In certain areas the progressive intellectuals themselves did not appreciate the force of the evolutionary-instrumentalist thought-pattern they were helping to create: many of them continued to believe, for example, that race and ethnic differences stemmed from immutable hereditary sources, a natural situation which environment was unlikely to affect. Nonetheless, the generalization holds that the academics and other theorists of the progressive era successfully changed their own minds, and the minds of many others, from the static, rationalist natural-law set so characteristic of the late nineteenth century to the processual, evolutionary, instrumentalist outlook of the twentieth. In doing so they created a popular metaphysic permitting receptivity to social and economic change. (And they also helped destroy the bases for rules about where change ought to stop.)

As natural law gave way to evolutionary pragmatism, laissez faire individualism gave way to a sense that society was an organism within which the individual members related (or should relate) to each other in structured ways: this was their second change in world view. It too was an incomplete revolution; laissez faire individualism disappeared no more completely than natural-law ideas. Nonetheless the progressive intellectuals mounted a variety of attacks on laissez faire. The National Civic Federation's cooperation with labor leaders to ameliorate labor problems and to create an economic society in which large corporations would not only be tolerated but would be accepted as the dominant form of business organization was one example, a secular and practical one. Croly's appeal for concerted action through politics and other institutional instruments to regain the "national Promise" was also secular but a little more mystical and all-embracing. Churchmen such as the Baptist Walter Rauschenbusch and the Catholic John A. Ryan looked forward to the realization of "the kingdom of God on earth," a transformation, as Rauschenbusch put it, of "human society into the kingdom of God by regenerating all human relations and reconstituting them in accordance with the will of God." [16] In these and the many other expressions by progressives that the problems and possibilities of society were indeed social and not individual, the thought was central, whatever the auspices of the expression or the detailed program set forth, that Americans would have to interact, to plan, to accept the fact that they were parts of larger wholes, to understand that society was something corporate, meaning literally, a body.

What form, what model, should that corporate society take? To many progressives the most available and concrete model was the business corporation, and they were satisfied when it appeared to them that society and government seemed more and more to be operating on "business principles." This attitude achieved its widest and bluntest acceptance in the 1920s, when President Coolidge made his undyingly crass remark that the business of America was business. During the progressive period itself, however, the new sense of society as something organic remained more protean and idealistic, less an installation of the business corporation as the model for other institutions than a yearning sense of the need for people and institutions to work together for ends, secular or religious, which transcended individuals. The concern of social thinkers of the late nineteenth century and the progressive era, as R. Jackson Wilson recently put it, was that "It became painfully clear that men were the products and not the wilfully compacting constituents of their species and their society. There was an urgent demand for concepts of man that gave him protective membership in a social community." [17] The terms "community" and "society," as used by the progressive theorists and planners, do not lend themselves to very precise definition, any more than Lyndon Johnson's "Great Society" of half a century later was defined other than by its energy and its results. But regardless of definition or differences of detail, their disenchantment with laissez faire was general. They were willing to accept, indeed they strongly advocated, social action through institutions, including government.

The third way by which progressives provided an escape from the intellectual confines of the late nineteenth century was in their discarding and redefining of the long-held belief that the role of *producer* was the fundamental one in economic life, in favor of the roles of *consumer,* and at times of *technician.* Many progressives, though not often the intellectuals, continued to exalt the independent entrepreneur. The producerite self-image and rhetoric still persisted among many agrarians and some radical laborites (for example, ex-Populists and Socialists). But even by the nineties, and more so after 1900, the spread of mass employment and more typically modern conditions of work had rendered old-fashioned producerism irrelevant to many people. Its withering away was already evident in the campaign of 1896 when Bryan's use of it brought little response from industrial workers in the East and the eastern Midwest. As ever-growing numbers of the labor force in the early twentieth century ceased to be their own bosses but instead were employees within large organizations, traditional producerism was ready for the graveyard of ideas which had worn away from continued friction with changed reality. It had become too narrowly agrarian. Redefined as the "work ethic," and expanded to include white-collar services as well as goods, it certainly continued to persist, but in a form more adequately describing the things that middle-class people did to achieve material success. The contribution of the progressives was not so much to give the *coup de grâce* to traditional producerism, for it was about to die anyway, but rather to provide a new self-image for white- and blue-collar workers alike. The Populists had argued that the producer was not getting his fair share, that only a union of the producing classes—"the people"—could secure that share. The progressives argued much the same point, but in different language: that unregulated monopolies were bilking the consumer through high profits and prices, and that corrupt political machines were soaking the consumer through wasteful expenditure dependent on high taxes. The "consumer" meant any user of goods and services, working-class or middle-class, rural or urban who was (or was in danger of) being victimized by large operators in large organizations. It was no longer important whether someone made something with his hands or brain, no longer necessary, for the establishment of good social credentials, to produce something. It was important instead to realize that the individual was part of an interconnected economy, and that the goods and services which that economy produced should reach him at a fair cost. A person functioned within that economy in any number of possible roles, blue collar or white collar or executive, but whatever his role he was part of "the people" insofar as that term had an economic aspect. The progressive political economists and sociologists such as Ross and Veblen did much to put this new idea across, and their technique—again borrowing upon some quite traditional terminology and adapting it to a new situation—was to rework the American antipathy to monopolies, distrust of oligarchy, and insistence on popular control of institutions, into a new kind of self-consciousness which made reform in business and government intellectually legitimate.

In sum, the progressive intellectuals and their allies among journalists, churchmen, and politicians became uneasy with the ideological legacy of the late nineteenth century and understood that some of it would have to go. They attacked, and the casualties were natural law, laissez faire individualism, and producerism. For these hoary notions the progressives substituted evolutionary pragmatism, a sense of society as organic, and consumerism. That done, the possibilities were greatly enhanced that change and experimentation would become acceptable; that social control could be undertaken; that the regulation of large units would ensue. The progressive intellectuals, for all their variety, did a great deal in the ten to twelve years following the end of the nineties to provide new ways of thinking about reality, ways which would permit action to take place with regard to that reality. They provided Americans with ways to cope.

They transmitted their ideas through many channels, including their own textbooks or book-length analyses, the teaching of graduate students, magazine articles, the Chautauqua circuit and other lecture platforms, and newspaper interviews. Their readers and listeners were consequently those who attended universities, churches, Chautauquas, and read books and serious articles—people who in class and ethnic terms were much like themselves, the respectable middle class. These readers and listeners formed a second-level leadership, which included businessmen, teachers, clergy, settlement house workers, politicians, and professionals. They did not possess the analytical power or seminal influence of an Ely, a William James, or a Herbert Croly, but they collectively made up a much larger body of people who might be called, in contradistinction to the intellectuals, the "working progressives": those concerned with at least one (often more) concrete social or political issue, who shared many of the presuppositions and ideas which the intellectuals made respectable, and who most often worked through structured social institutions to bring about the thousands of changes which progressivism entailed. Four of those institutions, and people who worked through them, need to be looked at: governments (considered in Chapter seven), organized religion, education, and the press.

In 1917 an ex-pastor from New York and Rochester, Walter Rauschenbusch, published his most ambitious work, *A Theology for the Social Gospel.* At the outset he asserted that "the social gospel has become orthodox"; it had already redefined the Christian idea of salvation to mean "the voluntary socializing of the Soul." [18] The great Baptist leader was somewhat optimistic in his claim, since many Americans at just that time regarded Billy Sunday as the outstanding religious spokesman in the country, and Sunday, like revivalists before him, preached individual not social regeneration. Moreover, the most pressing issue in American religion for many Protestants was the controversy then raging between fundamentalists and modernists. The Social Gospelers, nearly all of them active or passive modernists, did not have the whole of American religion to themselves. Nonetheless Rauschenbusch had a point, since most of the major Protestant denominations had committed themselves between 1901 and 1912 to "social Christianity" programs of analysis and active field work to improve social conditions. The Social Gospelers generally championed labor unions and social legislation affecting labor, industry, and urban life. They were progressivism's vanguard in organized religion, and although they may never have constituted a majority even in the most social-minded denominations, the Episcopalians, Congregationalists, and Unitarians, they were sufficiently numerous in leadership positions to give reform activity a religious sanction.

Filled with a sense of crisis about social problems, driven by crusading zeal, and confident about the techniques of the new sociology and social work, they sought to regenerate urban-industrial society. About immigrants they were ambivalent; some sought to convert the immigrants to Protestantism, others at least to Americanize them, others simply to improve their living conditions. The Social Gospel movement was, in the words of one of its most perceptive historians, "the reaction of Protestantism—markedly stimulated by socialism—to the ethics and practices of capitalism as brought to point in the industrial situation. In the large, social Christianity was not concerned with the problems of war, imperialism, race, democracy, or the use of force." [19] They were optimists, evolutionists, believers in the perfectibility of society as well as individuals. Many of them had been raised on a liberal theology that deemphasized scriptural literalism but stressed the brotherhood of man, and on that basis they had little quarrel with Darwinism. God was understood to be the immanent force producing evolutionary development, including the progressive development of society. The Social Gospel worked well with the prevailing progressive mood, and functioned as a kind of sanctified version of secular reform. As such, it permitted most of the leading Protestant denominations (and some Catholic and Jewish leaders who shared its ethical thrust) to operate as supportive rather than retardant factors in early twentieth-century social change.

Education, as a social institution, began to function in a similar way. In higher education, especially in the growing state universities and private graduate schools, the new social scientists had a forum, a laboratory, and a base of operations. In addition, education at the elementary and secondary levels became one of the principal arenas for progressive reform and for the transmission of cultural values, both traditional ones and those being revised by the progressive intellectuals. One of these intellectuals, John Dewey, was also the leading theoretician of "progressive education," and he had more impact than any other individual since Horace Mann in changing the character of American schools. Dewey applied the pragmatic test to curricula: what counted was the social utility of the subject matter and the most effective methods for getting it across. As in other areas where the pragmatic test was applied, the ultimate goals were not really in question. The school was to function in aid of—or where necessary instead of—the home as the inculcator of good socialization. Pupils in the public schools would learn good morals, good citizenship, and the skills necessary to permit them to contribute to the progress of society. Dewey worked out his ideas as head of the Laboratory School at the University of Chicago, building on the work of earlier pedagogues such as William T. Harris, G. Stanley Hall, and Francis Parker, and explicated his ideas in his most famous book, *The School and Society*, published in 1899. Schools were conceived to be microcosms of society; learning took place best in a community setting. Cooperative discovery and social interaction were to replace individual memorization. The curriculum did not become crudely utilitarian; there was a place for the arts and humanities. But whatever the subject matter, the child was learning in the best way possible, it was hoped, to allow him to function later for the benefit of society as well as himself.

The role of the public school as a socialization device, and indeed as a place to learn good morals, was not new; moral virtue had of course been a principal aim of the McGuffey readers.

Progressive education was thus more innovative in its method than in its aims, and in lesser hands than Dewey's and in less well-endowed settings than the Laboratory School it could become simply a device for drumming middle-class conformity into the heads of native or foreign-stock, rural or urban children. To some progressives the schools were the prime instrument of Americanization, the best hope, if any hope there was, of molding the children of less well-endowed nationalities and races into adults whose attitudes would at least be safe if not very serendipitous. These educators regarded parochial schools as divisive; parochial schools did not adequately inculcate American social values (as understood by public school administrators). Educators did the best they could to make public education, which became compulsory almost everywhere during the progressive years, into a key means for social control. In that way, and by running the schools "scientifically" and according to "sound business principles," they justified spending the taxpayers' money.[20]

The press had been a rapidly changing social institution since the mid-1880s, in large part as a result of technology—the linotype, high-speed electric presses, photographic reproduction—which greatly reduced production costs and made possible large-scale circulation of daily newspapers and weekly and monthly periodicals to the expanding urban readership. Before the end of the nineties the potential for mass-market journalism was yet to be realized; the subscription price of a genteel monthly like *The Century* was still four dollars in 1890, or about one percent of a factory worker's annual income. Hence factory workers seldom read *The Century*, nor did its editors expect them to. By 1900 this had changed: Hearst and Pulitzer had waged their circulation war, the modern metropolitan daily was a fact of life, and so was the mass-circulation weekly or monthly, aimed at a readership which did not have to be genteel, but only literate. Given this situation, the press functioned very effectively in the progressive period as a disseminator and agitator of reform, especially among its middle-class readership.

In journalism, the progressive urge manifested itself in what Theodore Roosevelt called "muckraking"—the investigation of corruption in business or politics, or of social problems such as white slavery or patent medicine frauds, and the publication of these investigations as single articles or, more often, series of exposés. Sometimes responsible and sometimes simply lurid, the muckrakers told the public some things it did not know—but didn't mind hearing. The public was willing to listen to the muckrakers' criticisms of society, sometimes *sotto voce* and sometimes shrill, and like good journalists anytime, the muckrakers and their publishers marched slightly, but only slightly, ahead of their readership. The most famous muckraking vehicle was Samuel S. McClure's monthly magazine, and the most famous single muckraking issue was *McClure's* of January, 1903, which contained the piece on Minneapolis in Lincoln Steffens' series on "The Shame of the Cities," another on labor union corruption by Ray Stannard Baker, and another by Ida Tarbell on the ruthless rise of the Standard Oil Company. For the next six to eight years, several mass-circulation magazines published muckraking articles by Steffens, Tarbell, Baker, and others including George Kibbe Turner (on vice and the liquor traffic), Charles Edward Russell (the beef trust, church ownership of tenements), Norman Hapgood (patent medicines), and David Graham Phillips (control of U.S. Senators by business interests). The obvious effect was to drum up mass political support for change. In some of the areas, change came forth.

At the time, the muckrakers seemed fresh, perhaps even radical. Certainly much of their information confirmed the worst suspicions of their uneasy readership. In retrospect they appear traditional, sharing most basic assumptions with readers (and publishers) who had just recently left the nineteenth century behind. Their impact was far less profound, much more transitory, than the progressive intellectuals'. An unscientific cross-section of widely circulated periodicals in 1903 suggests that muckraking had by no means taken over; more accurately, it was spice added to familiar fare. McClure just happened to have three exposés ready at publication time in January. More typical was *Munsey's Magazine*, which in the fall led off with an illustrated article on "The Equipage of the Millionaire," on the carriages of the rich, which smacked less of perfervid reform than of Veblen's "pecuniary emulation." The issue carried a profile of Joseph Folk, the reform prosecutor of St. Louis, but balanced that with another on Andrew Carnegie. *Everybody's*

Magazine for November ran a piece on the religious communitarian John Alexander Dowie, another on Barney Oldfield, the auto racer, and an appreciative feature on Mayor Seth Low's reform administration in New York. The *Atlantic* in August discussed banking trusts, but also included Lyman Abbott's "Why Women Do Not Wish the Suffrage." The break with the past, even the genteel journalism of the recent past, was not clean. As Robert Stinson has pointed out, Sam McClure himself continued to be imbued with the nineteenth-century success ethic of "work hard and you are sure to get ahead." [21] But the muckrakers nonetheless had a wide if crude impact in readying people for political and social change—indeed in making them demand change.

A couple of summary comments are in order before we move on from changes in ideas and institutions to changes in the context of life and the political response to them. In the first place it should be pointed out that the aim and the success of the progressive intellectuals and their clients among institutional opinion-makers was moderate. Theirs was not a radical critique of American society and culture and it did not bring radical results. By "radical" I mean here the social theories which were considered radical at the time, in America or industrialized Europe or both, and which were thus available *in theory* for application: Marxian socialism, anarcho-syndicalism, and the socialism of Debs and certain Christian ministers. These were not the choices of the progressive intellectuals, and certainly not of the businessmen and politicians and professionals who absorbed their ideas and came to promote specific adjustments. Instead they remained just as convinced as their counterparts in the nineteenth century of the moral rightness of American society and culture.

Consequently they promoted revision, not revolution. The results—a willingness to experiment (but not to level everything and rebuild from the ground up), to regulate large organizations and to reform government (but not tear them apart), to reintroduce social controls (while preserving the Bill of Rights)—amounted in some respects to sweeping problems under the rug. They and their followers did get rid of the most cumbersome of the nineteenth century's ideological baggage. They did provide the ideological tools for the reassertion of social control and the avoidance of the class war that so many observers in 1900 to 1905 thought was almost inevitable. But despite varying degrees of effort, they did not solve such problems as the increasing accumulation of power by large corporations, the crime and poverty in both cities and rural areas, the situation of the black one-eighth of the population, or the assimilation (or exclusion) of diverse ethnic and religious groups. They provided the intellectual tools to justify regulation and social control, but no more. Their contribution above all was to build the ideological superstructure which Americans needed in order to justify participation in reform activity. Very probably they would have failed if they had not built it in a familiar, middle-class shape. After all, the majority which became in one sense or another "progressive" by 1912 had refused to embrace Populism or Debs' socialism—and not only because these two movements were unable to break away from nineteenth-century rhetoric but because they appeared to represent certain social-economic classes exclusively. The progressive intellectuals and the institutions which helped disseminate their ideas served a critical function of ideological integration. They set American social thought on a liberal path for most of the rest of the twentieth century, making social revolution most unlikely, and insuring the dominance of bourgeois capitalism and middle-class morality in the country that had become the world's foremost industrial power.

6

Life and Labor,
1901–1916

The ideological revisions generated by the progressive intellectuals came none too soon. The demographic and economic facts of American life continued to change after the depression and recovery period of 1893–1901, if anything at a more rapid rate than during the interdepression years of the eighties. These changes evoked a continuing, though sporadic, response.

A quick overview of demographic and economic trends in the progressive years from the turn of the century to World War I reveals the following as outstanding. Total population, estimated by the Census Bureau at 77.6 million in 1901, rose to just over 100 million in 1915, an increase of just about one-third. The increase was fairly steady, at 1.5 to 2 million a year, which meant a rate faster than during the depression years of the nineties or during the World War years. A substantial part of the increase came from net foreign immigration, which continued through the period until the onset of the war in Europe in the summer of 1914 reduced it to a fraction of its previous level. Before then, however, annual arrivals reached higher levels than ever before or since (though in proportion to people already in the United States, not quite as great as in the Irish and early German wave of 1847–1857). In six different years more than one million immigrants arrived; in five of those years, however, over half a million departed.[1] The foreign-born and their children accounted for more than 35 percent of the total population on the eve of World War I. Aside from their sheer numbers, the most striking thing about the immigrants was their ethnic diversity: in 1897 the combined arrivals from Russia, Poland, Italy, and Austria-Hungary began to exceed those from Britain, Ireland, Scandinavia, and Germany. This switch from the "old" to the "new" immigration was never to be reversed. Ethnic homogeneity was a thing of the past.

The new immigrants overwhelmingly took up residence in urban areas, whether from choice or necessity, and they reinforced the rural-to-urban trend which was evident enough among the native stock. Still three-fifths rural and small-town in 1900, the American people became just over half urban in 1918 or 1919. As a consequence both of the location of immigrants and the urbanizing trend among the native white stock, new metropolises emerged, often of the satellite variety, in the Northeast and the East North Central states. That corner of the country, which amounted to less than one-seventh of the land area, included about half of the total population. Since large tracts of Michigan, Wisconsin, New York, and northern New England were thinly inhabited or near-wilderness, a very substantial number of Americans had direct if not daily experience with urban life. Another substantial number, in the South, the Great Plains, and farther west, did not. The map showing the electoral results of 1896, with the rural-symbol Bryan capturing three-fourths of the geographical area of the country but losing to the urban-symbol McKinley, whose victory basically came in the Northeast and East North Central states, reflected the demographic realities (and the sectional, rural-urban split) which continued to prevail during the first fifteen years of the twentieth century. The South in those years underwent an urbanization process as well, remarkable when compared to the overwhelmingly rural history of that region, but very unremarkable compared to the states to the north. The black minority, growing in numbers more slowly than the native white or immigrant components, remained as they had since Reconstruction days 85 to 90 percent Southern and rural—until the historic twentieth-century exodus got well under way after 1915.

The economic history of the period is one of general prosperity, with no relapse into inflation, panic, and depression according to the nineteenth-century pattern, although there were signs of that happening in 1903 (a year of "banker's panic"), 1907 (a real panic, but not followed by depression), and in 1913–1914. The slow recovery from the depression of the nineties was effectively complete by 1901, and after that came fifteen years of economic growth and prosperity which if not exactly utopian were more satisfactory and steady than during the interdepression period of

1879–1893 or any before it. And it ended not in panic and depression but in the boom days of World War I. Even agriculture, that chronic problem sector, benefited, although as usual the smaller, marginal farmer did not. But many of them had been "shaken out," as the economists' dismal phrase puts it, by the long downswing of 1887–1897. Those who remained on the land either sank into tenancy or did quite well despite the costs of modernized competition. Manufacturing and other nonfarm blue-collar sectors continued to outstrip agriculture greatly in rate of growth. Real wages of workers generally tended to increase. The composition of the labor force changed, not only in the direction of nonfarm workers and away from agriculture, but most strikingly in the expansion of white-collar jobs, a trend evident before 1893 but much more prevalent in the progressive period. Business consolidation and the average size of firms continued to increase, in spite of new antitrust laws, prosecutions, and antimonopoly sentiment among the public.

Such are the economic and population trends in the gross aggregate. The particulars need further discussion, for their own sake and to place them in the context of ideological and political change in the prewar years. The rural-to-urban trend was geographically concentrated in the New England, Middle Atlantic, and East North Central states, as already stated—essentially a belt from the west coast of Lake Michigan and the St. Louis area eastward to the Washington-to-Boston seaboard strip. It took several forms: the continued growth of the very largest cities (New York, Philadelphia, Chicago), the rise of satellites like Lowell, Camden, or Yonkers, and the emergence of national-market manufacturing towns like Dayton, Akron, or Grand Rapids. In other parts of the country metropolises also emerged, many more than before 1900, and often regional processing centers. In the South, Atlanta, Richmond, and Nashville reached metropolitan size (100,000 or more) by 1910, and four cities in Texas—Dallas, Fort Worth, Houston, and San Antonio—did so by 1920. In the West, Oakland had become a metropolitan satellite of San Francisco by 1910, while Portland, Seattle, and Spokane had become metropolises, based on trade or primary processing, by the same date. The opening of the Spindletop oil field in east Texas in

1901 and the expansion of world wheat markets, among other things, promoted this geographically diverse urbanization.

Urbanization, in the sense of an ever-increasing proportion of the population living in cities rather than in country villages or on farms, has been a constant feature of American historical demography. But its outstanding characteristic in the first twenty years of the twentieth century was the diffusion of the urban life experience, especially in the St. Louis-Chicago-Boston-Washington parallelogram. In the eighties and nineties the most rapid growth occurred among the three-million-plus giants; the 1900 census showed that New York, Philadelphia, and Chicago increased by more than 75 percent in the preceding decade, a rate more than twice that of all urban population, and nearly four times that of the general population. In the next two decades the largest cities grew more slowly than all urban population, but cities of half a million to a million, which then included Detroit and Los Angeles, and cities of 50 to 250 thousand, grew faster than urban or general population. As the urban experience became more and more the rule, at least in the northeastern parallelogram, so did contact between native and foreign stocks (immigrants and their children being overwhelmingly urban in that period), and so did experience with the problems of operating urban communities.

Cities had to be lighted, their streets paved, their water supply made clean and dependable, their police and fire departments effective for the prevention of damage to limb and property. Sewage had to be treated and disposed of. Given the separation between home and workplace which was a mark of urban-industrial life, intraurban transportation systems had become a necessity. None of these problems were simple, but more and more cities had to find out how to deal with them. During the progressive period the operation of cities was handled with varying degrees of success but also, in general, according to certain assumptions. Things had to be done cheaply and efficiently, at the lowest cost to the taxpayers (most of them middle-class) consistent with getting the job done. This assumption blended well with another, that government and its agencies be uncorrupt. Corruption was immoral, and it also cost money; hence the efforts, sporadic or continuing as the case may have been, to root out linkages between police, politicians, and vice elements; to reduce the power of political-party organizations (the "machines"), which seemed inevitably to involve such linkages; and to reconstitute urban administration by putting authority in the hands of nonpartisan elected commissioners and appointed efficiency experts. The traditional practice of granting franchises to private corporations to build and operate public utilities such as water works, gas works, or transportation lines, came under heavy attack, in some places as early as the 1890s. The taxpayers, as consumers of urban services, objected to paying the high prices these necessities involved when they were operated for private profit, and many middle-class people accepted the solution of "socializing"—that is, bringing under municipal ownership—these services despite the ideological odium involved. Taxes on corporations and on incomes, at the state and federal level, were other solutions advocated principally by middle-class urbanites who refused to let the rising cost of urban government be met chiefly by taxes on their real property. As C. K. Yearley wrote in his remarkable study of government finance in the Northeast, income and corporation taxes and municipal ownership of utilities were certainly "real reforms," but "they also promised to be a real relief to that small number of property holders who had long been convinced they were financing both the revels of the new wealth and the bread and circuses of the new democracy." The thrust toward efficiency as well as frugality, by devices such as city-manager and commission forms of city government, came from much the same people, who could not stand for their money as well as their power in their communities to be taken over by party politicians.[2]

Other changes in city life during the period cannot be ascribed solely to the self-seeking of middle-class businessmen and professionals, however. Humane and, often, religious motives propelled the settlement house movement. A sincere belief in the efficacy of the public schools to produce useful and moral citizens underlay a willingness to increase expenditure for elementary and secondary school expansion. A disgust with wretched overcrowding and lack of sanitation in New York's old-law tenements motivated Lawrence Veiller to push for the landmark tenement reform act of 1901.[3] Simple necessity, and a dawning understanding of the germ theory of disease transmission, caused large and small municipalities to create modern sanitation systems; the death rate from typhoid fever, which reached epidemic proportions in many cities in the opening years of the century, was cut in half by World War I. The eradication of poverty and disease was seldom objected to, then or at other times, and progressive-era Americans became willing out of humaneness or necessity to attack them as the urban experience made them more visible.

The generalization that the larger a city was, the more foreign-stock it was, held true in the early twentieth century as it had in the late nineteenth. Every ethnic group which was a part of the "new immigration," except for the East European Jews, was rural in origin, and all groups without exception settled in urban areas and into urban-located occupations after their arrival in the United States. The immigrant, when he arrived at Ellis Island or some other debarkation point, was asked to give his or her occupation. From the late nineties until the outbreak of World War I in Europe, only a very small fraction ($\frac{1}{2}$ to $1\frac{1}{2}$ percent per year) listed themselves as professional or technical. About the same proportion said they had been owners or managers of farms, and slightly more claimed to have been managers of businesses or public officials in the old country. Craftsmen and skilled manual workers accounted for a sixth to a tenth of the immigrants. People who had been domestic servants of various kinds, most of them presumably women, made up on the average about 9 percent. Laborers of various kinds other than farmers or miners, and with few or no skills, constituted over a third of the total immigration at the beginning of the century, but their proportion dropped fairly steadily until it levelled off at roughly 17 or 18 percent of the whole, in the four years just before World War I began in Europe. The decline reflected a reverse movement on the part of people who had been poorer peasants—that is, farm workers—in southern or eastern Europe.

This group was fairly small, less than one-eighth of the immigrant wave, before 1902, then dipped in 1903–1904 but thereafter increased to more than one quarter of the whole. Interestingly, the proportion of farm workers—all the time meaning tenants and poorer peasants, not owners or estate managers—

was highest, as a rule, in those years when the total numbers of immigrants was largest, and the proportion dropped in the relatively lighter years. The indication is that after the option of emigrating to America had become realistic and attractive—it took a few years after postdepression economic recovery before that option became clear—the southern and eastern European peasants were the occupational group in Europe most sensitive to the "pull" factors enticing them away from Poland or Russia or Italy or other places. The factors tending to push them out of their traditional homelands were more or less constant, or nearly so (although some temporary prosperity had to prevail to make departure financially possible), while increases in the apparent opportunity for jobs in America brought significant rises in the numbers of tenants and peasants who grabbed the main chance and went to the United States.

Contributing to the greatly increased proportion of farm workers emigrating between 1906 and 1914, and accounting for the much smaller proportion before 1906, was undoubtedly the accumulation of relatives, acquaintances, and fellow villagers already in the United States who wrote encouraging letters (or occasionally made return visits) to the effect that those still in southern Italy or the Polish provinces could actually put together something like a new home for themselves, and need not fear linguistic, cultural, or religious isolation. Much greater numbers of the European peasantry, therefore, as distinct from townspeople or the more skilled, entered the United States in the nine years just before World War I and tended to settle in city neighborhoods close to previous arrivals from their own village or district. Thus European localisms, what the Italians called "campanilismo" and the Yiddish-speakers "Lansmannshaft," persisted longer than they might have. The process also meant that the immigrant groups were less unified, more fragmented, than nonimmigrants could conceive of. National self-identification did mean something to Poles, Czechs, Hungarians, or other subject nationalities who had lived within the multi-national Russian or Austro-Hungarian empires, but for Italians and east-European Jews especially, nationality was less of a self-identifying factor than community, village, or even simply the extended family.[4] These kinds of immigrants, arriving in such circumstances, would indeed prove more resistant to assimilation than members of the "old immigration"—though often for reasons different from those suspected by native-stock reformers.

Another quarter, roughly, of the immigrants of 1902–1914 gave no occupation at all. These included the elderly, children under 14, many women, and a certain number of working-age males actually without occupation. Numbers of these people rose in 1913 and 1914, and their proportion to more than a third of total immigrants in the next two years, to a large extent because working-age males who had immigrated earlier had found a sufficient niche in the American scheme of things to import members of their families whom they had left behind. Between 1900 and 1913 over 80 percent of the immigrants every year were in the prime productive years of their lives, from the late teens through the early forties, and in every year from 1900 through 1913, two-thirds or more of the immigrants were male. And again, the proportions of males and prime-working-age entrants were highest, as a rule, in the years when total immigration was greatest.

To sum up, a rough but fair generalization would be that the typical member of the "new immigration," when it was at its high tide, was a young and able-bodied man who was leaving a provincial peasant area in southern or eastern Europe, who had some skills at farming, but who found himself in manufacturing, railroading, or mining in the United States—and who, if he was not part of the exodus of 200,000–400,000 who left the United States each year between 1908 and 1915, managed to gain a foothold and quite possibly eventually bring over the old, young, and female members of his family. Among the major immigrant groups, this pattern was probably very typical of the Italians, Poles, and less numerous Slavic groups. The East-European Jews departed from it in certain ways: they had been townspeople rather than peasants; more of them had manual or clerical skills of some kind; perhaps half of them, a much higher ratio than among the peasant non-Jews from the same areas, were female.[5] With this major exception, however, the early twentieth-century immigrant was an ex-peasant who transplanted himself first from an old country to a new one, and secondly from country to city, to work in occupations for which the existing technology did not require a high degree of skill or craftsmanship.

As had been the case with immigration that took place before the depression of the nineties, forces pushing people out of Europe were at least as important as forces pulling them into the United States. Again, high birth rates in Italy and elsewhere in the seventies and eighties were reflected in high numbers of emigrants fifteen to thirty years later, and this was a factor which obviously had very little to do with economic attractiveness in the United States. In eastern Europe, the commercialization and mechanization of agriculture increased farmworker productivity and made many farm laborers redundant. This process had been at work in the latter half of the nineteenth century in western Europe and by the turn of the century was operating to promote emigration from the east-central and eastern areas of Europe. For the nonfarming Jews living in the Russian Empire, the increasing likelihood of conscription into the Russian army and the spreading incidence of anti-Semitic propaganda and riots made emigration advisable, and Jews who were religiously orthodox and Jews who were secular socialists both did so. A higher proportion than among the Italian or Slavic immigrants had enough of the world's goods to qualify as middle class, and took enough possessions with them in many cases to resume in some form the mercantile occupations they had practiced in the old country. Again, however, their relatively small numbers made them exceptions.

The able-bodied ex-peasant male from Italy, Poland, Austria-Hungary, Greece, Serbia, and parts of the Ottoman Empire had a stimulating effect on the development of the American economy in that period. The presence of jobs in the United States pulled the immigrants westward and benefited them economically. But it is also necessary to observe that the immigrants shaped American economic development. As Brinley Thomas has stated, "The great injection of cheap labour from South [and] Eastern Europe after the turn of the century induced a 'widening' of the capital structure of the United States, enabled the country to take maximum advantage of the technical innovations of that time, and established the basis of its modern economic power." [6]

Diverse in religion and culture and language from each other as well as from the native-stock Americans, possessing few marketable skills and minimal education, the great majority of the new immigrants settled either in the largest cities of the Northeast and the eastern Midwest or else in the rising manufacturing cities in the 25,000–100,000 category in those regions. To a considerable extent they tended to cluster in certain neighborhoods within those cities, and it was this clustering, especially in New York and Chicago, that gave rise to the impression that they were residentially segregated in "ghettoes." Recent historical research has revealed that they were more dispersed than the term "ghetto" suggests, that their dispersal increased over time, and that in both of those respects their experience differed from that of the black migrants who arrived in Northeastern and Midwestern cities a short time later. Ethnic groups tended to overlap in given areas; a "Polish neighborhood" could be at the same time a "German neighborhood," and perhaps a Jewish and Greek and Japanese neighborhood as well. Rarely did a single ethnic group exclusively occupy or even dominate an area of several city blocks. Moreover, most ethnic groups were to be found in not one but several parts of largest cities, if not initially then within a few years of their arrival. For example, Rischin points out that in New York's Lower East Side, where 75 percent of the city's Jews lived in 1892, an out-migration to other parts of the city was already underway, and by 1916 only 23 percent of a much larger Jewish population lived there.[7] Dispersal was almost certainly slower for other groups, and the ethnic character of neighborhoods and districts in many large and small cities persisted well past the middle of the twentieth century. But ethnic "ghettoes," and the stigma attaching to the term, were a temporary phenomenon (to the extent that the term is appropriate at all) and diminished as the economic level of the foreign-stock rose.

The native-stock reaction to all of this was mixed. Although the proportion of foreign-born and foreign-stock people in the general population rose, the increase was hardly overwhelming, even in the Northeastern urban-industrial parallelogram. The new immigration, nonetheless, involved a much greater degree of ethnic and linguistic diversity and (except for the Irish of forty or fifty years earlier) a lower level of skills, capital, and previous urban experience. Employers did not need to be told that the ex-peasants of the Slavic countries and Italy were a cheap and effective labor source. But even they, in their role as citizens and taxpayers, worried about the economic costs of schools and city services and the social costs of a diverse and, according to the conventional wisdom of the day, perhaps unassimilable third of the population. To many intellectuals and professionals, the new immigration was a disaster; brought up to believe that social classes were stratified (with themselves near the top), their hostility was reinforced by the race theories of the time. Prevailing theory maintained that racial differences were ineradicable; that eugenics—selective breeding— would produce a better human; and to this better human, inferior races had nothing to contribute. Thus immigration restriction would obviously mean the first step toward the restoration of racial and ideological purity in American society.

These attitudes shaped the thought and action of the Boston-based Immigration Restriction League, an organization with an elite old-stock membership whose political spokesman was Senator Henry Cabot Lodge. Not all Boston Brahmins shared their viewpoint: Harvard's Charles W. Eliot, William James, and other Boston intellectuals rejected racism and the eugenics movement and ascribed the evident poverty and slum conditions among many immigrants to urbanism and industrialism rather than to any innate racial characteristics of the immigrants. In Chicago, native-stock progressive reformers, who formed the Immigrants' Protective League to help ease the immigrants' transition into American social and economic life in many practical ways, also rejected racism, blamed city conditions for the immigrants' problems, and attempted (without much success) to secure state and federal legislation on industrial safety, hours and working conditions, regulation of employment agencies, and other matters. They included altruistic, realistic, and highly competent women such as Jane Addams, the Abbott sisters, Sophonisba Breckinridge, and Emily Balch. These social-work progressives, in close touch with actual conditions among the immigrants, believed that the new-comers could contribute much to American life besides simple muscle. The immigrants also had to be Americanized; education, whether night schools for the workers or the public schools for their children, would best hasten assimilation of American cultural values.

Progressive churchmen taking part in the Social Gospel movement often supported the social workers and sociologists in the Americanization campaign, and for them the objectives of labor legislation for the immigrants' bodies and education for their minds were supplemented by mission work to provide Protestantism for their souls. As one church researcher wrote a few years later, "the evangelization of Catholic immigrants was undertaken by the Protestant churches in the belief that the ideals and principles of government and social life in America were derived from and supported by the spirit of Protestantism." [8] Billy Sunday and presumably his followers took a dimmer view; the immigrants and their Jewish or Catholic religion were a foreign element. Since saloons were especially disgraceful, prohibition seemed to such people the main legislative answer to social problems. The movement to restrict immigration by federal law gained sufficient strength in the mid-nineties for Congress twice to pass bills providing for literacy testing—frankly advocated by Lodge and other congressmen, mostly Republicans, as a way to keep out southern and eastern Europeans—only to see it twice vetoed by President Cleveland on the ground that the United States always had been, and always should be, the haven for Europe's oppressed. Support for literacy testing subsided for a while. Nativist legislation during the progressive period included a 1903 law excluding anarchists, and the "Gentlemen's Agreement" of 1907 excluding Japanese, but no general attack on the European new immigrants. After World War I began, however, literacy testing became law over President Wilson's veto, and national-origins quotas, an even more candidly racist barrier, soon followed.

The immigrants, in the meantime, struggled toward their main objectives of economic survival and, if lucky, prosperity. Family life was somewhat reshaped, but remained strong as it had been in Europe. Education at least at basic levels was eagerly sought after by the immigrants, and Catholic churches and Jewish congregations helped provide schools. Often rejected by the native-stock social institutions, immigrants formed thousands of their own ethnic and religious associations for a wide range of social and economic purposes. Many of them, dubbed "birds of passage," either found the United States an impossible place in which to gain a foothold, or, as part of a labor population floating across western Europe and between Europe and North or South America, never intended to stay: the outflow of foreign-born was a third to a half as large as the inflow. For the millions who did stay, however, enough evidence exists to allow the conjecture that perhaps they needed language, education, and jobs so badly that they were geographically more stable than the native-stock and Irish floating population of twenty or thirty years earlier. If so, immigration restrictionists need not have worried; social control, through very gradual assimilation, was coming anyway. Yet the numbers and ethnic variety of the newcomers was so great as to frighten many opinion-leaders among the white native-stock majority. To them, immigration was a problem.

For most of the period the Negro, that other alien within the gates, was of less immediate concern. Except for a few race riots (in 1906–1909 especially), and the almost routine announcement of lynchings across the South, the black minority could be forgotten about as it had been for most of the time since the zeal went out of Reconstruction thirty years before. There was even talk of the black minority eventually disappearing. Darwinist race theorists believed that the Negro was not fit enough to survive, and high mortality rates coupled with lower than normal birth rates produced a drop in the black proportion of the United States population from 12 percent in 1900 to 11 percent in 1910 to 10 percent in 1920. In any event, the black was a Southern "problem," as he had been always: nearly 90 percent lived in the South, nearly 85 percent in rural areas.

Just as the progressive period closed, this traditional pattern began to change. It would continue to change in both the rural South and the urban North, for another fifty years or more, as massive numbers of the Southern black peasantry moved into the larger cities of the Northeast, Midwest, and West. Little of this was noticeable until after 1915. The exodus began then, coinciding with the sudden dropoff in European immigration. It continued through World War I, slowed with the resumption of heavy immigration lasting from the spring of 1919 until the restriction laws took effect in 1921, and accelerated thereafter.

These facts reveal one of the major trends in American demographic history: the existence of a "substitution effect" as the main characteristic of black-immigrant population patterns. Both groups competed, at that time, for low-skilled urban-located jobs. Until and unless European immigration was reduced to a fraction of what it was in 1905–1914, black migration did not take place; World War I was the exceptional period that proved the rule. As Thomas said, "The peopleing of America by the 'huddled masses' of the Old World was a boon to the whites [in providing a cheap mass labor force for low-skill positions] and a curse to the blacks." [9]

Before the exodus began in 1915, the life of the American black was not greatly different from what it had been in the late nineteenth century, except that Jim Crow had reached maturity. In 1913, William E. Burghardt DuBois summed up the situation in an editorial in *The Crisis*, the monthly publication of the recently founded National Association for the Advancement of Colored People:

> . . . after fifty years of attempted liberty, the reactionary South and the acquiescent North come forward with this program: 1. The absolute disfranchisement of all citizens of Negro descent forever. 2. The curtailment and regulation of property rights by segregation. 3. Strictly limited education of Negro children as servants and laborers. 4. The absolute subjection of Negro women by prohibition of legal marriage between races. 5. The eventual driving of the Negro out of the land by disease, starvation or mob violence.

The indictment was bitter but scarcely overwritten. Whether one speaks of the 10 percent of the American black population scattered about Northern towns and cities, or the majority (before 1915) in the South, the pattern of segregation and subjection differed little except that it was mandated and enforced by law in the Southern states more thoroughly than in the North.

Jim Crow functioned in several areas of life. Perhaps the most overtly offensive manifestation to blacks and the true democrats among whites was the systematic deprivation of the right to vote, because that seemed so clearly to violate the letter as well as the spirit of the Fourteenth and Fifteenth Amendments. Between 1890 and 1908, every Southern state enacted laws disfranchising blacks, and in the process many poorer whites. The poll tax did the job on both groups. The story of its enactment varied from state to state, but generally it was instituted by dominant Democratic factions who were afraid that other factions might unseat them by recruiting the blacks and poorer whites. Often the fear was of a recrudescence of Populism. As Sheldon Hackney succinctly put it, "Progressives and other white Alabamians eliminated the theft of Negro votes by eliminating Negro voting." [10] Another disfranchisement device was a literacy requirement, enforced selectively by local registrars. Another was the white primary—the exclusion of blacks from voting in Democratic primary elections in states where winning the primary assured election because the Republican vote was so small. In Texas, according to Alwyn Barr, "The impulse toward . . . white primaries became statewide in the 1890s when growing Populist strength split the white vote and made it possible for a Negro minority to swing an election." [11] The device was effective in cutting off black votes and also those of many Mexican-Americans and poorer Anglos; voter participation in elections fell below 50 percent. In Virginia, where a new Constitution in 1902 was supposed to end "electoral corruption" and bring "good government" (by disfranchising blacks), the number of eligible black voters fell from 147,000 in 1901 to 21,000 in 1905, and the majority of the latter had not paid poll taxes. [12] By 1908 the black voter was a great rarity in the South, and would remain so for nearly sixty years.

If the laws and the courts could sanction deprivation of voting rights, then social and educational segregation was an easy matter. Southern and some Northern states legally forbade, increasingly after 1890, interracial marriage; interracial use of public transportation and public accommodations; common schools that were common to both races; interracial juries (unconstitutional on the face of it, but since jurors had to be voters, and blacks were disfranchised, Jim Crow juries became the rule). The Supreme Court chartered Jim Crow in 1896, in its now infamous *Plessy* v. *Ferguson* decision. The argument in the case was over the constitutionality of a Louisiana law of 1890 requiring segregated passenger cars on railways, but the Court suggested broader applications: "Laws permitting, and even requiring, their [the races'] separation in places where they are liable to be brought into contact do not necessarily imply the inferiority of either race to the other, and have been generally, if not universally, recognized as within the competency of the state legislatures in the exercise of their police power. The most common instance of this is . . . separate schools for white and colored children. . . ." Schools for blacks were, of course, separate, but not equal; why, asked white taxpayers, should we put money into them, since it was unlikely that the black child can learn much anyway? The consequence of this expectation of racial inferiority was indeed educational inferiority: a classic self-fulfilling prophecy. Teachers in Jim Crow schools were paid less, physical plants were second-rate; the gyms, shops, and libraries which progressive educators were urging for white schools were absent. In an age when blacks were being lynched at an average frequency of once or twice a week, and serious race riots occurred once a year, it was little wonder that school attendance by black children lagged well behind that of whites. The wonder is that despite all of these obstacles, the illiteracy rate among the black population, which had been about 80 percent in Reconstruction days, fell from 45 percent in 1900 to 31 percent in 1910 to 23 percent in 1920.

Although about 400,000 blacks left the South for Northern cities in the war years of 1915–1918, the lives of the more than eight million remaining in the South underwent little change; perhaps a good thing since most changes were for the worse. Endemic diseases sapped the strength and the lives of blacks and whites alike. Dr. Joseph Goldberger of the U. S. Public Health Service was just discovering and convincing people that pellagra, the hookworm disease which spread throughout the South (separately but equally) after 1902, was caused by a vitamin deficiency in the rural diet of meat, meal, and molasses. Some blacks apparently avoided pellagra because they were too poor to afford even that diet and had to subsist on fish, which happened to have the right nutrient.[13] Malaria and yellow fever were also common. For blacks, infant mortality and general death rates were higher and life expectancy lower, compared not only to whites in America but also to the peoples of Europe, including the Balkans. Black life expectancy rose substantially in the early twentieth century, from about 33 years to nearly 40 (life expectancy at birth, for the registration area of the Northeast and Midwest). But that was still about fifteen years less than the white population. Too many blacks died either in infancy—almost one-fourth of all deaths in 1900, which had to be a disruptive social factor—or in what would have been the prime productive years for personal and race improvement. In 1915 about 27 percent of all deaths among blacks occurred within the cohort aged 25 to 44 (the figure for whites in the same cohort was 16 percent).[14] In all the vital statistics—malnutrition, disease, infant mortality, early death—the black population was greatly disadvantaged in any competitive struggle toward middle-class or even white working-class standards. The black family, according to the sociologist E. Franklin Frazier, was unstable; marriage and divorce was often casual, illegitimacy high. Adult males tended to travel from place to place in search of jobs, and a pattern of father desertion evident in the South before 1915 was magnified, as was illegitimacy, by the institutional disruption attendant upon the northward migration.[15] Child and woman labor was much more common among blacks than among native or immigrant whites in Southern cities as well as in rural areas: another socially disruptive force. The possibility of acquiring yeoman status, an elusive dream since the end of slavery, dwindled further. Sharecropping, the mortgaging of crops before harvest or even before planting, and the convict lease system, all militated against property acquisition. The black Southern farmer often operated on an economy of barter, seeing few cash dollars for years at a time. The proportion of farms operated by tenants rather than by owners or part-owners was higher, but only slightly, among whites in the South than among whites in the rest of the country—about 30 compared to about 37 percent. Among Southern blacks, however, the tenancy rate was more than twice as high, and the proportion increased from 74.5 percent in 1900 to 76.3 percent in 1920.

When Southern blacks migrated north, then, they left little behind. The minority in the North was economically and legally better off, and the small black communities in New York, Chicago, and many smaller cities in the Northeast and Midwest were fairly stable in size and in social structure, though they were already segregated residentially to a greater degree than immigrant groups were. The exodus of 1915 and later tended to overwhelm the preexisting black communities, but the causes and benefits of migration were obvious. Labor depression in 1914, the devastation wrought by boll weevils to the cotton crop in 1915 and 1916, which destroyed the meager economic basis for tenants and sharecroppers, and on the other hand an increasing demand for able-bodied men at a time when immigration suddenly fell off, made the North doubly attractive.[16] The black migration of the twentieth century had begun. Together with foreign immigration, it was to be one of the two great diversifying trends in modern American demography.

Neither blacks nor whites overlooked entirely the miserable condition of the black minority. Several answers were proposed for "negro improvement." Booker T. Washington's "Atlanta Compromise" of 1895, and his efforts at Tuskegee Institute since the early 1880s, formed the most accommodating answer; Negroes would gradually fit into white economic life through vocational training, and perhaps in fifty years voting rights and legal equality would come, as the value of Negroes to the general society increased and was appreciated. W. E. B. DuBois disagreed. Himself the holder of a Harvard Ph.D. and over his (ultimately) 95-year life the author of many books on Negro history and life, DuBois declared that 10 percent of the black race was as talented as any whites, and this "talented tenth" deserved the best teachers, the best training, and equal opportunity. The difference between Washington's and DuBois' viewpoints was not the only one among black leaders at the time, but it was the outstanding difference.

In 1909, after a bloody race riot at Springfield, Illinois, DuBois joined with certain other blacks and a number of white progressives, often of the social-work wing of progressivism, including Jane Addams, William English Walling, Oswald Garrison Villard, John Dewey, and others, and founded the N.A.A.C.P. The new organization was to promote "full enjoyment of rights as citizens, justice in all courts, and equality of opportunity" for blacks. At a time when Booker Washington was just barely acceptable in the South, the DuBois-N.A.A.C.P. point of view was considered aggressively subversive in the region where most blacks lived. The National Urban League was founded the next year, and began a broad program of social work and housing improvement. But it too was effective mainly among migrants in the North, not among the rural peasantry in the South. These agencies, and men like DuBois (and Washington, let it be said), often in cooperation with white progressives, did improve to some extent the condition of the black minority. Yet in a day when ideas of race inferiority were rampant among the educated as well as the mass, when the absence of unions in Northern manufacturing industry and the segregation policies of craft unions made the condition of the black worker better solely by contrast with the deplorable state of Southern black farmers, and when the progressive President Wilson kept the federal services rigidly segregated, the work of amelioration was almost infinitesimal compared to the problem. The immigrant from Europe had no bed of roses in America during the progressive period; the black American had a bed of nails.

The demographic changes which happened to American society between 1901 and the coming of World War I were accompanied by, and interlinked with, economic changes of remarkable proportions. The growth of cities and of industry and the increase in urban population and urban-located jobs were obviously symbiotic. Mass employment, that untraditional kind of work situation already beginning to be apparent to the 1870s and which became ever more common during the last quarter of the nineteenth century, affected more and more people, whether men or women, white native or immigrant or black. By 1899, the four and a half million production workers in manufacturing were located in about 205,000 establishments, averaging about twenty-two workers per factory. The average rose gradually to about twenty-five per factory on the eve of World War I, and in 1919, after the expansion in size of firms brought on by wartime demand and consolidation, the average was about thirty-one workers per factory. Outside of manufacturing, in sectors such as trade and finance, the average was smaller, but in transportation and public utilities the mass-employment phenomenon was more pronounced. Concentration of business also meant concentration of workers. The experience of spending one's working hours, which usually meant ten to twelve hours per day on a six-day week, for an impersonal industrial corporation, as has been described so well by Herbert Gutman,[17] became the usual thing for millions of people. Whether they were native-stock, immigrant, or black, their urban-industrial situation was very different in most aspects of life-style from the rural-agricultural background in which they and their families had been raised. But wages in industry, as usual, rose faster than returns from farming, whether in Vermont or Illinois, Poland or Sicily, Georgia or Mississippi; despite the regimentation and boredom of so many jobs in manufacturing, mining, or clerking, the prospects were better than in farming.

In most years employment rates were very high. Only in 1908, just about the Panic of 1907, and in 1914–1915, just before wartime demand began, did unemployment surpass 7 percent. Demand for workers, white collar and blue collar, remained generally high; demand for farmers stabilized. Although the number of farms in the United States rose about 10 percent between 1900 and 1910, many of the new farms being Homestead patents in remoter parts of the West, the 1910 figure of 6.4 million farms represented the edge of a historic plateau. Twenty-five years later there were 6.8 million farms, the all-time high; the number has fallen ever since, to fewer than 3 million in 1970. Before World War I the historic peak in absolute numbers of farmers was passed (at 13.6 million in 1916), and had been stable for several years. In 1900 farm workers constituted about 38 percent of the work force; in 1920, about one-fourth, which indicated even more powerfully than the fact of 50 percent urban residence how thoroughly American society had become urban and industrial.[18]

While farming continued to be a decreasingly common way of earning a living, blue-collar and white-collar jobs proliferated. Craftsmen, foremen, and skilled workers of various kinds increased from 3 to 5½ million between 1900 and 1920; manufacturing operatives from 1½ to 3 million; unskilled or semiskilled manufacturing workers from 700,000 to over 2 million. Numbers of blue-collar workers rose from 36 to 40 percent of the work force, and in so doing continued a trend already apparent in the last three decades of the nineteenth century. A more startling development was the increase in white-collar workers—professionals, managers, clerical and sales people—of whom there were over 10 million in 1920, or about one worker in four. This development had begun to be apparent by the turn of the century, continued in the first decade, and accelerated between 1910 and 1920. A few examples of occupational increase from 1900 to 1910 to 1920 (thousands of people thus employed): accountants and auditors, from 23 to 39 to 118; college teachers and administrators, from 7 to 16 to 23; engineers, 75 to 154 to 267; nurses, from 12 to 82 to 149; operators of auto shops and service stations, from practically nobody to 5 to 56; bookkeepers, 232 to 447 to 616; stenographers, typists, and office secretaries, from 134 to 387 to 786; telephone operators, from 19 to 98 to 190; office machine operators, shipping clerks, bank tellers, and other clerical people, from 235 to 654 to 1,323.

These were all jobs that required a degree of literacy and numeracy, and it is no accident that during the early years of the century a minimal level of compulsory schooling, usually eighth grade or age 14 to 16, became universal. The movement toward making every American child complete the eighth grade, and high school if possible, had succeeded in securing laws to that effect in more than two-thirds of the states by 1900, and in the rest shortly thereafter. The impetus came partly from educational ideology, especially the argument that the populace had to be well schooled if democracy was to function, and also from the drive, supported not only by humanitarian reformers but also by labor leaders, to suppress child labor. It happened also to coincide with a marked increase in demand in the labor market for people possessing nonmanual skills. Indeed it is difficult to say which caused the other—whether the existence of a pool of literate and numerate people spurred the increase in the white-collar job market, or whether the need for such people provoked the rise in school attendance, school completion, and large numbers of aptly trained workers. One suspects that the latter was a bigger reason than the former, but in any event the spread of mass elementary and secondary education, and the great expansion of white-collar jobs and workers, were doubtless closely interlinked phenomena. And millions of these jobs were typically filled by women—secretaries, telephone operators, nurses, teachers, salesgirls, and others. In the first twenty years of the century the numbers of white women in the labor force almost doubled, to nearly seven million or about one-sixth of all workers.

What did all these workers earn? There has been some argument among economic historians as to whether real earnings increased; there is no doubt that dollar income rose, but the period was also inflationary. The most recent comprehensive study, by Albert Rees, finds that real wages did rise, especially after 1914. It is still doubtful, however, that income gains matched productivity gains; changes in real income were certainly not sufficient to produce wholesale changes in wealth distribution. At the turn of the century, the sociologist John Graham Brooks estimated that 1 percent of the population owned 55 percent of the wealth, and 50 percent of the population, none of the wealth. Accumulation to the extent of being able to buy a house or, a little later, a car, remained very difficult and depended in many cases on several members of a family being employed, daughters as well as sons. Many white-collar jobs paid better than factory work, railroading, or mining, certainly better than farming; and although wage rates for males generally were higher than for females, the rewards to a family with a working wife or daughter were very tangible. It helped, of course, if a worker was skilled, or if he belonged to a union (which were overlapping categories; the skilled-worker American Federation of Labor accounted for 70 to 80 percent of all union members during the period). Unionized workers in manufacturing earned on the average about twice as much per hour and worked about ten hours less per week than nonunion workers. In general, however, the mass-employment industries such as steel and the rapidly growing white-collar occupations were not unionized, and despite the explosion of union membership from half a million in the late nineties to over a million in 1901 to two million in 1907 and almost three million in 1917, more than 90 percent of the nonfarm labor force was nonunionized even by the outbreak of World War I. For working people of whatever category, increases in income, wealth, or property depended much more on the expansion of nonagricultural jobs, skilled or semiskilled, blue collar or white collar, than on unions or, certainly, government action. Improvements in the condition of labor were a product of market forces, involving structural changes in the demand for certain types of workers and involving changes in educational patterns to meet that demand.

A certain element among capitalists and employers, notably the several thousand who expanded the membership of the National Civic Federation after the Panic of 1907, believed that it was to their enlightened self-interest to cooperate with "responsible" union leadership such as Gompers of the A.F. of L., and thus to undercut the socialists, the radical laborites, and anti-big-business rhetoricians like Senator Robert M. La Follette. But the enlightened-cooperation viewpoint was not shared by smaller manufacturers or for that matter by large ones such as Charles Schwab of Bethlehem Steel, Elbert Gary of U.S. Steel, or Henry Ford. The leadership and membership of the National Association of Manufacturers spoke out constantly and vigorously against any labor organizations except perhaps those set up by companies themselves. Businessmen, large or small, regardless of product or service, were extremely reluctant to release any significant degree of control over one of the major variables in their operations, their labor costs. Almost always, and with the help of court injunctions and other devices to stop strikes and boycotts, or avoid collective bargaining, they successfully retained that control.

The merger movement in big business slowed after 1902. Consolidations did continue to occur and the major share of American business activity, especially in manufacturing, transportation, mining and refining, and to some extent marketing, came to rest among a few hundred large firms. The dominant trend was not so much toward monopoly, though that existed in a few industries, but toward oligopoly. In social terms, the difference was not crucial as to whether one huge firm or several very large ones controlled most or all of an industry. In either case new technologies could be employed more or less rapidly. Vertical integration of raw-materials sources, primary processing, transporting of materials and products, finishing of goods, and marketing them to wholesale if not retail distributors, could take place. Decision-making could be diffused throughout a hierarchical, bureaucratic structure. Pricing and output could be raised or lowered, and product innovations decided for or against, in response to market demand.

Specialists in finance, law, engineering, sales, and management itself would be required. "Big business" had already made an appearance in the interdepression years of 1878–1893 as the first large-scale organizations in American society, internally structured for a common purpose involving hundreds or thousands of people. The five or six years following the depression of the nineties brought rapid consolidation; the years from 1902 to the outbreak of World War I brought, chiefly, refinements in the management process; responses to new technology, products, and power sources, particularly electrical power and internal combustion engines; and a gradual decline in the importance of investment bankers and other finance capitalists.

Perhaps the last was a function of the aging and death of giants like J. Pierpont Morgan, Sr. (d. 1913) and E. H. Harriman (d. 1909), but it was more important in the long run that nonbanking companies themselves generated and retained capital in large enough amounts to permit their own reorganization and expansion, or to get capital from other nonbanking companies, as DuPont refinanced General Motors in 1915. The large, integrated business corporation remained, in the years before World War I (and for that matter until the 1930s), without parallel in complexity and almost without parallel in any sense, the prime contact which Americans had with large-scale organizations. Organizations of a voluntary kind, like churches, unions, or political parties, or governments, though in some important respects they became more complex during the progressive era or even slightly before, did not match the business oligopolies. The public response, whether by social theorists or by the mass of people, was vigorous but often uninformed and confused. Many progressives recognized no greater enemy than "the trusts." Business regulation by state or federal commissions, new antitrust laws, scores of antitrust prosecutions by the Justice Department, and ongoing voter approval of progressive antimonopoly candidates achieved a breadth and respectability unknown before 1900. Nevertheless the most famous antitrust prosecutions, while successfully "breaking up" Standard Oil and the sugar and tobacco trusts, simply changed them from monopolies to oligopolies with similar social consequences. Business leaders themselves understood no better than anyone else that they were in the grip of a social process, a structuring of society in such a way that large organizations were becoming dominant. On both the state and federal levels they sought either to control and minimize the efforts to regulate them, or more often, as was the case with the railroads, simply to oppose and fret at regulation.[19]

Quite probably the businessmen need not have bothered. The development of large-scale organizations in other areas of society, in the form of labor unions and, ultimately more importantly, the federal government, only just began during the progressive period. The efforts of progressive intellectuals to understand social changes and to generate ideological revisions sufficient to avoid reaction and revolution, were undoubtedly of major significance. These efforts underpinned progressive measures both in and out of law and government to regulate the most offensive and antisocial manifestations of big business, to reduce social frictions arising from urbanism and industrialism, and to bring about substantially effective social control in a population which was increasingly and dangerously heterogeneous. But they did not strike in any fundamental way at the substance or development of large-scale organization. Nor, in the long run, did they provide leads to Americans in the future as to how to do so.

7

Social Change Through
Law and Politics,
1901–1916

The response of progressive-era Americans to the demographic and economic change happening all around them, and the uses to which they put the ideas of the progressive intellectuals, were partial and selective. They were also nonradical and reaffirmative, as suggested earlier. The Populists, the Debsian socialists, the Bellamy Nationalists, and Henry George Single-Taxers, even semi-establishment political leaders like Robert M. La Follette, had all provided blueprints of greater or less detail for identifying and correcting the problems engendered by contemporary change, as those people saw and felt them. None of these blueprints found more than temporary acceptance and only among certain segments of the population. For political progressivism there was no single blueprint either. Instead there were several wide-ranging blueprints, parts of which were erected into political and legislative edifices, and a lot of little blueprints to achieve limited goals.

We are always forced to recognize, when considering progressive-era changes both inside and outside of government, the enormous diversity of "progressivism" and "progressives" as to chronology, geography, breadth of interest, and commitment to "reform" motivation. We have already observed the contribution of the progressive intellectuals, who were less important for their practical efforts in social work or economic legislation than for their ideological role in preparing Americans to think in such ways as to make change acceptable. Certainly this was true for their precursors; it may seem outrageous to those who think of history as past politics, but in terms of impact on social thought (and eventually, action), Charles Sanders Peirce was a more seminal figure than Rutherford B. Hayes, William James more than

William McKinley, Richard T. Ely certainly more than Henry George or even Bryan, John Dewey more than William Howard Taft or Robert La Follette. But our concern here is not with the intellectuals but with the many others who were more or less, on some issue or other, some time and place or other, progressives, who struggled to bring about change and to institutionalize it in government and politics. These were the people who had adopted, again thoroughly or superficially as the case may be, the evolutionary and progressive cast of mind.

It may be useful to make a few rough distinctions among them. There were those who worked actively with the urban poor, native and immigrant, and whose knowledge of urban and labor conditions was direct: the social workers, settlement house people, Social-Gospel clergy (some of them), and some teachers and academics and other professionals. The great majority were white native-stock, middle class in origin, and their motivation altruistic; preeminent among them was the secular saint of Chicago's Hull House, Jane Addams. Not primarily interested in social control but rather in social betterment, anxious to help people regardless of race or nationality or religion, the social-justice progressives spent most of their efforts working with what would later be called the "underprivileged"; their efforts in support of social legislation were important but, to them, secondary. They could be counted on to favor actively not only social-justice and labor reform laws, but changes in governmental structure, business regulation, and progressive politicians like Theodore Roosevelt. They understood Edward A. Ross's idea that sin was no longer individual, but social. They were not concerned with their own middle-class status but in helping others. They were the most thoroughgoing, perhaps "hard core," progressives, and those still active in the 1930s were the most likely of former progressives to support the New Deal.[1] They perceived a connection between political machines, corporate power, and urban conditions which clashed with their ideas of democracy and uplift, and the net result of their political efforts was less to bring about social justice, which occurred marginally, than to bolster the wide-ranging progressive coalition bringing about "good" (middle-class) government.[2]

The social worker–settlement house worker progressives were a highly visible, often revered group, but as is perhaps the case with altruists anytime, greater in virtue than in numbers. Probably larger and certainly more heterogeneous were those who sought social improvement but in a much less comprehensive way, often on a single issue such as workmen's compensation, tenement house reform, sanitation or other public health measures, and many others. The single-issue progressives often functioned in politics as pressure groups, crossing class or ethnic or party lines to form a coalition whose goal was specific. Single-issue progressivism has caused much trouble for taxonomy-minded historians because it was in single-issue struggles that many people participated who were "progressive" in few if any other ways. The foreign-stock element in progressivism was most often found here, coalescing with native-stock reformers to promote labor and welfare legislation, sometimes structural changes such as the income tax or direct election of senators, but seldom woman suffrage or prohibition, which remained ethnically sensitive issues. These people were part-time, in-and-out, progressives who, like the social workers, had some direct experience with urban conditions, were outraged, and, out of self-interest or altruism or both, tried to do something.

Progressivism also included some socialists or near-socialists, a mixed group including some Protestant clergy on the left wing of the Social Gospel movement, some seculars like Milwaukee's Socialist Mayor Victor Berger and his supporters (many of them foreign-stock), and of course Debs' Socialist party of America. Working from then-radical presuppositions, their political successes were at best sporadic. Journalists, especially the muckrakers, played an enormously important role in the progressive movement. But their contributions were characteristically fleeting and their analyses superficial, as Lincoln Steffens himself confessed years later. He and the other progressive-era newspapermen, magazine writers, and novelists saw some of the undemocratic and corrupt linkages between businessmen and politicians, but not all, and except for a very occasional Lippmann or Croly they did not philosophize. They were the provocateurs of many of the changes that took place, and without them and the new mass-circulation outlets for which they wrote much less would have got done. But their thrust and political effect were not radical.

The rest of the identifiable subgroups within the progressive mélange were less interested, or plainly not interested, in reform of the social-welfare kind. Their concerns were more abstract—the restoration of political democracy and equal economic opportunity in American life, as they saw it—and also more selfish and less globally humanitarian. In the large, their main concerns were to regulate big business, to restructure governments (especially city governments), and to accomplish such other reform as seemed available and appropriate for social efficiency and control. Among these people were social-register people of leisure and property, clergy, professionals, male and female "civic leaders," newspaper editors and publishers, and businessmen of various shapes and sizes, from those who owned and ran the main companies in company towns to local merchants or bankers, and at times the trustees or partners in nationally important firms: in short, the "white power structure," situated in hundreds of small, medium, or large cities, very heavily native-stock, with a considerable amount of status and wealth to maintain. Frequently high-minded, intelligent, and well-read, they nonetheless saw the present and future of America through their own upper- and upper-middle-class white native-stock prejudices. It was their support, awareness, and efforts that brought about many of the changes which filled the grab-bag called progressivism, and it was their sense that the main outlines of the social, economic, and political structure of the country should be preserved which prevented the grab-bag from containing very many measures of a directly social-welfare type. Whether in the Northeast or the Midwest or the South, these were the people in a position to bring about political and legislative responses to social and economic changes, and they did bring them about. But the changes were to be selective, limited responses.

Many of these responses occurred before 1901, and in many ways the political-structure, middle-class-democracy, social-control progressives were direct descendants of the mugwumps of the late Gilded Age. In certain states where contact with industrial and urban conditions happened early, such as New York and Massachusetts, or where aggrieved groups coalesced into an angry citizenry with vigorous leaders, as in Wisconsin, the progressive movement for practical purposes manifested itself in the 1890s.

Primitive outcroppings in such areas as railroad regulation, the Australian ballot, primary elections, and of course prohibition were even evident in the reform-resistant soil of the eighties. Indigenous progressivism in the South began in earnest by 1900, partly as a response to freak events like the Galveston tidal wave of that year, which provoked restructuring of inept city government, and more widely as a response to agrarian protest. In the Midwest and Northeast several forces coalesced after 1901, and particularly after 1905, to produce the vigorous political progressivism which lasted until American entry into World War I. These forces were the frightening prospects of the merger movement, the revelations of the muckrakers, the growing social and intellectual respectability of reform, the charisma of Theodore Roosevelt and a few dozen governors, senators, and mayors, and the gradual development of concrete reform proposals.

Of the constituent groups which comprised "the progressive movement," the upper-middle-class people interested above all in political structures made that ten or twelve years into an era of "reform" and governed the shape and limits of the reforms that took place. The social-work progressives, Social Gospelers, journalists, intellectuals, foreign-stock participants, and certainly the millions of white-collar and blue-collar workers and their families who voted for either of the two progressive candidates, Woodrow Wilson or Theodore Roosevelt, in 1912 (70 percent of the total vote), were integral parts of the movement and gained many of their objectives. But the most impressive results came to those concerned about regulating big-business excesses, restructuring unresponsive governments, and reintegrating society.

The changes which the progressive era brought to American society through legislation and government were too numerous to describe in detail in this brief space, but the main areas where progressive efforts made a difference should be sketched. These areas were party politics and the suffrage; the regulation (or lack of it) of new forms of business enterprise; labor relations; problems of urbanization; and finally, the practice and conduct of government, especially the progressives' efforts to make it more efficient and bureaucratic.

The thrust of progressivism in regard to political parties was to reduce the power, or reputed power, of existing organizations. This was usually done on the grounds that the Republican or Democratic politicians running those organizations were self-serving; were involved in unholy alliances with powerful and often shadowy business combines seeking tax, franchise, or other favors; or were unresponsive to social and economic change or ideals. The progressive attack on political organizations came at all levels of government: At the city and county levels the hope was to secure new city charters vesting power in boards of commissioners and in appointed city managers and other experts. In state governments, as in Theodore Roosevelt's New York, Woodrow Wilson's New Jersey, Hazen Pingree's Michigan, Robert La Follette's Wisconsin, Hiram Johnson's California, Joseph Bristow's Kansas, even James K. Vardaman's Mississippi and elsewhere, progressives struggled for dominance through factional fights within the political party which was normally in the majority, or if the balance was close, within both. Progressives struck at party organizations even at the loosely organized national level, notably in the spectacular episode when Theodore Roosevelt led the progressive wing of the Republican party out of the Old Guard-dominated convention of 1912 to support his personal candidacy on the Progressive ticket. The "Bull Moose" campaign of Roosevelt and the insurgent senators, congressmen, editors, and others who joined him was in many ways the paradigm of political progressivism—it was progressive with a capital "P" in name; proposed a comprehensive platform for business regulation, governmental restructuring, and (to some extent) welfare; and not least, was headed by a vastly popular personality—probably the most popular American politician between Jackson and Franklin Roosevelt—who appeared unwilling to sacrifice his reform ideals to party loyalty. But Theodore Roosevelt was not the only charismatic leader of the time; all of the gentlemen just mentioned shared the quality to some degree. Many (though not all; Wilson was an exception) rose through the ranks of party organizations in their states and had been loyal regulars in the 1890s, staunchly fighting the Populists. They were archprotagonists of reform, to be sure, but often emerged as reformers for the first time by putting together some of the old mugwumps with middle-class citizens, who were concerned about state or local tax and franchise issues or were upset about corruption in business and government, into personal factions of their own which would bring them nominations for significant offices. Such was roughly the case with La Follette. As Thelen has shown, he jumped in front of a parade that was already about to march. In the South, ambitious politicians often put together a winning faction from economically pressed farmers or businessmen who wanted stiffer regulation of railroads or any corporations from outside their state, and prohibitionists. A change began to take place in public expectations about the presidency and state governorships, and the men who held them: the voters wanted action and voted for those who seemed to produce it.

The executive branches of state and federal governments were strengthened by this movement in favor of loyalty to personalities rather than to party organizations. The reasons lay partly in the mass-circulation press, the new mass medium of the time, which tended (though not as much as television several decades later) to focus on news-making leaders. Beyond that, however, the strengthening of personal politics and the simultaneous weakening of parties derived from increasing voter preoccupation with issues which the press, the leaders themselves, and non-office-holding progressives promoted in the public mind. Also, progressive-era politicians could take more chances in raising issues: unlike the elections of the eighties in which the extremely close electoral balance between the major parties taught each of them to avoid divisive issues and noisy leaders in favor of retaining their coalitions intact, the years after 1894 and 1896 were, in national politics and in many states outside the Democratic South, years of Republican dominance.

In the congressional elections of 1894, as noted earlier, the Republican party managed to turn its traditional tendency toward activism (as compared to the Democrats) to good advantage. G.O.P. leaders soft-pedalled, as much as they could, the *moralist* activism of the late eighties and early nineties, when their party laid itself open to charges of nativism, anti-Catholicism, and prohibitionism, and thereby suffered great losses in the elections of 1890 and 1892. They advertised themselves to the voters in 1894 as the party of *economic* activism, the party that would do something about the depression while the Democratic negativist Cleveland dallied with Wall Street bond syndicators, tried to lower the tariff, and refused to send aid to drought-stricken farmers in Texas. The appeal worked. The G.O.P. gained 117 seats in the House of Representatives, the greatest gain ever by one party in one election, and began a string of victories in congressional elections that lasted with only four exceptions (1910–1916) through 1928. From 1895 through 1909, the Republicans enjoyed majorities of never fewer than thirteen House seats (usually thirty to sixty) over the combined opposition, as well as a proportionate command in the Senate.[3]

The sources of Republican voting strength were widely distributed. Outside the South, Republican victories came in urban counties as dependably, sometimes more dependably, as in rural ones. Except for 1912, when the Republicans split between Taft and Theodore Roosevelt, and except for two states in 1916, Republican presidential candidates captured every state in the Northeast and East North Central urban-industrial parallelogram in every presidential election from 1896 through 1920. And in those states, it was not a matter of Democratic big cities being outnumbered by the still preponderant rural and small-town counties. Indeed McKinley, Roosevelt, Taft, and Charles Evans Hughes in 1916 generally succeeded in the larger cities, including Chicago, Philadelphia, Detroit, Los Angeles, even Boston and New York, as well as in the proliferating smaller cities. The voters were looking for leaders and party programs who would provide some active response to the urban-industrial changes which the voters increasingly perceived and increasingly believed should be rectified. McKinley and certainly Theodore Roosevelt had wide appeal as presidential candidates, while in states and counties all over the Northeast and Midwest in the first decade of the century the more progressive leaders and factions took over local Republican organizations. As long as the Democrats continued to renominate Bryan, as they did in 1900 and 1908, and the lackluster Judge Alton B. Parker in 1904, they were saddled with the image of agrarianism and negativism, and were thus at a severe disadvantage both demographically and ideologically. In national elections through the period, the Democrats won only when two things happened, usually simultaneously: when the Republicans split into "Old Guard" and insurgent factions, and the Democratic candidates appeared themselves to be "progressive."

This seldom happened. The popular vote cast for Democrats running for Congress exceeded the Republican vote only in 1910 and 1914, and then only by about one hundred thousand, below one percent of the total. Even in the Bull Moose year of 1912, the combined Republican and Progressive congressional vote was 55 percent of the total and Woodrow Wilson went to the White House on 42 percent of the presidential vote. In 1916, despite the advantage of incumbency, Wilson was reelected on less than a majority (49.25 percent) of the popular vote, and a margin of only 23 electoral votes despite his secure base in the Solid South. Democratic congressional candidates in 1916 kept a thin control of the House on 46.3 percent of the popular vote. The Democrats remained the minority they had become in the depression of the nineties, and they were still unable to broaden their minority base in the South by detaching urban-located, blue- and white-collar people from the G.O.P. Only later would the Democratic party gain wide support among poorer people both rural and urban, native or foreign stock. In the Northeast and Midwest, where the demographic current was running toward the cities, the progressive Republicans appeared to the voters more willing, and in fact were, to employ the instruments of government to restructure the electorate and certain governmental institutions and to continue the prosperity that returned with McKinley in the late nineties.

In the South, the Democrats' only stronghold, the most successful state and local politicians avoided repetitions of the agrarian unrest of the nineties through a combination of appeals to white supremacy, progressive regulation of corporations, reform of state institutions, and prohibition. For Southern Democratic progressives, prohibition became a rallying point, and in Texas, those Democrats who supported Woodrow Wilson in national politics were often those most supportive of prohibition in the state. In the Wilson period "the dry adherents developed attitudes and principles that would form the basis for the views of the old-stock, prohibitionist, and rural wing of the Democrats [nationally] after 1920."[4] Southern Democratic progressivism most certainly existed, but insofar as it integrated white supremacy and prohibition within itself, it traveled a different route from Northern Democratic progressivism, such as it was, as developed by governors Woodrow Wilson in New Jersey and David Walsh in Massachusetts. The New Deal coalition between Solid South and Northern urban-industrial voters was still twenty years away, and before it happened the split between the Northern and Southern wings became sufficiently complete to produce the epic confrontation at the Democratic nominating convention of 1924, when the delegates took 104 ballots to produce a candidate who won less than 29 percent of the popular vote. So, with the few exceptions noted (and they tend to prove the rule), the combination of Republican party labels and progressive rhetoric and issues proved to be a generally successful one in the Northeast, Midwest, and West from the time of McKinley to World War I.

In this discussion of political progressivism two points have been stressed thus far. In the urban-industrial Northeast and Midwest, the Republican party and its Progressive offshoot were usually the partisan vehicles for governmental response to social problems and received voter support in urban as well as rural areas. In cities large and small, those voting progressive were middle class or were hoping to become middle class, whether they were blue- or white-collar. Secondly, the most prominent progressive politicians at the state and national levels rose through party factional struggles but portrayed themselves as independent of entrenched party bosses. They were in fact not free of partisanship or party machinery, but were creating a new kind of politics centering not on ethnocultural issues—except in the subtle sense that much of what they proposed would have reinstituted democracy and morality as they defined those terms—but instead, on broadly appealing issues of economic reform and governmental restructuring. In the process of doing all this, the political progressives achieved their victories among an electorate that was declining in numbers proportionately and sometimes even absolutely. They were not winning over great masses of previously silent or noncommittal voters. Rather, voters were losing their attachment to party organizations, whether Republican or Democratic, as organizations were made to seem disreputable. Much of the

Republican success in elections may be explained by the fact that the Republican party contained reformers as well as machine men, while the Democratic party presented mostly the latter. The issue-orientation of the Republican progressives, whether those who stayed within the fold or those who bolted to follow Roosevelt, undoubtedly had a broad appeal in itself. But their antibossism, and many of the structural changes which they advocated, tended to undermine party loyalties and increase the respectability of nonpartisanship.

Progressivism, by its stress on national problems and issues, also tended to reduce voter participation. One of the paradoxes of recent American political history is that voter participation was never higher than in the eighties and early nineties, when great national issues were scarce and popularly unappealing, and never lower than in the progressive era and the twenties, when great national issues abounded. The explanation for this seeming paradox is that in neither period did many voters perceive those great national issues as directly affecting or benefiting them. Progressivism was a middle-class movement in its leadership, its program, and its effects; for those who were not, or not yet, middle class the party organizations against which the progressives inveighed had done some tangible good. With the weakening of party organizations came a decline in participation by organization-oriented voters.[5]

The popular vote in the election of 1896 climaxed a period of high voter participation. Even more than in the three preceding presidential elections, the first Bryan-McKinley campaign brought out the voters. Bryan's national total was about a million larger than Cleveland's had been in either 1888 or 1892. But it was slightly smaller than the combined vote for Cleveland and the Populist, James B. Weaver, in 1892, and 600,000 smaller than McKinley's total. McKinley won by the largest plurality since 1872, and drew more than a million and a half votes beyond Benjamin Harrison's total of 1892. The new voters of 1896, the product of expanding population, of high interest, and of strenuous efforts to get out the vote, supported the Republican. Political historians often cite Bryan's margin of defeat in 1896 as evidence of the emergent Republican majority, which is worth noting, but they should add the fact that no Democratic presidential candidate, before Wilson in his 1916 reelection campaign, received as many popular votes as Bryan did in 1896. Republican presidential candidates after 1896 added to McKinley's winning total of 7.1 million, but only by about a half million despite population expansion. Democratic totals declined slightly, Republicans' increased somewhat, in 1900 through 1912.[6] As a proportion of the voting-age population, voter participation decreased, slowly in 1900 and then more rapidly in the next three presidential elections. In 1912, the year of the four-way race between Wilson, Roosevelt, Taft, and Debs, the election which is generally regarded as the high-water mark of political progressivism,[7] voter participation was lower than in any presidential election since universal manhood suffrage was theoretically instituted after the Civil War. Votes cast in 1912 for congressional candidates were fewer than in 1908, 1900, or 1896. The total presidential vote rose substantially after 1912, as a consequence of woman suffrage in many states in 1916 and then nationally in 1920; but without that infusion of female voters (who split on party lines much like males, i.e. a majority voted Republican) participation might well have declined further. It would be a gross exaggeration to say that progressivism was not a popular movement. It was. But it is also evident that it was a politics revolving around issues and personalities rather than party loyalty and organization, a movement arousing much middle-class interest but not including certain classes of people at least in the fundamental political act of casting a ballot.

Blacks were the largest group of nonparticipants. Jim Crow was in the saddle throughout the South; new election laws and, where necessary, changes in state constitutions systematically disfranchised blacks everywhere in the region after the first few years of the new century had passed. Southern progressivism was lily-white, both among the dominant Democrats and the minority Republicans. Poll taxes served also to disfranchise poorer whites, and with the exception of momentary if traumatic episodes like the Ferguson governorship in Texas (1915–1917) no political leaders or factions paid attention to the marginal and tenant farmers, black or white. Nor did they need to; their position was safe behind the newly erected electoral barriers.

Another group of nonparticipants, less often noticed than the blacks because efforts to prevent them from voting were less systematic, were recent immigrants. In 1875 about two-thirds of the states permitted nonnaturalized immigrants to vote, provided that they had declared their intention to become citizens in the future. As the foreigners grew more numerous and more "foreign," laws or constitutional amendments gradually ended alien suffrage. Several states acted in the nineties, four more during the progressive period, four more during World War I. Measures to tighten residency requirements for voting, of which the withdrawal of alien suffrage was one, became law, with the result that newer immigrants were not drawn into American political life as readily as the Irish, Germans, and Scandinavians had been a few decades earlier. Progressivism had a considerable amount of support from foreign-stock politicians, Republican and Democratic,[8] but the foreign stocks in question were very rarely those of the new immigration. The new immigrants at that time included a disproportionate share of the poorest and least skilled and were overwhelmingly urban. But progressivism was not primarily concerned with them, except as problems. Those progressives who were interested in the electoral process aimed at reducing "corruption" and the power of the "bosses," which usually meant reducing the foreign-born vote. The "bosses" themselves, often of older foreign stocks who had only recently achieved power, were not anxious to organize the newer immigrants even if the reformers and the election laws had permitted it. In any event the political assimilation of the newer immigrant groups, en masse, had to wait for a later day. It was not part of progressivism. By 1918 alien suffrage was a rarity.

The progressives were nonetheless dedicated, sincerely as well as vocally, to the reinvigoration and extension of popular democracy. It was just a question of reinvigoration for whom, and extension to whom. Blacks, tenant farmers, and newer immigrants did not qualify, but the native-stock and older foreign-stock middle class, or those on their way to becoming middle class, did. States in both South and North revised their constitutions to restrict the franchise to the presumably competent, to circumscribe carefully home rule for cities (on the mythical assumption that cities spawned political bosses and rural areas did not), and to establish boundaries of legislative and congressional districts so that large cities were underrepresented. Once the middle-class progressives defined the franchise to exclude marginal and minority groups, they could proceed to revise the machinery of government so as to reduce further the power of party organizations. The direct primary, whereby candidates for office were nominated by public ballot of those identifying themselves as members of a party rather than by "bosses" in caucus or convention, became the law in Southern states at about the turn of the century, along with black and poor-white disfranchisement. Wisconsin adopted the direct primary in 1903 and other non-Southern states did so thereafter. The initiative and referendum, whereby a mass petition from voters could initiate legislative action, or require a legislative enactment to be resubmitted to the voters, were written into about twenty state constitutions, especially in the West and Midwest, within a dozen years after South Dakota did so in 1899. The election of United States senators by direct popular vote, replacing the 1787 Constitutional provision that state legislatures elect senators, was resisted by the Senate and by conservative political organizations, but preferential primaries forced the idea ahead, and in early 1913 the Seventeenth Amendment, providing for direct popular election of senators, was ratified. Also during the period, the movement to extend the suffrage to women developed strength, along with other progressive measures to assure property rights to women and to ease restrictions on women suing for divorce. In 1900 a majority of the states allowed women some voting rights, but only after 1910 did full suffrage become a fact. By 1914, Kansas and nearly all of the Mountain and Pacific states had enacted it; New York did so in 1917; and the rest followed during World War I or in compliance with the Nineteenth Amendment, which was ratified in 1920.

Progressivism's overall thrust, with regard to governmental structure and the suffrage, was to solidify the democratic sources of power in middle-class hands. Various restrictions on the suffrage for some groups, while others simultaneously or subsequently received extensions of it, were not paradoxical developments at all. Underlying both was the purpose of making sure that uncontrollable political machines, uncontrollable mass movements like Populism, and racial or ethnic groups whose electoral presence was actually or potentially dangerous, would be excluded, and that the right people would be included. In several important ways the progressives achieved this purpose very well. They weakened party organizations, and they focused voters' attention on "broad national issues" which they, and not machines, could deal with best. But the cost was high in terms of democratic theory. Progressivism's structural reforms diminished the power and the political interest of many people, certainly institutionalized Jim Crow, probably retarded immigrant assimilation, and created, through nonpartisan independency, political alienation. To a large extent the efforts of the progressives, only partly by design, simply enhanced the political strength of the native-stock white middle class, and did little else.

In the area of business regulation the progressives orated, gyrated, and occasionally acted. The issues involved were many, and because of the continuing strength of the rhetoric of economic democracy, equal opportunity, and antimonopoly, ideological positions whose origins went far back into the American past and which required (or at least received) only a modicum of updating, the progressives made the regulation of private enterprise one of their major concerns. Regulation was also a matter on which coalitions were rather easily built. Many different groups had a concrete as well as an abstract stake in it. The main thrust, as in political-structure and suffrage changes, came from progressivism's middle-class leadership, in this case including many businessmen themselves. But labor unions frequently had a direct concern, farmers and shippers stood to benefit from regulation of common carriers, taxpayers large or small were becoming quite aware by 1900 that the costs of government might well be borne by new sources of wealth, and anyone regardless of residence or occupation who considered himself a "consumer" had an interest in helping see to it that what he consumed was safe and cheap. The groundwork for business regulation had already been laid by the turn of the century. "Trust" was a household word in the nineties; even the Republican platform of 1896 criticized "domestic monopoly"; and corporation taxes were being written into law in New York and some other states. The merger movement of 1897–1902 frightened many middle-class and working-class observers, and they gobbled up the report in John Moody's 1904 book, *The Truth about the Trusts*, that the business and capital of the country was rapidly coming under the control of two vast "supertrusts" headed by J. P. Morgan and John D. Rockefeller. The "public interest" was threatened—"public" again being defined as the actual and incipient middle class, who were deeply and generally suspicious of large organizations, locally or nationally, and who sought the restoration of small-unit competition. The "public interest" to many of them also meant a recognition of labor problems and the need for legislative correctives, though enthusiasm was limited toward the idea that labor unions should play a decision-making role in industry.

The scope of progressivism's concern with business regulation was broad because "big business" touched so many people and groups. The matter also combined ideology and self-interest, always a volatile mixture. Regulation involved many businessmen, themselves progressives of various shades. Their positions varied according to which business they were in, what their competitive standing was, and whether they operated in the South, the Southwest, or the North, or in large or small cities. No single "business community" existed but rather a congeries of individuals and groups, expressing themselves through organizations such as boards of trade and chambers of commerce and manufacturer's associations which had nineteenth-century origins, as well as more recently founded trade associations and national groups such as the National Civic Federation, the U. S. Chamber of Commerce, and the National Association of Manufacturers. The N.A.M. was antiunion, but still qualified as "progressive"; so, on the opposite pole, did most unions. The specifics were different, but the rhetorics of public (or at least national) interest and private enterprise were similar. To many businessmen and nonbusiness progressives, big business had to be regulated stringently, the trusts probably destroyed. To others, following Herbert Croly's lead, the large organizations were by no means bad in and of themselves and simply required federal watchdogs to insure that they continued to serve the national interest. To yet others it was only important, philosophy aside, that businesses as well as governments operate "cleanly and efficiently."

Given so many kinds of progressives, their concerns not surprisingly varied. Among them were railroad regulation, public utilities regulation, tax policy, antitrust and tariff policy, banking reform, and the stimulation of enterprise. The regulation of railroads by state governments had roots well back into the nineteenth century, most prominently after the Civil War in the Granger laws *circa* 1870, and in state boards of railway commissioners thereafter and through the nineties. Variously affected business groups had backed federal intervention through the creation of the Interstate Commerce Commission in 1887. Effective (or annoying) only in rare cases during the nineties as regulators of railroad rates and practices, federal and state commissions received broad new powers from state legislatures and the U. S. Congress, especially between 1903 and 1910. The I.C.C. and state government agencies proscribed or increasingly scrutinized rebating, pooling, and above all rate-making, to the extent that the railroads surrendered a substantial part of their control over rates, as a result of the Hepburn Act of 1906 and Mann-Elkins Act of 1910. Later they lost a measure of control over their labor costs. Large manufacturers and other major shippers who had made their own rate deals with the roads, and the railroad managements themselves, opposed or tried to soften such legislation. But antimonopoly sentiment was too strong, and the roads had too many traditional enemies among small shippers such as farmers, merchants, and small businessmen. Insurgent Midwestern Republicans like senators La Follette or Albert Cummins of Iowa fixed on railroad regulation as a popular issue, helped make it so, and welded together previously disgruntled but voiceless groups into a progressive coalition fighting on behalf of the "public interest," i.e. stringent regulation. Perhaps the roads were actually not rapacious —there is some evidence that, whatever the reasons, the railroads' services and capital investment declined after 1907. In any event, the progressives' efforts to control consumer prices by means of regulatory commissions did work.[9] The last major federal law of the progressive period, the Adamson Act of September 1916, supported the demands of the railway brotherhoods for an eight-hour day without pay reduction; progressivism in its twilight further limited the self-determination of the railroad corporations.

It did not nationalize them, however, as some progressives wished. The government federalized the roads as a wartime necessity, but then returned them to private control in 1920, with a "fair return" guaranteed to them.

Regulation or municipal ownership of public utilities, and the limiting of the terms of street railway and other franchises, appealed both to property owners who otherwise would have had to pay higher taxes, and to the general public (including workers) who used the street railways, gas, and water. In Milwaukee, Detroit, and a few other cities in the nineties, and in many more after 1900, demand rose for public services such as roads, trolley lines, schools, sanitary water and sewer systems, and the efficient management of all aspects of urban government. Progressive leaders at the state and local level had an issue, or really a set of issues, which evoked a broad popular response and which they argued in several rhetorically appealing ways—antimonopoly, antibossism, anticorruption, economy, public service. The resulting reforms in municipal government, including the commission and manager forms of government as well as better and cheaper services, operated to secure and promote the interests of middle-class property owners. Higher-income voting districts voted most strongly for these changes. Samuel P. Hays has provided evidence that "municipal reform in the early twentieth century involves a paradox: the ideology of an extension of political control [to the general public] and the practice of its concentration" in the hands of business and professional elites in a community.[10] Changes in the tax laws of the states and the federal government also resulted from the employment of popularly resonant rhetoric by progressive political leaders. Taxes on corporations, and income and inheritance taxes on the wealthy, were not difficult to sell; it was easy to demand that the bloated corporations should be deflated and the rich should be soaked. The force for change was again, in political terms, a coalition of various groups of people, or at least urban people, under middle-class leadership. The results benefited efficiency- and economy-minded middle-class business and professional people most of all, creating a tax system which, as Yearley said, "enshrined in the basic institutions of the land, for better and for worse, middle-class definitions of democracy, efficiency, and stability." [11] In the years just before World War I, the federal government got the bulk of its revenue from customs duties and excise taxes on alcohol, both passed on to the consumer; state governments got most of their revenues from property taxes, also passed on through rents to the majority who did not own real property. Both systems, therefore, were regressive. Also, the first federal income tax law enacted under the Sixteenth Amendment, in 1913, provided an effective tax rate of only one percent at the $25,000 per year level, and made a negligible difference in class structure and income distribution.

Trust-busting, it is true, did take place during the progressive period. The Sherman antitrust law of 1890, severely limited by the courts during the 1890s and quite ineffective in preventing or influencing the merger movement of 1897–1902, was resuscitated by the Justice Department during the presidencies of Roosevelt and (even more so) Taft. Prosecutions led to the dissolution in 1911 of Standard Oil and American Tobacco in their existing forms. But though the forms changed, the substance did not. In its decisions, the Supreme Court stated that a "rule of reason" must apply in antitrust prosecutions: that is, the restraint of trade in question must not be unreasonable—a quality which remained mysterious and undefined. The implication was that some monopoly practices were reasonable and lawful. A new antitrust law seemed called for, and early in his administration Woodrow Wilson, true to his campaign pledges, asked Congress to pass the Clayton antitrust act. After months of parliamentary maneuvering, the Clayton act, much emasculated, passed together with an act creating a Federal Trade Commission to prevent "unfair methods of competition." Further prosecutions followed, until antitrust policy was suspended during World War I, but neither prosecution nor commission regulation had much effect in changing the structure of large corporate enterprise. The Wilsonians took a generally dimmer view of big business than Roosevelt or Herbert Croly had done, as was natural in view of their more Southern and agrarian electoral base, but the results were far from radical. The first measure of the Wilson administration upon taking office in 1913 was to lower the

tariff, which had long been criticized as "the mother of trusts."
However, this law, the Underwood-Simmons Act, made little
difference to the structure of industry.

In banking and finance, the progressive era produced one
far-reaching innovation: the Federal Reserve System, enacted by
Congress in 1913. Until then the United States had been an
exception among industrially advanced countries in that it lacked a
central bank. The money, banking, and credit system—"system"
was an overly flattering word—had operated with some success in
the late nineteenth century, but less in the early twentieth, out of
large banks with regional or national influence and, often less
importantly, the U. S. Treasury. Populists and their Bryanite
successors had for years denounced the "money power" of the
great private banks, and when the Democrats gained control of
Congress in 1911, a special committee headed by Congressman
Arsène Pujo of Louisiana began a two-year investigation of the
"money trust" which supposedly (and probably) nourished many
other massive businesses with money and credit. The Pujo committee uncovered many self-serving deals among bankers, grilled J.
Pierpont Morgan on the witness stand, found that a carefully
defined "money trust" did exist, and generated a potent wave of
public and congressional pressure for thoroughgoing banking
legislation. By then, most of the bankers did not object to that. The
Panic of 1907 had frightened them and led them in the next two to
five years to develop a reform plan of their own, which would have
turned over control of the whole system to the largest private
banks. Pujo and the Bryanites had in mind public control. After an
intense factional struggle, Congress passed the Federal Reserve Act
which established twelve regional banks owned by their private
member banks, empowered to issue currency, but governed by a
board of public appointees. The act was a compromise less
favorable to farmers, small businessmen, and smaller banks than
they then believed. The position of the largest investment and
commercial banks was not greatly reduced, and the Federal
Reserve began functioning as an effective regulator only after its
powers were broadened twenty years later during the early New
Deal.

Federal and state governments continued during the progressive period to stimulate private enterprise, as they had done before, but in a greater variety of ways. Federal and state aid to transportation, generously given for canals and railways in the nineteenth century, helped build good roads in Midwestern states around the turn of the century and after. Federal and state matching money introduced the federal highway system (the U. S. routes) in 1916. The Wilson administration put federal money and backing into agriculture, vocational education, rural free delivery and other postal improvements, and not insignificantly, into expanding and upgrading the army and navy. The military buildup began in earnest in Theodore Roosevelt's first term, and continued under Taft and Wilson, intensifying after World War I began in Europe in 1914. In many ways, the progressive era brought changes and new functions for state, local, and federal government. People were now willing to use government in new ways; they were accepting activism. For the most part, the activist changes resulted from pressures generated by progressive politicians to promote the "public interest," which usually meant middle-class interest. And although the progressives' efforts were not markedly beneficial for racial and ethnic minorities, or the propertyless, or the rural and urban masses with low incomes, they did satisfy many members of the public who wanted assurance that reform of the worst excesses of the industrial system was taking place. The progressives did not succeed, however, in reversing the trend toward oligopoly. The period brought no basic change in the trend toward large organizations in business enterprise; indeed the communications media and the transportation network encouraged further the development of advertising and marketing on a nationwide scale.

Progressive efforts toward calmer labor relations produced even less structural change than in the regulation of business. Those progressives most interested in reform of local government or railroad rates were not immediately concerned with labor problems except insofar as strikes and attendant violence threatened to harm property or halt production. The social-worker progressives and some of the more practical of the intellectuals were aware of labor problems and saw more clearly than most people how inadequate income, poverty, industrial accidents, and maldistribution of wealth shortened or ruined many lives. They also feared that intolerable conditions might propel workers toward socialism or anarchism. To those progressives, labor reform legislation was not only humanitarian but in society's enlightened self-interest. Foreign-stock politicians and churchmen and others among the smaller, fringe groups within the progressive movement were often directly involved with industrial problems. To them, legislation which would improve working conditions, wages, and hours was the major concern. As several recent writers have shown, labor legislation in the progressive era resulted from many individual instances of interclass and interethnic cooperation.[12] Politicians in both major parties supported it. Some amelioration of labor problems did take place, on the state level from the nineties onward, and in federal law from 1914 to 1916 especially. Humanitarians and labor leaders helped curb (though not end) child labor in many states, and the Keating-Owen Act of 1916 prohibited the interstate shipment of goods made by child labor. Workmen's compensation for industrial accidents also appeared on state statute books and, in the Kern-McGillicuddy Act of 1916, as federal law. New laws required employers to put safety devices on dangerous machines, required railroads to use safety couplers and warning signals, and limited the workday for women on grounds of health and safety. These and other laws to get rid of the worst, most obvious abuses came into being in the Northeast, Midwest, and West. As legal doctrine gradually shifted away from nineteenth-century (or more ancient) concepts such as "freedom of contract" and the fellow-servant rule (which in effect placed the blame for an industrial accident on the worker), the courts began to uphold many of the new statutes.

The courts, and employers and many progressives, were much less willing to entertain the idea of labor organization and collective bargaining. It was one thing to legislate away sickening abuses, especially if their continuation fed the viruses of radicalism, but it was quite another to permit unions a legal position which reduced employer control over labor costs and other aspects of production and marketing. The final version of the Clayton antitrust act contained a provision exempting unions from the "restraint of trade" prohibition, but the Supreme Court disallowed the provision a few years later. For skilled workers, organized in craft unions affiliated with the A.F. of L., some gains in wages, hours, and working conditions did result from the pragmatic "market unionism" policy of Samuel Gompers and other union leaders. On isolated occasions the more radical unions, even the Industrial Workers of the World, conducted strikes whose results were partially successful for the workers. But the class-war rhetoric of the I.W.W., clashing with the deep-seated fears of socialism among the middle class, provoked increasingly successful attempts at forcible government suppression of the I.W.W., and the government's popular antisubversive campaigns during World War I destroyed it. Prosperity after the recession of 1913–1914, bringing with it full employment, certainly contributed more than middle-class progressives did to keep the lid on labor trouble. The urban industrial worker was not a prime beneficiary of the progressive movement.

The middle-class, stabilizing thrust of progressivism was nowhere more evident than in legislation touching on social institutions. The spread of compulsory public education has already been discussed in Chapter six; it derived from the belief that mass education was essential in a democracy, from the demand for people with white-collar skills, and from the felt necessity to Americanize immigrants and inculcate in both native and foreign stocks the principles of moral citizenship. The schools were, and many progressives meant them to be, a prime agent of social control. Education worked indirectly and over a long time span, however, if it worked at all. In the meantime more direct measures to purify and to control society were suggested and applied. The muckrakers brought it to popular attention that meats, processed cereals, patent medicines, and many other consumer items were harmful. Rotten meat had caused widespread sickness and death in the army during the Spanish-American War. Some packaged cereals contained bits of glass. Patent medicines, even soft drinks, were often laced with alcohol, opium, morphine, or other narcotics. The evils seemed obvious and preventable, and Congress passed sumptuary legislation to control them—notably, the Pure Food and Drug Act of 1906 and subsequent amendments to it and the 1914 Harrison Act regulating narcotics. By that time the movement to prohibit the sale of alcoholic beverages, one of the key ethnocultural issues which devastated the Republicans in 1890, had gained tremendous momentum. Congress in 1913 passed the Webb-Kenyon Act, allowing states to regulate interstate commerce by keeping out liquor shipments, and by 1915 eleven states were completely dry and every one of the others had local option laws. Thirty of them were completely dry by the end of World War I. The Eighteenth Amendment, effectuated in 1920, institutionalized something already in effect in much of the country. The prohibition movement had far less support in the largest cities than in more rural areas both in and out of the South, but prohibition was not simply an outcropping of rural reaction. To some people it was a religious imperative, to others a device to purify local governments in which liquor interests corrupted police and politicians, to others just another proscription of an unhealthy drug, to others an aspect of antimonopoly. As its best historian has said, "To the old-stock, middle-class progressive, prohibition was a way of uplifting and Americanizing the lower classes; to the urban [foreign-stock] masses, it was an intolerable interference with their personal liberty." [13] So it had been, in fact, since the 1880s. But only in the progressive period, and specifically in the latter part of it which coincided with the Democratic Wilson administration—for middle-class progressivism was by no means an exclusive Republican preserve—did those prime native-stock ethnocultural issues of the late nineteenth century, prohibition and woman suffrage, finally win.

Censorship and obscenity laws proliferated at the same time. Local societies for the suppression of vice, the most famous of which was Anthony Comstock's in New York, managed to have offensive (to them) books and periodicals removed from libraries. The anti-vice societies were even delegated what amounted to police powers over the U. S. mails. Again a culture conflict: intellectuals who liked modern art and literature were outraged at being told what to see or read; foreign-stock groups at being told what to think or do. Certain progressives, however, whose fear of foreign and base influences increased during the Wilson years and culminated during World War I, who had been told that most prostitutes were foreign-born, who were upset about vice districts, saloonkeepers, police graft and politicians anyway, were willing to embrace censorship as they did prohibition: it had to be done to keep America moral. In that culture conflict of the late progressive period, the native-stock middle-class ideology prevailed. The cumulative force of all the agencies seeking social stability and control, its vigor growing from the time when Theodore Roosevelt began to use the White House as his "bully pulpit" to preach social righteousness, went over the top in World War I to produce prohibition, the suppression of socialists and radical laborites, "pure" education, and the promise of a pure, ideologically unified society.

Another watchword, not unrelated to social purity, captured the minds of many progressives in responsible positions in business and government: the ideal of efficiency. The most ballyhooed formulation of the ideal was the system of "scientific management" developed by the engineer Frederick Winslow Taylor, the inventor of time and motion studies. Americans, long enamored of science and respectful of management, would have given Taylor a hearing just because of his system's label, but bureaucrats in business and government were even more impressed when they discovered that Taylorism really did increase worker productivity by analytically simplifying the steps needed to accomplish tasks. Taylorism saved money and increased output. It also typified the growing conviction among progressives that, as Jean Quandt put it in a slightly different context, "society was not a loose collection of self-sufficient individuals but an organic whole made up of interrelated parts." [14] This was no news to the directors and managers of major corporations whether in manufacturing, insurance, railroading, or marketing; the development of a series of techniques for operating very large firms, so that they continued to produce profitably instead of becoming dinosaurs dragged down by their own colossal weight, had been going on at least since the creation of the Standard Oil Trust in the early eighties. Ever since then, large firms had been creating auditing, accounting, comptrolling, diffused decision-making, budgeting, long-range planning, divisional structures, and other modern procedures—what might be called the "software" of large-scale enterprise. These devices were obviously useful and successful in business. Progressive reformers, whether businessmen or academics or politicians, simply assumed that devices that worked for business would work in public administration. To them and many Americans since, large organizations were large organizations; seldom did they question whether business, government, school systems, or other organizations had different basic purposes and therefore whether the model of scientific business management might be inappropriate to other institutions.

Instead, the search for efficiency on business principles became a major "industry" within progressivism and would continue to be so during the twenties. The nonpartisan fact-finding board and its more potent counterpart, the regulatory commission, were particular pets of progressives in government. Staffed by trained experts and clerks who were supposed to see to it that the public interest was served efficiently and honestly, and probably more economically than partisan politicians and their organizations would do, boards and commissions were introduced (especially after 1910) in state and local governments as well as the federal. It was expected that governments could and should be more businesslike, in the literal sense: operated in the manner of, using the procedures of, large businesses. The application of business methods to the federal government accelerated during World War I when the need to mobilize quickly the manpower, agriculture, transportation, and manufacturing capacities of the country could be met only by powerful nonpartisan, expert boards using modern management techniques. In general, the devices worked, from the standpoint of efficiency. After the war the boards were demobilized but the ideas behind them stayed, and in 1921 Congress passed the first Budget and Accounting Act creating a federal budget, a General Accounting Office, and a Comptroller General to head it.[15] Schools of business and public administration proliferated; the "efficiency expert" and the governmental "consultant" became widely known if somewhat suspicious figures; progressivism lasted into the twenties not as a crusade to reform society and government and to solve the problems of industrialism and urbanism, but as a drive to extend efficiency and businesslike methods into schools, the executive branches of governments, and public administration generally. But that is another story. We need to note here only that by the eve of World War I, progressivism—a certain kind of progressivism—had successfully eased the social crisis of 1893–

1901. The answer was not the Populists' answer, not the utopian visions of Henry George or Edward Bellamy, not that of the Debsian socialists, not the stringent trustbusting of La Follette and other insurgents, certainly not a continuation of the laissez faire negativism of the late nineteenth century. The answer had lain in piecemeal legislative attacks on the worst, most scabrous social ills, a recognition of the legal and political rights of women and the suppression of those rights for others, the regulation but by no means the restructuring of large business organizations, the continuous weakening of political party organizations and party loyalties, and the gradual introduction of businesslike, efficient methods into nonbusiness institutions. All of which amounted to the minimal reforms which were necessary to avert radical change and to secure the ideological, political, and social dominance of the expanding middle class.

8

Looking Backward,
1916–1876

Forty years separated the America of the Centennial celebration from the America about to send its boys to France to fight the Kaiser. During that forty years, Americans had, as has often been said, grown up in the country and moved to the city; which also meant that they dropped their plows and went to work in factories and offices. In many respects the changes had been vast, for those four decades brought the United States through the most upsetting phase of the urban-industrial revolution that had transformed western and central Europe a little earlier and is just now happening in many parts of the world today. The changes in America by 1916 were also incomplete in some important respects, and it is worth summarizing and making explicit the outstanding differences between the two Americas of 1876 and 1916 to see with some precision just how far the changes had or had not gone.

In the first place the two societies were visually very different. The mansard roofs of the old State-War-Navy building were still there, but taste since decreed the neo-Gothic immensity of Ralph Adams Cram's Cathedral of St. John the Divine in New York, the decreasingly decorated limestone slabs of office and government buildings, and the reinforced concrete factory. Frank Lloyd Wright was already past his prairie-house phase, and the glass and steel boxes of Walter Gropius' Bauhaus style were to come to the United States in just a few years. The Model T Fords were commonplace, and three hundred thousand miles of highway, almost none of which existed at the end of the nineties, were there to run them on.

Americans were just about to cross the line between a rural and urban majority. Two-thirds had lived in country villages or small towns at the time of the Centennial; half still did so by World War I. The United States was still a fairly rural country by World War I in sheer numerical terms, but cities of over 100,000—over sixty compared to about fifteen in the mid-seventies—flourished in all regions, even the South. The urban experience was rare at the Centennial, quite common forty years later.

The work force was very differently distributed. In 1916 farmers peaked in absolute numbers, and had receded from half of the gainfully employed at the Centennial to one-fourth. They were about to be outnumbered by white-collar workers, the most rapidly expanding category after 1900 and especially 1910. Outnumbering both, at about 40 percent of all workers, were factory operatives, miners, railroadmen, and other blue-collar workers.

The numbers of foreign-born had increased, though the proportion of them to total population had risen only marginally. Nonetheless, about a third of the population was of foreign stock, and the ethnics were much more varied than the Irish, Germans, and British who made up the great majority of foreign-stock Americans in the seventies. The drive to stabilize ethnic variation by immigration restriction was gaining greater force in 1916–1917 than it ever had, and was about to become law.

The black minority had changed little in social, economic, and geographical position in the forty years since the end of Reconstruction. Almost 90 percent still lived in the South, most of them on farms, more and more of them tenants and sharecroppers. More than half, however, were at least literate; even segregated schools were an improvement over the systematically imposed ignorance of the slave regime. In social terms, however, the black minority was more segregated and suppressed in 1916 than in 1876. The great migration out of the South to Northern and Midwestern cities had just begun; thirty to fifty thousand Southern Negroes per year were trying to find a better life, and in comparison to what they left, they succeeded.

The legal position of women had changed considerably, especially after 1900. Suffrage was a fact in most states and in three more years would be constitutionalized. Women's rights to hold and dispose of property had been extended, and divorce laws eased. Millions of women had entered the work force, taking advantage particularly of the newly opened, white-collar job opportunities. Family structure, however, had not changed radically with the exceptions that more common residence in cities cut down the average numbers of children per family, and reduced infant mortality made the funerals of children a less common thing than in the nineties and before.

Economic life had changed in striking ways. In the nonfarm sectors, large organizations were dominant. Although combination slowed after the merger movement of 1897–1901, and numbers of medium-size firms increased, the contrast with 1876 was great. Mass employment, beginning then, was common by World War I; mass unions, however, especially in metals and durable-goods industries, were twenty years in the future. Gross national product was five to six times greater; even before World War I began in Europe, the United States was producing more than France, Germany, and Britain combined. In the seventies American output had been smaller than each. At the time of the Centennial, railroad and other development, farm and nonfarm, had depended heavily on the importation of capital from Britain and Europe; by 1916, thanks in part to those countries' needs for capital to fight the war, the United States was the world's leading exporter of capital. Although governments and businesses still had a great deal to learn about management techniques and how firms might be organized efficiently, bureaucratic structures and modern business procedures had been developed extensively in large firms and were gradually being applied elsewhere. In 1876 these techniques, as well as office machines, telephones, and the other accoutrements of modern business, were as yet unapplied or were even nonexistent.

In social thought, evolutionary pragmatism and a sense of society or community, primitive as it still was, had replaced the individualism, producer identification, and natural-law mind-set of the seventies. To a partial yet socially successful extent, social thought and attitudes had undergone a kind of paradigm shift, to use Thomas Kuhn's term,[1] and in a vast number of small ways, in education, business, labor relations, city administration, state and federal governments, and other institutions, people were proceeding with the "normal science" of applying the new paradigm. To suggest the paradigm shift with illustrative figures: note the difference between Rutherford B. Hayes and Woodrow Wilson; between the social philosophies of William Graham Sumner and those of Croly or Lippmann; between William McGuffey and John

Dewey. Laissez faire negativism had by no means disappeared, however, and neither, despite evolutionary theory, had racist ideas about blacks, Asians, and newer immigrants.

Another change, though not much reflected in social theory or popular ideology, had taken place in America's world position. The army and navy, used in the seventies mainly to fight Indians and to patrol coasts, had expanded to world rank, especially after the Spanish-American War. Martial attitudes and the popularity of military training units increased as World War I began in Europe; the accelerating rate of progressive social control domestically seemed to be paralleled by an accelerating acceptance of militarism. Also, the United States had acquired substantial possessions as booty from the Spanish-American War. The country also decided, through executive and judicial action, that most of them would be treated as dependent colonies, their residents not to be admitted to full citizenship, rather than as territories which would ultimately become states. Hawaii, acquired in 1898 but independently of the war, did receive territorial status; white Americans controlled the government. In Puerto Rico and the Philippines the "natives" did. A sizable antiimperialist minority in Congress and around the country opposed the acquisitions and claimed that the Constitution had to follow the flag—that is, that the inhabitants of those areas had to be granted the same rights that American citizens possessed since a republic by its nature could not have colonials. Their arguments failed. In foreign policy, notably as applied to small countries in the Caribbean and Central America, order and efficiency proved to be much more potent ideals than democracy: Theodore Roosevelt instituted, and Taft and Wilson continued, the policy of making disorderly republics including Cuba, Haiti, Panama, Santo Domingo, and Nicaragua into "protectorates" of the United States. The inconsistency between protectorates and colonies on the one hand, and sending troops in 1917 to make the world safe for democracy on the other hand, was not widely appreciated. But there had never been any law against illogicality.

Another difference between the Centennial years and the eve of World War I was the development of the early mass media: the inexpensive, widely circulated newspaper and magazine press. In the seventies the closest thing to a mass medium was the small group of weekly and monthly periodicals such as the *Nation* or the *North American Review*, or church publications, reaffirming in fact and fiction the genteel notions of their middle- and upper-class readerships. The rural majority received its intellectual nourishment chiefly from books and from locally oriented weekly newspapers. In the eighties and nineties, journalistic entrepreneurs like Joseph Pulitzer and William Randolph Hearst began to exploit new technology to produce cheap, mass-circulation newspapers. S. S. McClure, Frank Munsey, and others did the same with magazines, and when the Wilson years arrived, the public was accustomed to wire-service news, display advertising, daily stock market reports, and comic strips. The newspapers of 1916 look, in most respects, like newspapers which a reader in 1976 would expect. The papers of 1876 look archaic.

In 1916 the country's elementary and secondary schools enrolled over twenty-two million children, nearly two million of them in nonpublic (mostly parochial) schools, compared to nine million in 1876. Well over half a billion dollars, eight times the expenditure of 1876, kept the schools running. High schools, a rarity in the seventies, had become common enough that attendance and graduation was a realistic hope, if not yet the usual fact, at least for white children in nonfarm areas. College was still an experience reserved for a well-to-do elite, or for struggling preprofessionals, despite the expansion of state universities. But colleges and universities granted nearly fifty thousand degrees in 1916, compared to about twelve thousand annually through the 1870s, and women earned about 30 percent of them. Graduate education and the training of experts and professionals scarcely existed in the seventies; in the fifteen years or so before World War I, graduate and professional schools established atop or beside increasingly elective-ridden liberal arts colleges became the common format and would remain so through the twentieth century.

Social mobility, other than that which was strictly geographical, rose after the depression of the nineties for most groups. The middle class was expanding, thanks to the creation of millions of white-collar jobs. People from farm backgrounds, people whose parents and grandparents had been artisans or mechanics, members of various immigrant groups, even some thousands of Negroes after the northward migration began, fought their way upward in the social scale. The climb was difficult, and property was not easily acquired; prevailing wage rates made saving a lifelong grind. Farmers and workers did not have to be reminded of the "work ethic" and other "middle-class" values; those values were essential to upward mobility, even to survival. Competitiveness, acquisitiveness, getting ahead, were common aspirations in the seventies, and for the next forty years and beyond. After the depression of the nineties, however, the opportunities to succeed were more numerous than before. Upward mobility was not easy; but it was just a little easier. Poverty and propertylessness, nonetheless, were still very widespread even with the coming of wartime prosperity after 1915.

In all these and other ways, America looked different on the eve of World War I from what it had looked like at the time of the Centennial of 1876. It *was* different. The society had made its transition through the most painful stages of urbanization and industrialization—and with remarkably minimal damage to social structure and idea patterns. Some key ideas and beliefs appropriate to an agrarian society had had to be jettisoned. They had become more aware that they were going to have to exercise much more conscious control over their society as well as the perhaps inferior or untrustworthy new groups that it contained by then. And they did exercise controls, through social legislation, through restructuring of governmental institutions, through immigration restriction, prohibition, and watchfulness toward "subversives." The changes were incomplete; many people, urban and rural alike, were trying hard to make old ideas work in a social and economic context that had shifted mightily in forty years and would continue to shift. But the minimum and essential changes did happen, at a cost of putting some major dents in democratic ideals, a cost which Americans in the progressive era were willing to pay. In so doing they averted class war and social revolution that seemed to them to impend at the end of the crisis of 1893–1901, and they set American society on most of the paths which it would follow for the next fifty years.

Notes

1. AMERICAN SOCIETY AT THE CENTENNIAL

1. *Indianapolis Sentinel*, June 15, July 4, 1876.

2. *Indianapolis Sentinel*, July 5, 1876. The next quotation is from the same paper for July 4.

3. Joel Barker, "Colorado Mail Service, 1859–85," *Colorado Magazine* 49 (summer 1972): 225.

4. Venola Lewis Bivans, "The Diary of Luna E. Warner, a Kansas Teenager of the Early 1870's," *Kansas Historical Quarterly* 35 (autumn 1969): 276–311; (winter 1969): 411–42.

5. Lillian B. Miller, "Engines, Marbles, and Canvases: The Centennial Exposition of 1876," in *Lectures 1972–1973: 1876, The Centennial Year* (Indianapolis: Indiana Historical Society, 1973), pp. 15, 20–21. This whole essay bears reading as an intelligent reassessment of the art and sculpture of the seventies.

6. Francis Parkman, *The Discovery of the Great West: La Salle*, ed. William R. Taylor (New York: Rinehart & Co., 1956), pp. 65–66.

7. The proportion in 1850 was 29.8 percent mechanical, 70.2 percent animate. By 1920 the proportions were 95.1 percent mechanical (by then including automotive power), 4.9 percent animate. See U.S., Bureau of the Census, *Historical Statistics of the United States, Colonial Times to 1957* (Washington, D.C.: U.S. Government Printing Office, 1960), series S 1, 3–5.

8. Alan Gowans, *Images of American Living: Four Centuries of Architecture and Furniture as Cultural Expression* (Philadelphia: J. B. Lippincott Co., 1964), p. 332. In this discussion of architecture I am indebted for a number of facts and ideas to Gowans (esp. chapters 5–7), and to another excellent social history of architec-

ture, Wayne Andrews' *Architecture, Ambition and Americans: A Social History of American Architecture* (New York: Free Press, 1964), esp. chapter 5.

9. John B. Jackson, *American Space: The Centennial Years, 1865–1876* (New York: W. W. Norton, 1972), p. 119.

10. *Indianapolis Sentinel*, July 5, 1876.

11. Henrietta M. Larson, *Jay Cooke, Private Banker* (Cambridge: Harvard University Press, 1936), pp. 177–78.

12. Wl. Woytinsky, *Die Welt in Zahlen* (Berlin: Rudolf Mosse Buchverlag, 1925), 1: 82, 104.

13. Census Bureau, *Historical Statistics*, series B 19, 23, 84–91, 158–60, 164–68; idem, *Pocket Data Book, USA 1971* (Washington, D.C.: U.S. Government Printing Office, 1971), pp. 8–9.

14. *Indianapolis Sentinel*, July 4, 1876.

15. Custer continued to call himself a Major General, which he temporarily was during the Civil War. But his permanent rank was Lieutenant Colonel. Custer's vanity was seldom surpassed among U. S. Army officers, except perhaps by Douglas MacArthur.

16. Henry G. Waltmann, "Circumstantial Reformer: President Grant and the Indian Problem," *Arizona and the West* 13 (winter 1971), 323–42.

17. David F. Musto, *The American Disease: Origins of Narcotic Control* (New Haven, Yale University Press, 1973), p. 2. This book, the best treatment of the history of narcotics use and control in the United States, points out further that "The unregulated patent medicine craze in the United States hit its peak in the late nineteenth century—a time when the opiate content in these medicines was probably also at its highest" (p. 3).

18. Ninety-six years later the burglary and bribery took place before the actual election, in connection with the nominating process and the campaign.

19. Walter T. K. Nugent, *Money and American Society 1865–1880* (New York: Free Press, 1968), esp. chapters 19 and 20.

20. For more detailed descriptions of Jay Cooke's involvement with the Northern Pacific, see Larson, *Jay Cooke*, esp. chapters 14–19. See also Bray Hammond, "The North's Empty Purse, 1861–1862," *American Historical Review* 67 (October 1961): 1–18.

21. Bureau of the Census, *Historical Statistics*, series P 13, K 267, 271, 303; Jeffrey G. Williamson, "Late Nineteenth Century American Retardation: A Neoclassical Analysis." *Journal of Economic History* 33 (September 1973): 581–607. Williamson's analysis includes citations from the works of Easterlin (1960), Gallmann (1966), and Lebergott (1964) on aspects of late nineteenth-century economic trends.

22. Richard A. Easterlin, "Interregional Differences. . . ." Appendix A in *Trends in the American Economy in the Nineteenth Century* (Princeton: Princeton University Press [National Bureau of Economic Research], 1960).

23. Woytinsky, *Die Welt*, 1:147.

24. Figures are taken from U. S., Bureau of the Census, *Tenth Census* . . . (1880), and *Eleventh Census* . . . (1890, parts I [Population] and II [Manufacturing]).

2. VALUES AND INSTITUTIONS, 1878–1893

1. Census Bureau, *Historical Statistics*, series Y 241–250.

2. One exception being the Civil Rights Act of 1875, an exception which proves the rule since it simply recognized that civil rights were general to *all* citizens. Even that pitifully minimal assertion rendered it practically inoperative; it was thrown out by the U. S. Supreme Court in 1883.

3. See for example Harold D. Woodman, "Chicago Businessmen and the 'Granger' Laws," *Agricultural History* 36 (April 1962): 16–24; Edward A. Purcell, Jr., "Ideas and Interests: Businessmen and the Interstate Commerce Act," *Journal of American History* 54 (December 1967): 561–78.

4. Adam Smith, *An Inquiry into the Nature and Causes of the Wealth of Nations*, ed. J. R. M'Culloch (Edinburgh: Adam and Charles Black, 1863), p. 1. Smith went on to say, "According, therefore, as this produce, or what is purchased with it, bears a greater or smaller proportion to the number of those who are to consume it, the nation will be better or worse supplied with all the necessaries and conveniences for which it has occasion. But this proportion must, in every nation, be regulated by two different circumstances; first, by the skill, dexterity, and judgment with which its labour is generally applied; and, secondly, by the proportion between the number of those who are employed in useful labour, and that of those who are not so employed."

5. A recent reprinting (Signet Classics, New American Library of World Literature, 1962) states that an estimated 122 million copies of the McGuffey Readers sold between 1836 and 1920.

6. Women and children were not generally perceived as minority groups; most Mexican-Americans had yet to arrive; Hispano-Americans in the Southwest are not considered at this point. "Native" in this context refers to British-stock persons, not to American Indians.

7. The occasionally positive perception of Chinese civilization, and thus the possession of a degree of innate virtue by Chinese immigrants, gave them a slight advantage over American blacks. As Luther W. Spoehr says, the prevailing idea in the Gilded Age was that a "good" black was such because he had been improved by white culture. Spoehr, "Sambo and the Heathen Chinee: California's Racial Stereotypes in the Late 1870s," *Pacific Historical Review* 42 (May 1973): 185–204.

8. For a remarkably incisive discussion of the nature and results of white American cultural policies toward Indians earlier in the century, see Bernard W. Sheehan, *Seeds of Extinction: Jeffersonian Philanthropy and the American Indian* (Chapel Hill: University of North Carolina Press, 1973). See also Waltmann's article, "Circumstantial Reformer. . . ."

9. Judith L. Everson, "The Rhetoric of the Abolitionist Remnant, 1870–1877" (Ph.D. dissertation, Indiana University, 1973).

10. Borrowing the title of C. Vann Woodward's famous book (3d ed., New York: Oxford University Press, 1974) on the development of Southern racial segregation after the Civil War.

11. Anthropology thus performed a reactionary social function in the late nineteenth century. In contrast, sociology—an even newer social science—functioned in a basically progressive way: see the final portion of this chapter. For an excellent discussion of the positions of American anthropologists on race differences, read John S. Haller, Jr., *Outcasts from Evolution: Scientific Attitudes of Racial Inferiority, 1859–1900* (Urbana: University of Illinois Press, 1971). The quote is from p. 209. Haller also says that "The subject of race inferiority was beyond critical reach in the late nineteenth century. Having accepted science and its exalted doctrinaires, American society betrayed no sentiment, popular or otherwise, that looked to a remodeling of its social or political habits of race. . . . [Even] the most sententious critics of the nineteenth century's concept of the survival of the fittest in a struggle for existence considered the structure of race inferiority as outside the framework of their discussions" (p. 210).

12. The title of chapter 4 of *The Origin of Species*. To jump ahead for a moment: it was the millions-of-years part of the argument, involving as it did a literal contradiction of the biblical story of creation, and the idea that man had evolved from lower, less elaborate organisms (cf. Darwin's *The Descent of Man*, 1871), that bothered theologians, preachers, and churchgoers, and produced the enormous impact of Darwinism on religious thought and action. The applications of Darwinism to political economy and social relations were not the issue for those people, though perhaps in the Christian churches they should have been.

13. Milton Millhauser, "In the Air," in *Darwin*, ed. Philip Appleman (New York: W. W. Norton & Co., 1970), pp. 36–40.

14. A standard and insightful work on this subject is Richard Hofstadter's *Social Darwinism in American Thought*, rev. ed. (Boston: Beacon Press, 1955). See especially chapters 2 and 3, on Spencer and Sumner.

15. Ernest R. Sandeen, *The Roots of Fundamentalism: British*

and American Millenarianism, 1800–1930 (Chicago: University of Chicago Press, 1970), esp. chapters 6–10; Stephen C. Scholl, "The Decline of Millennialism in American Protestant Theology" (Ph.D. dissertation, Indiana University, 1974).

16. An example of this way of thinking occurs in the biography of Frances Willard, the long-time president of the Women's Christian Temperance Union. The author sketches Willard's deep roots in small-town Midwestern Methodism. Willard, she says, invented the W.C.T.U. motto, "God and Home and Native Land," and an 1889 general meeting of the organization complained that 800 newspapers were printed in the United States in a foreign language, and "most of them contained ideas relating to the home, women, temperance, and the Sabbath . . . that were European and revolutionary, not American or Christian." Mary Earhart, *Frances Willard: From Prayers to Politics* (Chicago: University of Chicago Press, 1944), p. 190 and passim.

17. Paul R. Messbarger, *Fiction with a Parochial Purpose: Social Uses of American Catholic Literature, 1884–1900* (Boston: Boston University Press, 1971).

18. Lawrence A. Cremin, *The Transformation of the School: Progressivism in American Education, 1876–1957* (New York: Alfred A. Knopf, 1961), p. 16, paraphrasing one of Harris's reports to the St. Louis school board.

19. Henry Steele Commager, foreword to *McGuffey's Fifth Eclectic Reader* (New York: New American Library, 1962), p. viii. A very similar summation appears in Ruth Miller Elson, *Guardians of Tradition: American Schoolbooks of the Nineteenth Century* (Lincoln: University of Nebraska Press, 1964).

20. In addition to books and articles already cited, I am indebted to the following: William H. Issel, "Modernization in Philadelphia School Reform, 1882–1905," *Pennsylvania Magazine of History and Biography* 94 (July 1970): 358–83; Richard E. Dudley, "Nebraska Public School Education, 1890–1910," *Nebraska History* 54 (spring 1973): 65–91; Charles E. Strickland, "The Child, the Community, and Clio: The Uses of Cultural History in Elementary School Experiments of the Eighteen-Nineties," *History*

of Education Quarterly 7 (winter 1967): 474–92; Marvin Lazerson, "Urban Reform and the Schools: Kindergartens in Massachusetts, 1870–1915," *History of Education Quarterly* 11 (summer 1971): 115–43.

21. Paraphrase in Winton U. Solberg, *The University of Illinois 1867–1894: An Intellectual and Cultural History* (Urbana: University of Illinois Press, 1968), p. 83.

22. John Barnard, *From Evangelicalism to Progressivism at Oberlin College, 1866–1917* (Columbus: Ohio State University Press, 1969), passim; Thomas D. Clark, *Indiana University: Midwestern Pioneer* (Bloomington: Indiana University Press, 1970), vol. 1, esp. chapters 10 and 11; Solberg, *University of Illinois*, chapters 3–8; Howard H. Peckham, *The Making of the University of Michigan, 1817–1967* (Ann Arbor: The University of Michigan Press, 1967), p. 75 and passim; Guy Lewis, "The Beginnings of Organized Collegiate Sport," *American Quarterly* 22 (summer 1970): 222–29.

23. R. Jackson Wilson, *In Quest of Community: Social Philosophy in the United States, 1860–1920* (New York: John Wiley and Sons, 1968), chapter 2, is a fine essay on Peirce's significance as a social philosopher.

24. Benjamin G. Rader, *The Academic Mind and Reform: The Influence of Richard T. Ely in American Life* (Lexington: University of Kentucky Press, 1966), p. 37.

25. As stated by Rader, *Academic Mind*, p. 82. On academic freedom battles see David Thelen, "The Academic Freedom Crisis of the 1890s and the Process of Change," paper delivered at the annual meeting of the Organization of American Historians, Washington, April, 1972.

26. Rader, *Academic Mind*, passim; Wilson, *In Quest*, passim; Charlotte G. O'Kelly and John W. Petras, "Images of Man in Early American Sociology, part II: The Changing Concept of Social Reform," *Journal of the History of the Behavioral Sciences* 6 (October 1970): 317–34.

3. LIFE AND LABOR, 1878–1893

1. This is true using the census definition of urban, i.e. people living in incorporated places of 2,500 or more, thus excluding people living on farms or in country villages.

2. The most reliable figures are for Massachusetts only, but they parallel general trends.

3. Brinley Thomas, *Migration and Economic Growth: A Study of Great Britain and the Atlantic Economy*, 2d ed. (Cambridge: At the University Press, 1973), pp. 117, 168–72.

4. Jack E. Eblen, "An Analysis of Nineteenth-Century Frontier Populations," *Demography* 2 (1965): 399–413; Hope T. Eldridge, "A Cohort Approach to the Analysis of Migration Differentials," *Demography* 1 (1964): 212–19; Warren S. Thompson and P. K. Whelpton, *Population Trends in the United States* (New York: McGraw-Hill Book Co., 1933), passim.

5. W. I. Hair, *Bourbonism and Agrarian Protest: Louisiana Politics 1877–1900* (Baton Rouge: Louisiana State University Press, 1969), esp. chapter 5; Kenneth W. Porter, "Negro Labor in the Western Cattle Industry," *Labor History* 10 (summer 1969): 346–74; C. Horace Hamilton, "The Negro Leaves the South," *Demography* 1 (1964): 273–95.

6. Alwyn Barr, "Occupational and Geographic Mobility in San Antonio, 1870–1900," *Social Science Quarterly* 51 (September 1970): 396–403.

7. Paul J. Lammermeier, "The Urban Black Family of the Nineteenth Century: A Study of Black Family Structure in the Ohio Valley, 1850–1880," *Journal of Marriage and the Family* 35 (August 1973): 440 (thanks to Robert G. Barrows for bringing this to my attention); E. Franklin Frazier, *The Negro Family in the United States*, rev. and abridged ed. (New York: Citadel Press, 1948), p. 87 and passim.

8. Reynolds Farley, "The Demographic Rates and Social Institutions of the Nineteenth-Century Negro Population: A Stable

Population Analysis," *Demography* 2 (1965): 386–98; Paul Demeny and Paul Gingrich, "A Reconsideration of Negro-White Mortality Differentials in the United States," *Demography* 4 (1966): 820–37.

9. Stephan Thernstrom and Peter R. Knights, "Men in Motion: Some Data and Speculations about Urban Population Mobility in Nineteenth-Century America," *Journal of Interdisciplinary History* 1 (autumn 1970): 7–35; the quote is from p. 17. Also, Brinley Thomas, *Migration*, chapter 6 on Irish migration. For Indianapolis see Robert G. Barrows, "A Demographic Analysis of Indianapolis, 1870–1920," (Ph.D. dissertation, Indiana University, 1976).

10. Clarence D. Long, *Wages and Earnings in the United States, 1860–1890* (Princeton: Princeton University Press for the National Bureau of Economic Research, 1960), passim; Charles Hoffman, *The Depression of the Nineties: An Economic History* (Westport, Conn.: Greenwood Publishing Corp. 1970), passim, for wage and income information; also, Census Bureau, *Historical Statistics*, series D on labor.

11. Alfred D. Chandler, Jr., "The Beginnings of Big Business in American Industry," *Business History Review*, spring 1959; reprinted in *New Perspectives on the American Past*, ed. Stanley N. Katz and Stanley I. Kutler (Boston: Little, Brown and Co., 1969), I: 31.

12. Chandler, p. 31 and passim; George Heberton Evans, Jr., *Business Incorporations in the United States, 1800–1943* (New York: National Bureau of Economic Research, 1948), pp. 11, 31, and passim. I have also benefited from passages in John F. Stover, *American Railroads* (Chicago: University of Chicago Press, 1961); and Douglass C. North, *Growth and Welfare in the American Past: A New Economic History* (Englewood Cliffs, N.J.: Prentice-Hall, 1966).

13. Hair, *Bourbonism*, p. 49 and chapter 3, passim.

14. Homer E. Socolofsky, "Land Disposal in Nebraska, 1854–1906: The Homestead Story," *Nebraska History* 48 (autumn 1967): 225–48.

15. For a strikingly cogent discussion of the socialization of American workers to industrial conditions, and a successful effort to treat labor history as something broader than the history of trade unions, see Herbert G. Gutman, "Work, Culture, and Society in Industrializing America, 1815–1919," *American Historical Review* 78 (June 1973): 531–88.

4. DEPRESSION AND SOCIAL CRISIS, 1893–1901

1. Paul Kleppner, *The Cross of Culture: A Social Analysis of Midwestern Politics 1850–1900* (New York: Free Press, 1971); Richard Jensen, *The Winning of the Midwest: Social and Political Conflict 1888–1896* (Chicago: University of Chicago Press, 1971); Samuel T. McSeveney, *The Politics of Depression: Political Behavior in the Northeast, 1893–1896* (New York: Oxford University Press, 1972).

2. Sheldon Hackney, *Populism to Progressivism in Alabama* (Princeton: Princeton University Press, 1969), p. 122; Alwyn Barr, *Reconstruction to Reform: Texas Politics 1876–1906* (Austin: University of Texas Press, 1971), esp. chapter 9. Lewis L. Gould, *Progressives and Prohibitionists: Texas Democrats in the Wilson Era* (Austin: University of Texas Press, 1973), distinguishes Hogg carefully from the Texas progressives of the Wilson period. The point here is that Hogg and his faction were something different from either Bourbons or Alliancemen.

3. Lorenzo D. Lewelling papers, Kansas State Historical Society, Topeka.

4. Lloyd Wendt and Herman Kogan, *Bosses in Lusty Chicago: The Story of Bathhouse John and Hinky Dink* (Bloomington: Indiana University Press, 1967), p. 91.

5. Hoffmann, *Depression of the Nineties*, chapters 1 and 2.

6. As McSeveney has shown with regard to key Eastern states; see McSeveney, *The Politics of Depression*, chapter 4.

7. Stover, *American Railroads*, p. 135.

8. Ernest Ludlow Bogart, *Economic History of the American People*, 2d ed. (New York: Longmans, Green, 1937), p. 580.

9. See Clifton K. Yearley, *The Money Machines: The Breakdown and Reform of Governmental and Party Finance in the North, 1860–1920* (Albany: State University of New York Press, 1970), and David P. Thelen, *The New Citizenship: Origins of Progressivism in Wisconsin 1885–1900* (Columbia: University of Missouri Press, 1972).

5. VALUES AND INSTITUTIONS, 1901–1916

1. They were discussed above, pp. 61–65.

2. See David Thelen, "The Academic Freedom Crisis of the 1890s and the Process of Change," pp. 1, 4.

3. Rader, *Academic Mind*, p. 175.

4. A partial list drawn from Rader's biography: John R. Commons, Albion Small, Edward Alsworth Ross, Frederick C. Howe, Newton Baker, Davis R. Dewey, Albert Shaw, Edwin H. Bemis, Thomas Nixon Carver. Ely also had contact as a graduate teacher with Frederick Jackson Turner, Woodrow Wilson, and J. Franklin Jameson. Ibid., pp. 21, 22, 26, 27.

5. Henry F. May, *The End of American Innocence: A Study of the First Years of Our Own Time, 1912–1917* (Chicago: Quadrangle Paperbacks, 1964), p. 180.

6. Edward A. Ross, *Seventy Years of It: An Autobiography* (New York: D. Appleton-Century Co., 1936), p. 291.

7. For an excellent discussion of Ross' idea of community, and his connections in this regard with C. S. Peirce and other thinkers, see Wilson, *In Quest of Community*, chapter 4.

8. Quotes from John R. Commons, *Races and Immigrants in America* (New York: Macmillan Co., 1908), pp. 12, 20–21, 41, 126, 154.

9. William James, *Pragmatism: A New Name for Some Old Ways of Thinking. Popular Lectures on Philosophy* (New York: Longmans, Green, 1907), esp. pp. 51, 200, 201.

10. Dewey's statement, made in 1908, appears in *American Ideas: Source Readings in the Intellectual History of the United States*, ed. Gerald N. Grob and Robert N. Beck (Glencoe: Free Press, 1963), II: 73–74.

11. See James Weinstein, *The Corporate Ideal in the Liberal State, 1900–1918* (Boston: Beacon Press, 1968), passim.

12. See James Gilbert, *Designing the Industrial State: The Intellectual Pursuit of Collectivism in America, 1880–1940* (Chicago: Quadrangle Books, 1972), passim.

13. Herbert Croly, *The Promise of American Life* (New York: Macmillan Co., 1910), chapter 1 and p. 454.

14. Walter Lippmann, *Drift and Mastery: An Attempt to Diagnose the Current Unrest* (New York: Mitchell Kennerley, 1914), p. 267.

15. In his dissent in *Lochner v. New York*, when the majority of the court voided a New York law limiting bakery workers to a sixty hour week, on the ground that to do so limited their freedom of contract. It should be added that when the progressives attacked and undermined "natural law," they were not directly concerned with the abstract idea of nature, but rather the conservative, rationalistic application of it, particularly in political economy, which was so deeply imbedded in thought and attitudes in the Gilded Age. Natural law in the abstract is ahistorical; in theory it can be put to revolutionary uses as well as to conservative ones; to wit, Thomas Jefferson and the signers of the Declaration of Independence, when they wrote the idea of natural rights into their revolutionary document. The progressives used it for neither conservative nor revolutionary purposes, but instead tried to erode it with pragmatic philosophy and empirical social science. They did not kill it, but did severely wound it.

16. Walter Rauschenbusch, *Christianity and the Social Crisis* (New York: Macmillan Co., 1908), p. xiii.

17. Wilson, *In Quest of Community*, p. 30. Of the several recent books detailing the development of the concepts of "community" or "corporatism," I have found Wilson's the most helpful, particularly his chapter on Peirce, and I am indebted to it at several points.

18. Walter Rauschenbusch, *A Theology for the Social Gospel* (New York: Macmillan Co., 1917), pp. 2, 99.

19. Charles Howard Hopkins, *The Rise of the Social Gospel in American Protestantism, 1865–1915* (New Haven: Yale University Press, 1940), p. 319.

20. Raymond E. Callahan, *Education and the Cult of Efficiency* (Chicago: University of Chicago Press, 1962).

21. Robert W. Stinson, "S. S. McClure and His Magazine: A Study in the Editing of *McClure's*, 1893–1913" (Ph.D. dissertation, Indiana University, 1971); idem, "S. S. McClure's 'My Autobiography': The Progressive as Self-Made Man," *American Quarterly* 22 (summer 1970); 203–12.

6. LIFE AND LABOR, 1901–1916

1. Over a million arrived in 1905–1907, 1910, 1913, 1914; over 500,000 left in 1908, and 1911–1914 inclusive.

2. C. K. Yearley, *The Money Machines*; Samuel P. Hays, "The Politics of Reform in Municipal Government in the Progressive Era," *Pacific Northwest Quarterly* 55 (October 1964): 157–69.

3. Roy Lubove, "Lawrence Veiller and the New York State Tenement House Commission of 1900," *Mississippi Valley Historical Review* 47 (March 1961): 659–77.

4. Edward C. Banfield, *The Moral Basis of a Backward Society* (New York: Free Press, 1958), is an intriguing analysis of self-identification among southern Italians. Banfield's observations were made in the early 1950s, but very probably the cultural pattern had changed little in that area in the intervening forty or fifty years.

5. Facts noted by Moses Rischin in *The Promised City: New York's Jews 1870–1914* (Cambridge: Harvard University Press, 1962), p. 81.

6. Brinley Thomas, *Migration*, p. 174.

7. Rischin, *Promised City*, p. 93.

8. Theodore Abel, *Protestant Home Missions to Catholic Immigrants* (New York: Institute of Social and Religious Research, 1933), p. 103. See also Barbara M. Solomon, *Ancestors and Immigrants* (Cambridge: Harvard University Press, 1956), esp. pp. 151–81; Henry B. Leonardo, "The Immigrants' Protective League of Chicago, 1908–1921," *Journal of the Illinois State Historical Society* 66 (autumn 1973): 271–84; William G. McLoughlin, *Billy Sunday Was His Real Name* (Chicago: University of Chicago Press, 1955).

9. Brinley Thomas, *Migration*, pp. xxvi, 330.

10. Sheldon Hackney, *Populism to Progressivism in Alabama* (Princeton: Princeton University Press, 1969), p. 146 and chapter 8.

11. Alwyn Barr, *Reconstruction to Reform: Texas Politics, 1876–1906* (Austin: University of Texas Press, 1971), p. 199.

12. Allan W. Moger, *Virginia: Bourbonism to Byrd, 1870–1925* (Charlottesville: The University Press of Virginia, 1968), pp. 182, 192. See also Paul Lewinson, *Race, Class and Party: A History of Negro Suffrage and White Politics in the South* (New York: Oxford University Press, 1932), esp. chapter 5.

13. Elizabeth W. Etheridge, *The Butterfly Caste: A Social History of Pellagra in the South* (Westport, Conn.: Greenwood Publishing Co., 1972), pp. 4, 59, and passim.

14. Again for the Registration Area. See Census Bureau, *Historical Statistics*, series B95–100. Also in Census Bureau, *Negro Population 1790–1915* (Washington: Government Printing Office, 1918; reprinted by Arno Press and the *New York Times*, 1968), p. 304.

15. E. Franklin Frazier, *The Negro Family*, chapters 13 and 14.

16. Emmett J. Scott, *Negro Migration during the War* (New

York: Arno Press and the *New York Times*, 1969 [first published 1920]), chapter 2.

17. Gutman, "Work, Culture, and Society," pp. 531–88.

18. In most countries the work force in agriculture declines rapidly after reaching the 25 percent point. In the United States it continued to fall over the next fifty years to about 4 percent in 1970, when it was still about 25 percent in the U.S.S.R.

19. Here I follow Albro Martin, *Enterprise Denied: Origins of the Decline of American Railroads 1897–1917* (New York: Columbia University Press, 1971) and others rather than Kolko. Though evidence exists for certain industries that business leaders reshaped regulation efforts to make regulation less irksome, more often they failed.

7. SOCIAL CHANGE THROUGH LAW AND POLITICS, 1901–1916

1. Otis L. Graham, Jr., *An Encore for Reform: The Old Progressives and the New Deal* (New York: Oxford University Press, 1967), chapter 3, discusses these people. Later (p. 145) Graham says that former progressives who either supported the New Deal, or criticized it for not going farther, generally had a background of "city slums encountered early, work in urban areas begun early and continued, and, in most cases, a conspicuous dedication to the ethical if not the theological teachings of Christianity." I have adapted Prof. Graham's typology of progressives and am indebted to his excellent book.

2. Miss Addams described a Hull House campaign against a "notoriously corrupt" alderman, admitting that "we doubtless depended too much upon the idealistic appeal for we did not yet comprehend the element of reality always brought into the political struggle in such a neighborhood where politics deal so directly with getting a job and earning a living. We soon discovered that approximately one out of every five voters in the nineteenth ward at that time held a job dependent upon the good will of the

alderman. . . . When [the alderman] protected a law breaker from the legal consequences of his act, his kindness appeared . . . like the deed of a powerful and kindly statesman. When Hull-House on the other hand insisted that a law must be enforced, it could but appear like the persecution of the offender. We were certainly not anxious for consistency nor for individual achievement, but in a desire to foster a higher political morality and not to lower our standards, we constantly clashed with the existing political code." Jane Addams, *Twenty Years at Hull-House* (New York: Signet Classics, 1960; first published 1910), pp. 222–23.

3. Samuel T. McSeveney, *The Politics of Depression: Political Behavior in the Northeast, 1893–96* (New York: Oxford University Press, 1972), chapter 4.

4. Lewis L. Gould, *Progressives and Prohibitionists: Texas Democrats in the Wilson Era* (Austin: University of Texas Press, 1973), p. 27. Gould later points out that prohibition was an ethnocultural issue, one "around which men could debate the nature and direction of their society" (p. 55). "What gave prohibition its intensity as a public question were its larger social and political implications. The movement affirmed older cultural values in a time of flux and uncertainty. Drys evoked memories of smaller communities untainted with urban ills. They spoke for time-honored Protestant folkways and rejected the newer nation of the immigrant, the liberated woman, and the city political machine." The issue may, however, have helped rural Democrats accept the idea of government activism (pp. 289–91).

5. The paradox also resulted, more than incidentally, from the disfranchisement of blacks and aliens as a result of progressive-era legislation, matters to be discussed in a moment.

6. Combining the Republican and Progressive votes in 1912.

7. Because the two Progressive candidates, Wilson and Roosevelt, won 70 percent of the votes; because the Roosevelt schism and campaign sharpened the philosophical issues between the New Nationalist and New Freedom varieties of progressivism; and because Debs, the Socialist, captured over 900,000 votes and a historically high (for a Socialist) 6 percent of the total.

8. As John D. Buenker, in numerous articles, and J. Joseph Huthmacher, in "Urban Liberalism and the Age of Reform," *Mississippi Valley Historical Review* 49 (September 1962): 231–41, and elsewhere, have shown.

9. Albro Martin, *Enterprise Denied*, p. 95. This defense of the railroads condemns the stringent regulation of 1903–1910 as "archaic progressivism" which ignored the complex realities of railroad management and severely damaged both the roads and the economy they served. See also ibid., pp. xii–xiii, 17, 128, 345, 359.

10. Hays, "Politics of Reform," p. 166.

11. Yearley, *The Money Machines*, p. 279. Yearley is at pains to show the diffuseness of tax reform and the fact that no ideological or economic interest group got all it wanted. Space limitations force me to oversimplify his subtle argument, which he summarized on pp. 269–79.

12. John D. Buenker, "The Progressive Era: A Search for a Synthesis," *Mid-America* 51 (July 1969): 175–93, and elsewhere; Forrest A. Walker, "Compulsory Health Insurance: 'The Next Great Step in Social Legislation,'" *Journal of American History* 56 (September 1969): 290–304; Irwin Yellowitz, "The Origins of Unemployment Reform in the United States," *Labor History* 9 (fall 1968): 338–60; Milton Derber, "The Idea of Industrial Democracy in America, 1898–1915," *Labor History* 7 (fall 1966): 259–86; and Lawrence M. Friedman and Jack Ladinsky, "Law and Social Change in the Progressive Era: The Law of Industrial Accidents," *Columbia Law Review* 67 (January 1967), 50–82, which also appeared in *New Perspectives on the American Past*, ed. Katz and Kutler, II: 172–202.

13. James H. Timberlake, *Prohibition and the Progressive Movement 1900–1920* (Cambridge: Harvard University Press, 1963), p. 154.

14. Jean B. Quandt, *From the Small Town to the Great Community: The Social Thought of Progressive Intellectuals* (New Brunswick: Rutgers University Press, 1970), p. 23.

15. Barry Dean Karl, *Executive Reorganization and Reform in*

the New Deal: The Genesis of Administrative Management 1900–1939 (Cambridge: Harvard University Press, 1939), p. 164.

"LOOKING BACKWARD," 1916–1876

1. Thomas S. Kuhn, *The Structure of Scientific Revolutions* (Chicago: University of Chicago Press, 1962).

Bibliography

An exhaustive bibliography on all aspects of American history from the 1870s to World War I would number some thousands of items. Thus the following list is quite selective, and includes only those items which appear in the footnotes or which otherwise proved particularly helpful and stimulating. For a comprehensive, recent survey of writing in American history, especially writings which appeared between 1960 and 1972, the reader may consult William H. Cartwright and Richard L. Watson, Jr., eds., *The Reinterpretation of American History and Culture* (Washington, D.C.: National Council for the Social Studies, 1973). The essays most relevant to the subject of this book are John W. Blassingame, "The Afro-Americans: from Mythology to Reality," pp. 53–79; Rudolph J. Vecoli, "European Americans: From Immigrants to Ethnics," pp. 81–112; Raymond A. Mohl, "The History of the American City," pp. 165–205; Walter T. K. Nugent, "Politics from Reconstruction to 1900," pp. 377–399; J. Carroll Moody, "The Transformation of the American Economy, 1877–1900," pp. 401–424; Robert H. Wiebe, "The Progressive Years, 1900–1917," pp. 425–442.

Statistical data were taken preeminently from U. S., Bureau of the Census, *Historical Statistics of the United States, Colonial Times to 1957* (Washington, D.C.: Census Bureau, 1960). Also, Census Bureau, *Pocket Data Book, USA 1971* (Washington, D.C.: U. S. Government Printing Office, 1971); Wl. Woytinsky, *Die Welt in Zahlen*, 7 vols. (Berlin: Rudolf Mosse, 1925ff.); B. R. Mitchell, comp., *European Historical Statistics 1750–1970* (London: Macmillan Press Ltd., 1975); Warren S. Thompson and P. K. Whelpton, *Population Trends in the United States* (New York: McGraw-Hill, 1933); Census Bureau, *Negro Population 1790–1915* (Washington: U. S. Government Printing Office, 1918; reprinted, Arno Press and the *New York Times*, 1968).

1. AMERICAN SOCIETY AT THE CENTENNIAL

Ambrose, David C. "The Major Reasons for Army Desertions at Fort Davis, Texas, 1882–1885." *Panhandle-Plains Historical Review*, 45 (1972), 38–45.

Andrews, Wayne. *Architecture, Ambition, and Americans: A Social History of American Architecture.* New York: Free Press, 1964.

Barker, Joel. "Colorado Mail Service, 1859–85." *Colorado Magazine*, 49 (summer 1972), 219–37.

Bivans, Venola Lewis. "The Diary of Luna E. Warner, a Kansas Teenager of the Early 1870s." *Kansas Historical Quarterly*, 35 (autumn 1969), 276–311, (winter 1969), 411–42.

Bloch, Herman D. "The National Labor Union and Black Workers," *Journal of Ethnic Studies*, 1 (spring 1973), 13–21.

Easterlin, Richard A., "Interregional Differences. . . ." In *Trends in the American Economy in the Nineteenth Century.* Princeton, N.J.: Princeton University Press for the National Bureau of Economic Research, 1960.

Farnham, Wallace D. " 'The Weakened Spring of Government': A Study in Nineteenth Century American History." *American Historical Review*, 68 (April 1963), 662–80.

Gould, Lewis L. "The Republican Search for a National Majority." In H. Wayne Morgan, ed., *The Gilded Age* (Syracuse: Syracuse University Press, 1970), 171–87.

Gowans, Alan. *Images of American Living: Four Centuries of Architecture and Furniture as Cultural Expression.* Philadelphia: J. B. Lippincott Co., 1964.

Hammond, Bray. "The North's Empty Purse, 1861–1862." *American Historical Review*, 67 (October 1961), 1–18.

Jackson, John B. *American Space: The Centennial Years, 1865–1876.* New York: W. W. Norton, 1972.

Larson, Henrietta M. *Jay Cooke, Private Banker.* Cambridge: Harvard University Press, 1936.

Marcus, Irwin M. "Labor Discontent in Tioga County, Pennsylvania, 1865–1905: The Gutman Thesis, a Test Case." *Labor History*, 14 (summer 1973), 414–22.

Miller, Lillian B. "Engines, Marbles, and Canvases: The Centennial Exposition of 1876." In *Lectures 1972–1973: 1876, The Centennial Year* (Indianapolis: Indiana Historical Society, 1973), pp. 2–28.

Musto, David. *The American Disease: Origins of Narcotic Control.* New Haven: Yale University Press, 1973.

Nugent, Walter T. K. *Money and American Society, 1865–1880.* New York: Free Press, 1968.

Parkman, Francis. *The Discovery of the Great West: La Salle.* William R. Taylor, ed.; New York: Rinehart and Company, 1956.

Persons, Warren M., Pierson M. Tuttle, and Edwin Frickey. "Business and Financial Conditions following the Civil War in the United States." *Review of Economic Statistics*, Supp., prelim. vol. 2 (1920), 1–55.

Waltmann, Henry G. "Circumstantial Reformer: President Grant and the Indian Problem." *Arizona and the West*, 13 (winter 1971), 323–42.

Williamson, Jeffrey G. "Late Nineteenth-Century American Retardation: A Neoclassical Analysis." *Journal of Economic History*, 33 (September 1973), 581–607.

Wishart, David J. "Age and Sex Composition of the Population on the Nebraska Frontier, 1860–1880." *Nebraska History*, 14 (spring 1973), 107–19.

2. VALUES AND INSTITUTIONS, 1878–1893

Appleman, Philip, ed. *Darwin.* New York: W. W. Norton, 1970.

Barnard, John. *From Evangelicalism to Progressivism at Oberlin College, 1866–1917.* Columbus: Ohio State University Press, 1969.

Blodgett, Geoffrey. *The Gentle Reformers: Massachusetts Democrats in the Cleveland Era.* Cambridge, Mass.: Harvard University Press, 1966.

Carter, Paul. *The Spiritual Crisis of the Gilded Age.* Dekalb: Northern Illinois University Press, 1971.

Clark, Thomas D. *Indiana University: Midwestern Pioneer.* Bloomington: Indiana University Press, 1970.

Cremin, Lawrence A. *The Transformation of the School: Progressivism in American Education, 1876–1957.* New York: Alfred A. Knopf, 1961.

Dudley, Richard E. "Nebraska Public School Education, 1890–1910." *Nebraska History,* 54 (spring 1973), 65–91.

Earhart, Mary. *Frances Willard: From Prayers to Politics.* Chicago: University of Chicago Press, 1944.

Elson, Ruth Miller. *Guardians of Tradition: American Schoolbooks of the Nineteenth Century.* Lincoln: University of Nebraska Press, 1964.

Everson, Judith L. "The Rhetoric of the Abolitionist Remnant, 1870–1877." Ph.D. dissertation, Indiana University, 1973.

Fine, Sidney. *Laissez Faire and the General-Welfare State: A Study of Conflict in American Thought, 1865–1900.* Ann Arbor: University of Michigan Press, 1956.

Galambos, Louis. "AFL's Concept of Big Business: A Quantitative Study of Attitudes toward the Large Corporation, 1894–1931." *Journal of American History,* 57 (March 1971), 847–63.

Gilbert, James. *Designing the Industrial State: The Intellectual Pursuit of Collectivism in America, 1880–1940.* Chicago: Quadrangle Books, 1972.

Gleason, Philip. *The Conservative Reformers: German-American Catholics and the Social Order.* Notre Dame: University of Notre Dame Press, 1968.

Haller, John S., Jr. *Outcasts from Evolution: Scientific Attitudes of Racial Inferiority, 1859–1900.* Urbana: University of Illinois Press, 1971.

Hofstadter, Richard. *Social Darwinism in American Thought,* rev. ed. Boston: Beacon Press, 1955.

Hoogenboom, Ari. *Outlawing the Spoils: A History of the Civil Service Reform Movement, 1865–1883.* Urbana: University of Illinois Press, 1961.

Issel, William H. "Modernization in Philadelphia School Reform, 1882–1905." *Pennsylvania Magazine of History and Biography,* 94 (July 1970), 358–83.

Lazerson, Marvin. "Urban Reform and the Schools: Kindergartens in Massachusetts, 1870–1915." *History of Education Quarterly*, 11 (summer 1971), 115–43.

Lewinson, Paul. *Race, Class, and Party: A History of Negro Suffrage and White Politics in the South.* New York: Oxford University Press, 1932.

Lewis, Guy. "The Beginnings of Organized Collegiate Sport." *American Quarterly*, 22 (summer 1970), 222–29.

May, Henry F. *Protestant Churches and Industrial America.* New York: Harper and Brothers, 1949.

McAvoy, Thomas T. *The Great Crisis in American Catholic History, 1895–1900.* Chicago: Henry Regnery Co., 1957.

McFarland, Gerald W. "Partisan of Nonpartisanship: Dorman B. Eaton and the Genteel Reform Tradition." *Journal of American History*, 54 (March 1968), 806–22.

McGuffey's Fifth Eclectic Reader. Henry Steele Commager, ed.; New York: New American Library, 1962.

Messbarger, Paul R. *Fiction with a Parochial Purpose: Social Uses of American Catholic Literature, 1884–1900.* Boston: Boston University Press, 1971.

O'Kelly, Charlotte G. and John W. Petras. "Images of Man in Early American Sociology, Part II: The Changing Concept of Social Reform." *Journal of the History of the Behavioral Sciences*, 6 (October 1970), 317–34.

Peckham, Howard H. *The Making of the University of Michigan, 1817–1967.* Ann Arbor: University of Michigan Press, 1967.

Purcell, Edward A., Jr. "Ideas and Interests: Businessmen and the Interstate Commerce Act." *Journal of American History*, 54 (December 1967), 561–78.

Quandt, Jean B. *From the Small Town to the Great Community: The Social Thought of Progressive Intellectuals.* New Brunswick, N.J.: Rutgers University Press, 1970.

Rader, Benjamin G. *The Academic Mind and Reform: The Influence of Richard T. Ely in American Life.* Lexington: University Press of Kentucky, 1966.

Rousmaniere, John P. "Cultural Hybrid in the Slums: The College Woman and the Settlement House, 1889–1894." *American Quarterly*, 22 (spring 1970), 45–66.

Sandeen, Ernest R. *The Roots of Fundamentalism: British and*

American Millenarianism, 1800–1930. Chicago: University of Chicago Press, 1970.

Scholl, Stephen C. "The Decline of Millennialism in American Protestant Theology." Ph.D. dissertation, Indiana University, 1974.

Sheehan, Bernard W. *Seeds of Extinction: Jeffersonian Philanthropy and the American Indian.* Chapel Hill: University of North Carolina Press, 1973.

Smith, Adam. *An Inquiry into the Nature and Causes of the Wealth of Nations.*

Solberg, Winton U. *The University of Illinois, 1867–1894: An Intellectual and Cultural History.* Urbana: University of Illinois Press, 1968.

Spoehr, Luther W. "Sambo and the Heathen Chinee: California's Racial Stereotypes in the Late 1870s." *Pacific Historical Review,* 42 (May 1973), 185–204.

Sproat, John G. *The Best Men: Liberal Reformers in the Gilded Age.* New York: Oxford University Press, 1968.

Strickland, Charles E. "The Child, the Community, and Clio: The Uses of Cultural History in Elementary School Experiments of the Eighteen-Nineties." *History of Education Quarterly,* 12 (winter 1967), 474–92.

Thelen, David. "The Academic Freedom Crisis of the 1890s and the Process of Change." Paper delivered at Organization of American Historians meeting, Washington, D.C., April 1972.

Tomsich, John. *A Genteel Endeavor: American Culture and Politics in the Gilded Age.* Stanford: Stanford University Press, 1971.

Veysey, Lawrence R. *The Emergence of the American University.* Chicago: University of Chicago Press, 1965.

White, Morton. *Social Thought in America: The Revolt Against Formalism.* Boston: Beacon Press, 1957.

Wilson, R. Jackson. *In Quest of Community: Social Philosophy in the United States, 1860–1920.* New York: John Wiley and Sons, 1968.

Woodman, Harold D. "Chicago Businessmen and the Granger Laws." *Agricultural History,* 36 (April 1962), 16–24.

Woodward, C. Vann. *The Strange Career of Jim Crow,* 3d ed. New York: Oxford University Press, 1974.

3. LIFE AND LABOR, 1878–1893

Barr, Alwyn. "Occupational and Geographic Mobility in San Antonio, 1870–1900." *Social Science Quarterly*, 51 (September 1970), 396–403.

Barth, Gunther. *Bitter Strength: A History of the Chinese in the United States, 1850–1870.* Cambridge: Harvard University Press, 1964.

Bieder, Robert E. "Kinship as a Factor in Migration." *Journal of Marriage and the Family*, 35 (August 1973), 429–39.

Bleser, Carol K. R. *The Promised Land: The South Carolina Land Commission, 1869–1890.* Columbia: University of South Carolina Press, 1969.

Calcott, Margaret L. *The Negro in Maryland Politics, 1870–1912.* Baltimore: Johns Hopkins University Press, 1969.

Chandler, Alfred D., Jr. *Strategy and Structure: Chapters in the History of the Industrial Enterprise.* Cambridge, Mass.: M.I.T. Press, 1962.

————. "The Beginnings of Big Business in American Industry." *Business History Review*, 33 (spring 1959), 1–30.

———— and Louis Galambos. "The Development of Large-scale Economic Organizations in Modern America." *Journal of Economic History*, 30 (March 1970), 131–49.

Chudacoff, Howard P. "A New Look at Ethnic Neighborhoods: Residential Dispersion and the Concept of Visibility in a Medium-sized City." *Journal of American History*, 60 (June 1973), 76–93.

Demeny, Paul and Paul Gingrich. "A Reconsideration of Negro-White Mortality Differentials in the United States." *Demography*, 4 (1966), 820–37.

Dinnerstein, Leonard and Frederick Cople Janer, eds. *The Aliens: A History of Ethnic Minorities in America.* New York: Appleton-Century-Crofts, 1970.

Dunbar, Willis F. *Kalamazoo and How it Grew . . . and Grew. . . .* Kalamazoo: Western Michigan University Press, 1969.

Dykstra, Robert R. *The Cattle Towns.* New York: Alfred A. Knopf, 1968.

Eblen, Jack E. "An Analysis of Nineteenth-Century Frontier Populations." *Demography*, 2 (1965), 399–413.

Eldridge, Hope T. "A Cohort Approach to the Analysis of Migration Differentials." *Demography*, 1 (1964), 212–19.

Evans, George Heberton, Jr. *Business Incorporations in the United States, 1800–1943.* New York: National Bureau of Economic Research, 1948.

Farley, Reynolds. "The Demographic Rates and Social Institutions of the Nineteenth-Century Negro Population: A Stable Population Analysis." *Demography*, 2 (1965), 386–98.

Fite, Gilbert C. *The Farmers' Frontier, 1865–1900.* New York: Holt, Rinehart and Winston, 1966.

Frazier, E. Franklin. *The Negro Family in the United States*, rev. abridged ed. New York: Citadel Press, 1948.

Gallman, Robert E. "Changes in Total U. S. Agricultural Factor Productivity in the Nineteenth Century." *Agricultural History*, 46 (January 1972), 191–210.

Gutman, Herbert G. "Work, Culture, and Society in Industrializing America, 1815–1919." *American Historical Review*, 78 (June 1973), 531–88.

Hair, William I., Jr. *Bourbonism and Agrarian Protest: Louisiana Politics, 1877–1900.* Baton Rouge: Louisiana State University Press, 1969.

Hamilton, C. Horace. "The Negro Leaves the South." *Demography*, 1 (1964), 273–95.

Higgs, Robert. *The Transformation of the American Economy, 1865–1914: An Essay in Interpretation.* New York: John Wiley and Sons, 1971.

————. "Railroad Rates and the Populist Uprising." *Agricultural History*, 44 (July 1970), 291–97.

Hoffmann, Charles. *The Depression of the Nineties: An Economic History.* Westport, Conn.: Greenwood Press, 1970.

Hopkins, Richard J. "Occupational and Geographic Mobility in Atlanta, 1870–1896." *Journal of Southern History*, 34 (May 1968), 200–213.

Juhnke, James C. *A People of Two Kingdoms: The Political Acculturation of the Kansas Mennonites.* Newton, Kansas: Faith and Life, 1975.

Klein, Maury and Kozo Yamamura. "The Growth Strategies of Southern Railroads, 1865–1933." *Business History Review*, 41 (winter 1967), 358–77.

Lammermeier, Paul J. "The Urban Black Family of the Nineteenth Century: A Study of Black Family Structure in the Ohio Valley, 1850–1880." *Journal of Marriage and the Family*, 35 (August 1973), 440–56.

Long, Clarence D. *Wages and Earnings in the United States, 1860–1890*. Princeton, N.J.: Princeton University Press for the National Bureau of Economic Research, 1960.

Modell, John and Tamara K. Hareven. "Urbanization and the Malleable Household: An Examination of Boarding and Lodging in American Families." *Journal of Marriage and the Family*, 35 (August 1973), 467–79.

Nordin, Dennis S. "A Revisionist Interpretation of the Patrons of Husbandry, 1867–1900." *Historian*, 32 (August 1970), 630–43.

North, Douglass C. *Growth and Welfare in the American Past: A New Economic History*. Englewood Cliffs, N.J.: Prentice-Hall, 1966.

Porter, Kenneth W. "Negro Labor in the Western Cattle Industry." *Labor History*, 10 (summer 1969), 346–74.

Rees, Albert. *Real Wages in Manufacturing, 1890–1914*. Princeton, N.J.: Princeton University Press, 1961.

Rice, Lawrence D. *The Negro in Texas, 1874–1900*. Baton Rouge: Louisiana State University Press, 1971.

Rischin, Moses. *The Promised City: New York's Jews, 1870–1914*. Cambridge, Mass.: Harvard University Press, 1962.

Rolle, Andrew F. *The Immigrant Upraised: Italian Adventurers and Colonists in an Expanding America*. Norman: University of Oklahoma Press, 1968.

Smith, Claude P. "Official Efforts by the State of Mississippi to Encourage Immigration, 1868–1886." *Journal of Mississippi History*, 32 (November 1970), 327–42.

Socolofsky, Homer E. "Land Disposal in Nebraska, 1854–1906: The Homestead Story." *Nebraska History*, 48 (autumn 1967), 225–48.

Stover, John F. *American Railroads*. Chicago: University of Chicago Press, 1961.

Thernstrom, Stephan and Peter R. Knights. "Men in Motion: Some Data and Speculations about Urban Population Mobility in Nineteenth-Century America." *Journal of Interdisciplinary History*, 1 (autumn 1970), 7–35.

Thomas, Brinley. *Migration and Economic Growth: A Study of Great Britain and the Atlantic Economy*, 2d ed.; Cambridge: At the University Press, 1973.

Vecoli, Rudolph J. "*Contadini* in Chicago: A Critique of *The Uprooted*." *Journal of American History*, 51 (December 1964), 404–17.

Ward, David. *Cities and Immigrants: A Geography of Change in Nineteenth-Century America.* New York: Oxford University Press, 1971.

Warner, Sam B., Jr. *Streetcar Suburbs: The Process of Growth in Boston, 1870–1900.* Cambridge: Harvard University Press and M.I.T. Press, 1962.

Wells, Robert V. "Demographic Change and the Life Cycle of American Families." In Robert I. Rotberg and Theodore K. Rabb, eds. *The Family in History: Interdisciplinary Essays.* New York: Harper and Row, 1971.

Yearley, Clifton K. *The Money Machines: The Breakdown and Reform of Governmental and Party Finance in the North, 1860–1920.* Albany: State University of New York Press, 1970.

4. DEPRESSION AND SOCIAL CRISIS, 1893–1901

Barr, Alwyn. *Reconstruction to Reform: Texas Politics 1876–1906.* Austin: University of Texas Press, 1971.

Bogart, Ernest Ludlow. *Economic History of the American People*, 2d ed. New York: Longmans, Green, 1937.

Cooper, William J., Jr. *The Conservative Regime: South Carolina 1877–1900.* Baltimore: Johns Hopkins University Press, 1968.

Goodwyn, Lawrence C. "Populist Dreams and Negro Rights: East Texas as a Case Study." *American Historical Review*, 76 (December 1971), 1435–56.

Gould, Lewis L. *Wyoming: A Political History, 1868–1896.* New Haven, Conn.: Yale University Press, 1968.

————. *Progressives and Prohibitionists: Texas Democrats in the Wilson Era.* Austin: University of Texas Press, 1973.

Hackney, Sheldon. *Populism to Progressivism in Alabama.* Princeton, N.J.: Princeton University Press, 1969.

Hammarberg, Melvin. "Indiana Farmers and the Group Basis of Late Nineteenth-Century Political Parties." *Journal of American History,* 61 (June 1974), 91–115.

Jensen, Richard. *The Winning of the Midwest: Social and Political Conflict, 1888–1896.* Chicago: University of Chicago Press, 1971.

Kleppner, Paul. *The Cross of Culture: A Social Analysis of Midwestern Politics, 1850–1900.* New York: Free Press, 1970.

Lamar, Howard R. *Dakota Territory, 1861–1889: A Study of Frontier Politics.* New Haven: Yale University Press, 1956.

Marcus, Robert D. *Grand Old Party: Political Structure in the Gilded Age, 1880–1896.* New York: Oxford University Press, 1971.

Martin, Albro. *Enterprise Denied: Origins of the Decline of American Railroads, 1897–1917.* New York: Columbia University Press, 1971.

McSeveney,Samuel T. *The Politics of Depression: Political Behavior in the Northeast, 1893–96.* New York: Oxford University Press, 1972.

Moger, Allan W. *Virginia: Bourbonism to Byrd, 1870–1925.* Charlottesville: University Press of Virginia, 1968.

Morgan, H. Wayne. *From Hayes to McKinley: National Party Politics, 1877–1896.* Syracuse: Syracuse University Press, 1969.

Nugent, Walter T. K. "Some Parameters of Populism." *Agricultural History,* 40 (October 1966), 255–70.

Parsons, Stanley B. *The Populist Context: Rural versus Urban Power on a Great Plains Frontier.* Westport, Conn.: Greenwood Press, 1973.

Rogin, Michael. "California Populism and the 'System of 1896.' " *Western Political Quarterly,* 22 (March 1969), 179–96.

Thelen, David P. *The New Citizenship: Origins of Progressivism in Wisconsin, 1885–1900.* Columbia: University of Missouri Press, 1972.

Wendt, Lloyd and Herman Kogan. *Bosses in Lusty Chicago: The*

Story of Bathhouse John and Hinky Dink. Bloomington: Indiana University Press, 1967.

Wright, James E. *The Politics of Populism: Dissent in Colorado.* New Haven: Yale University Press, 1974.

5. VALUES AND INSTITUTIONS, 1901–1916

Note: Some of the works cited for chapter two also apply here.

Bowers, William L. "Country-Life Reform, 1900–1920: A Neglected Aspect of Progressive Era History." *Agricultural History*, 45 (July 1971), 211–21.

Buenker, John D. *Urban Liberalism and Progressive Reform.* New York: Scribner's, 1973.

———. "The Progressive Era: A Search for a Synthesis." *Mid-America*, 51 (July 1969), 175–93.

Callahan, Raymond E. *Education and the Cult of Efficiency.* Chicago: University of Chicago Press, 1962.

Carlson, Robert A. "Americanization as an Early Twentieth-Century Adult Education Movement." *History of Education Quarterly*, 10 (winter 1970), 440–64.

Commons, John R. *Races and Immigrants in America.* New York: Macmillan Co., 1908.

Croly, Herbert. *The Promise of American Life.* New York: Macmillan Co., 1910.

Feldman, Egal. "Prostitution, the Alien Woman, and the Progressive Imagination." *American Quarterly*, 19 (summer 1967), 192–206.

Fox, Bonnie R. "The Philadelphia Progressives, A Test of the Hofstadter-Hays Thesis." *Pennsylvania History*, 34 (October 1967), 372–94.

Graham, Otis L., Jr. *An Encore for Reform: The Old Progressives and the New Deal.* New York: Oxford University Press, 1967.

Grob, Gerald N. and Robert N. Beck. *American Ideas: Source Readings in the Intellectual History of the United States.* Glencoe, Ill.: Free Press, 1963.

Hopkins, Charles Howard. *The Rise of the Social Gospel in American Protestantism, 1865–1915*. New Haven, Conn.: Yale University Press, 1940.

Israel, Jerry. *Building the Organizational Society*. New York: Free Press, 1972.

Janick, Herbert. "The Mind of the Connecticut Progressive." *Mid-America*, 52 (April 1970), 83–101.

Karl, Barry Dean. *Executive Reorganization and Reform in the New Deal: The Genesis of Administrative Management, 1900–1939*. Cambridge, Mass.: Harvard University Press, 1963.

Levine, Daniel. *Varieties of Reform Thought*. Madison: State Historical Society of Wisconsin, 1964.

Lippmann, Walter. *Drift and Mastery: An Attempt to Diagnose the Current Unrest*. New York: Mitchell Kennerley, 1914.

May, Henry F. *The End of American Innocence: A Study of the First Years of Our Own Time, 1912–1917*. Chicago: Quadrangle Paperbacks, 1964.

McGovern, James R. "The American Woman's Pre-World War I Freedom in Manners and Morals." *Journal of American History*, 55 (September 1968), 315–33.

Rauschenbusch, Walter. *Christianity and the Social Crisis*. New York: Macmillan Co., 1908.

———. *A Theology for the Social Gospel*. New York: Macmillan Co., 1917.

Ross, Edward A. *Seventy Years of It: An Autobiography*. New York: D. Appleton-Century Co., 1936.

Stinson, Robert W. "S. S. McClure's *My Autobiography:* The Progressive as Self-made Man." *American Quarterly*, 22 (summer 1970), 203–12.

———. "S. S. McClure and his Magazine: A Study in the Editing of *McClure's*, 1893–1913." Ph.D. dissertation, Indiana University, 1971.

Weinstein, James. *The Corporate Ideal in the Liberal State, 1900–1918*. Boston: Beacon Press, 1968.

6. LIFE AND LABOR, 1901–1916

Note: Some of the works cited for chapter three also apply here.

Abel, Theodore. *Protestant Home Missions to Catholic Immigrants.* New York: Institute of Social and Religious Research, 1933.

Allswang, John M. *A House for all Peoples: Ethnic Politics in Chicago, 1890–1936.* Lexington: University Press of Kentucky, 1971.

Banfield, Edward C. *The Moral Basis of a Backward Society.* New York: Free Press, 1958.

Chandler, Alfred D., Jr. "The Structure of American Industry in the Twentieth Century: A Historical Overview." *Business History Review*, 43 (autumn 1969), 255–98.

Etheridge, Elizabeth W. *The Butterfly Caste: A Social History of Pellagra in the South.* Westport, Conn.: Greenwood Press, 1972.

Haller, Mark H. "Urban Crime and Criminal Justice: The Chicago Case. *Journal of American History*, 57 (December 1970), 619–35.

Hays, Samuel P. "The Politics of Reform in Municipal Government in the Progressive Era." *Pacific Northwest Quarterly*, 55 (October 1964), 157–69.

Higgs, Robert. "Race, Skills, and Earnings: American Immigrants in 1909." *Journal of Economic History*, 31 (June 1971), 420–28.

Higham, John. *Strangers in the Land: Patterns of American Nativism, 1860–1925.* New Brunswick, N.J.: Rutgers University Press, 1955.

Kingsdale, Jon M. "The 'Poor Man's Club': Social Functions of the Urban Working-Class Saloon." *American Quarterly*, 25 (October 1973), 472–89.

Leonardo, Henry B. "The Immigrants' Protective League of Chicago, 1908–1921." *Journal of the Illinois State Historical Society*, 66 (autumn 1973), 271–84.

Lubove, Roy. "Lawrence Veiller and the New York State Tenement House Commission of 1900." *Mississippi Valley Historical Review*, 47 (March 1961), 659–77.

McLaughlin, Virginia Y. "Patterns of Work and Family Organization: Buffalo's Italians." In Robert I. Rotberg and Theodore K. Rabb, eds. *The Family in History: Interdisciplinary Essays.* New York: Harper and Row, 1971.

McLoughlin, William G. *Billy Sunday Was his Real Name.* Chicago: University of Chicago Press, 1955.

Scheiner, Seth M. *Negro Mecca: A History of the Negro in New York City, 1865–1920.* New York: New York University Press, 1965.

Scott, Emmett J. *Negro Migration during the War.* New York: Arno Press and the *New York Times*, 1969.

Solomon, Barbara M. *Ancestors and Immigrants.* Cambridge, Mass.: Harvard University Press, 1956.

Spear, Allan H. *Black Chicago: The Making of a Negro Ghetto, 1890–1920.* Chicago: University of Chicago Press, 1967.

7. LAW AND POLITICS, 1901–1916

Note: Some references may be found under chapters four, five, and six.

Abrams, Richard. *Conservatism in a Progressive Era: Massachusetts Politics, 1900–1912.* Cambridge, Mass.: Harvard University Press, 1964.

Addams, Jane. *Twenty Years at Hull-House.* New York: Signet Classics, 1960.

Allen, Howard W. "Geography and Politics: Voting on Reform Issues in the U. S. Senate, 1911–16." *Journal of Southern History*, 27 (May 1961), 216–32.

————, Aage R. Clausen, and Jerome M. Clubb. "Political Reform and Negro Rights in the Senate, 1909–1915." *Journal of Southern History*, 37 (May 1971), 191–212.

Bernstein, Barton J. and Franklin A. Leib. "Progressive Republican Senators and American Imperialism 1898–1916: A Reappraisal." *Mid-America*, 50 (July 1968), 163–205.

Burner, David. *The Politics of Provincialism: The Democratic Party in Transition, 1918–1932.* New York: Alfred A. Knopf, 1968.

Caine, Stanley P. *The Myth of a Progressive Reform: Railroad*

Regulation in Wisconsin, 1903–1910. Madison: State Historical Society of Wisconsin, 1970.

Chrislock, Carl H. *The Progressive Era in Minnesota, 1899–1918.* St. Paul: Minnesota Historical Society, 1971.

Crooks, James B. *Politics and Progress: Urban Progressivism in Baltimore, 1895–1911.* Baton Rouge: Louisiana State University Press, 1968.

Derber, Milton. "The Idea of Industrial Democracy in America, 1898–1915." *Labor History,* 7 (fall 1966), 259–86.

Friedman, Lawrence M. and Jack Ladinsky. "Law and Social Change in the Progressive Era: The Law of Industrial Accidents." *Columbia Law Review,* 67 (January 1967), 50–82.

Huthmacher, J. Joseph. "Urban Liberalism and the Age of Reform." *Mississippi Valley Historical Review,* 49 (September 1962), 231–41.

Lowi, Theodore. *At the Pleasure of the Mayor: New York City Patronage, 1889–1958.* New York: Free Press, 1965.

Timberlake, James H. *Prohibition and the Progressive Movement, 1900–1920.* Cambridge, Mass.: Harvard University Press, 1963.

Walker, Forrest A. "Compulsory Health Insurance: 'The Next Great Step in Social Legislation.'" *Journal of American History,* 56 (September 1969), 290–304.

Yellowitz, Irwin. "The Origins of Unemployment Reform in the United States." *Labor History,* 9 (fall 1968), 338–60.

Index

Abbott, Lyman, 142
Abbott sisters, 154
Abilene, 77
abolitionists, 22, 51
academic freedom disputes, 64, 120
acquisitiveness, 45, 63, 201
Adamson act, 185
Addams, Jane, 154, 161, 170
advertising, 189, 200
agrarianism, 118
agricultural depression of 1887–1897, 78, 98, 109, 146
agriculture, 146; federal aid for, 189; in 1878–93 period, 87–90; recovery after 1896, 111
Akron, 146
Alabama, 21, 98, 158
Alaska, 112
Alger, Horatio, 45–46
alien suffrage, 181
Altgeld, John Peter, 106
American Economic Association, 121–22
American Federation of Labor, 91, 118, 129, 165–66, 191
American Historical Association, 133
American Indians, xiii. *See also* Indians.
American Railway Union, 106
American Tobacco Company, 86, 187
Americanization, 125, 138, 140, 154–55, 191–92. *See also* social control.
anarchism, 190
Angell, James B., 61
anti-Catholicism, 175
antigambling laws, 96
antimonopoly, 41, 45, 107, 136, 146, 167, 183–87, 192
anthropology, 52, 206
antitrust laws, 45, 185
Appalachia, 5

arc light, 33
architecture, 9–10
army, 199
Asians, 42, 46, 49–50, 199
assimilation of immigrants, 150, 181, 183; of minorities, 46–55
Astor, John Jacob, 17
athletics, intercollegiate, 61
Atlanta, 146
Atlanta Compromise, 52, 161
Atlantic, 142
Australia, xi
Australian ballot, 173
Austria–Hungary, 16, 20, 31, 72, 144, 150, 152

Baker, Ray Stannard, 141
Balch, Emily, 154
Bakunin, 102
Baltimore, Council of, 58
Baltimore & Ohio Railroad, 85, 113
bank failures in 1893–94, 104
bankers' panic of 1903, 145
banking, investment, 27, 87, 113, 167
banking reforms, 185
banks, laws concerning, 115, 188
Barr, Alwyn, 158
Bauhaus style, 196
Beard, Charles A., 125–26, 133
Belgium, 70
Bell, Alexander Graham, 33
Bellamy, Edward, 64, 115, 126, 169, 195
Belmont, house of, 106
Bemis, E. H., 62
benevolent and protective associations, 82
Bennett law, 96, 115
Berger, Victor, 171
Bessemer-Kelly process, 85
Bethlehem Steel Company, 166